JIM BUTLER

BRIDAL PROFIT EXPLOSION

12 KEYS

TO HELP YOU MAKE A
QUANTUM LEAP IN YOUR
BRIDAL BUSINESS

Bridal Training
&
Marketing Systems

Butler, James K.,
Bridal Profit Explosion: 12 Keys to Help You Make a Quantum Leap in Your Bridal Business/ Jim Butler

ISBN 978-0-578-05529-9
1. Business 2. Success

Printed in the United States of America

To my beautiful wife Heather,
and my five precious children
who are each my eternal inspiration

CONTENTS

Introduction & Self-Assessment

The bridal business is such a fun and wonderful business! It is exciting to be a part of one of the most meaningful days in people's personal lives. We have the opportunity day in and day out to make people's dreams come true and have a lot of fun in the process. But, make no mistake about it. This is a business, and a very challenging one at that. It can quickly spiral out of control without careful attention to the many facets and critical factors that can make or break you. In this book, I will talk straight with you about the things you may have been ignoring, what you should be paying attention to and giving you the strategies that will help your business grow.

I don't want you to make the same mistakes my wife and I did when we opened our business in the fall of 2001. We made a lot of mistakes and learned a lot of things along the way. I truly want you to be as successful as you want with your bridal store and I sincerely believe that what you are about to read will change your life.

I know that you may not agree with everything you read in this book. But I would like you to read it with an open mind and seriously consider what I have to say about succeeding in the bridal industry.

You may be wondering, "Who is Jim Butler and why should I listen to what he has to say?"

That's a fair question and one I will try to answer briefly here. I was born in upstate New York. My father is a farrier (shoes horses) and educator who taught at several universities and colleges when I was growing up. My mother stayed in the home raising me and my six siblings (I was born third). I have to be honest that I never really saw myself being an entrepreneur when I was growing up in west Texas and northwest Missouri. You'll see why as you read on.

I graduated from college with a microbiology major and a chemistry minor. I always thought I would go to medical school and work on developing vaccines in the field of immunology. While I was in college, I met my wife Heather. When I graduated from college, I couldn't get a job in my field to support my family. I ended up working in construction for a while and hated it. I couldn't afford to go back to school and so I wound up in sales so I could pay the bills and support our young daughter Madeline who was born thirteen months after we got married.

In a word, I stunk at sales. I was terrible at it. We nearly starved as I spun my wheels trying to figure out what would work. I quickly learned that there were books that had been written on selling. I couldn't afford them, but I went to a local Barnes and Noble and read books with a note pad each night before coming home. I took copious notes of ideas I could try in my next day's sales efforts. As I started to implement what I was learning and along with the coaching of my sales manager and the top sales people in the office, I started to make improvements. The week before Madeline was born I had one of my best sales weeks ever and beat everyone else at the office in total sales. I even got an award for selling the most that week. I became excited about what I was learning and studied with even more diligence. My first year in selling I read over 60 books. I was on fire and very excited about business and selling. Even though I didn't know much about business, I was excited by what I was learning and found that I enjoyed selling and business much more than the science I had been studying in school.

After Madeline was born, I worked for my father selling his one-on-one farrier training and coaching programs and helped him write many articles for horse industry publications. I also did a lot of research and helped him outline and write two books (one on creative thinking and the other on business). I loved the process of writing and owe a lot to my father for teaching me how to distill a lot of information into a few key ideas.

After working for my father for a year and a half I helped start an interactive marketing agency called Impact Media which grew to be one of the top 100 interactive advertising agencies (#84) in the United States. I was their Director of Business Development (and their top sales person) with millions of dollars in sales with such clients as Fidelity Investments, Hewlett Packard, IBM, Upper Deck and Toyota. I also worked with many of the top advertising agencies in the country including Ogilvy, J. Walter Thompson, Brodeur Worldwide and DNB Media. This company was publicly acquired twice during the .com era.

My wife had a good friend who was in the bridal business and Heather actually worked at her store while we were dating and going through college. We ended up starting our bridal business together in Mesa, Arizona. In July of 2006, I began Bridal Training and Marketing Systems to help other bridal retailers learn many of the secrets we had learned as we grew our business. I have since helped many of the most respected and largest bridal stores across the country to grow their sales and shatter their previous sales records.

I now speak several times a year to groups of hundreds of bridal stores and wedding professionals and offer training and coaching to improve their businesses. Today Heather and I have five children (two girls and three boys). We also own and operate a wholesale bridal company, Bridal Manufacturing Designs which creates three bridal lines and two prom lines for bridal stores across the United States and Canada. I have personally consulted with dozens of bridal stores and even conducted individualized training in their stores.

I'm not saying this to brag. It has been a long process and a lot of work to get here. We have had many individuals who have helped us along the way. I just want you to understand where I'm coming from so that you'll listen to the secrets I'll share with you that can transform your business. My hope is that by sharing with you my story about the mistakes we made when we opened our store, I'll be able to help you objectively see your business so that you can make a quantum leap in your business as a result.

To start, I would like you to answer a few questions to assess where you are now. If you want to create a road map and outline where you are going, it is critical to understand where you are starting from. On the pages that follow I have put together a 10 area, 101 question self-assessment quiz that can help you see where your business is at right now. Answer each of the questions honestly. At the end of the exercise, I'll show you how you can score it to see what grade your business currently has. After reading the book and implementing what I'll teach you, you should take the test again to see how you are doing at implementing these fundamentals into your business. Let's get started.

BUSINESS CHECKUP EXERCISE

MISSION/VISION/PURPOSE

Mission / Vision /Purpose	Oops	Sometimes	Mostly	Always
1. We have our finger on the pulse of the market at all times.				
2. We are moving in a clear direction and every strategic decision supports that direction.				
3. We have a good knowledge of our competition and their practices and how we stand out from them.				
4. Our business is going in the direction that we originally intended and/or in a direction we are happy with.				

Mission / Vision /Purpose	Oops	Sometimes	Mostly	Always
5. Vision, mission, goals, and strategies are well known by all.				
6. We have clarity and consistency of our goals.				
7. I am proud of myself as both a business owner and as a human being.				
8. I am happy with the amount of money I make.				
9. I do not stay awake at night worrying about my business.				
10. The brides and prom girls coming into our store have a positive perception about our mission and purpose.				

SALES

Sales	Oops	Sometimes	Mostly	Always
1. We analyze our mistakes when sales don't happen and learn from them.				
2. Sales information is readily available and closely monitored.				
3. We track our brides, our close ratios and the number of transactions per bride continuously. If our bridal consultants aren't where they need to be (closing percentages), we help them become better or replace them quickly.				
4. Every bridal consultant knows and achieves their sales goals per hour, week, and month.				
5. Every member of the team recognizes and works to help achieve daily, weekly, and monthly sales goals.				

Sales		Oops	Sometimes	Mostly	Always
6.	Our bridal consultants follow a system that allows them to stays in touch with brides in the marketing funnel.				
7.	Regular sales training is offered and implemented to every member of our staff.				
8.	Our bridal consultants have a system in place to prioritize the brides they are working with.				
9.	Our bridal consultants are professional and have the experience necessary to excel at selling.				
10.	We evaluate and make changes to our sales training based on changes in the marketplace.				

MARKETING

Marketing		Oops	Sometimes	Mostly	Always
1.	I have a complete marketing plan for the year.				
2.	I adhere to the marketing plan throughout the year (with some adjustments).				
3.	Our marketing plan is a result of input and involvement from key managers and staff.				
4.	Our marketing plan guides the actions of our staff to achieve our financial goals and objectives.				
5.	We have a contingency plan to adjust for external changes that can affect our business (what our competitors do, etc.).				

Marketing		Oops	Sometimes	Mostly	Always
6.	Our marketing plan contains specific and measurable objectives for each sales event.				
7.	We track the effectiveness of our marketing collateral and promotions to ensure that advertising expenditures are wisely made.				
8.	We only advertise when we can test and measure the results.				
9.	Our marketing pieces are evaluated carefully before they are sent out to ensure that they will grab and hold the attention of our brides and cause them to act.				
10.	There is accountability for implementation of our marketing plan.				
11.	We have quality marketing materials that build our brand, not a manufacturer's brand.				

LEADERSHIP

Leadership		Oops	Sometimes	Mostly	Always
1.	Our store manager and assistant managers (if you have them) have strong leadership capabilities.				
2.	We have a strong culture of developing leaders around us at our store.				
3.	We provide learning resources to our staff members to help them develop their leadership qualities.				
4.	I continuously offer hope and encouragement in our staff's ability to reach our store goals.				

Leadership	Oops	Sometimes	Mostly	Always
5. I set and enforce high standards at our store.				
6. I reward production and results, not laziness and mediocrity.				
7. I foster an environment where rotten attitudes, selfishness, and gossip cannot take root and spread.				
8. I stop investing in staff members who aren't growing.				
9. I create new opportunities that motivate and excite each member of our team based on their motivational style.				
10. I evaluate our team members often and replace 'C' players with 'A' players.				

TEAM

Team	Oops	Sometimes	Mostly	Always
1. There is a synergy among all of the members of the team.				
2. Everyone is listened to and encouraged to speak up and make recommendations.				
3. The team always remains positive and does not tolerate negativism among its members.				
4. The team sees change as positive and is always ready for challenges.				
5. My team members are accountable and never make excuses for performance.				

Team	Oops	Sometimes	Mostly	Always
6. Deadlines are taken seriously and managed by the team leaders.				
7. Every member of the team enjoys their work.				
8. Every member of the team does complete work, nothing is redone or substandard.				
9. Team communication is effective and duplication of work does not occur.				

CUSTOMER SERVICE

Customer Service	Oops	Sometimes	Mostly	Always
1. We follow an overall team approach to create loyal brides who refer us to their friends.				
2. We evaluate the timeliness and efficiency with which we handle customer complaints and make adjustments.				
3. We stay in touch with our brides once they have purchased and encourage additional business (accessories, bridesmaids, etc.).				
4. We always ask our brides for referrals.				
5. We act on the feedback we receive from our brides and prom girls to make improvements.				
6. We measure our customer satisfaction and train our bridal consultants to make improvements based on what is learned.				

Customer Service	Oops	Sometimes	Mostly	Always
7. We have a training system in place for handling customer service issues and complaints.				
8. We provide rewards or incentives to those on our staff who provide superior customer service.				
9. We have an ongoing program to regularly communicate with our brides and prom girls (newsletter, Facebook, Twitter, etc.)				
10. When someone commits to do something for a bride, are there systems in place to ensure that it happens?				
11. We send written notes of appreciation to every bride who buys from us.				
12. We survey those brides who don't buy from us in order to improve our offerings and service.				

PRODUCTIVITY

Productivity	Oops	Sometimes	Mostly	Always
1. I spend time on my highest value activities.				
2. Our bridal consultants and employees are very productive and fully utilized.				
3. I have time to do the things I want to do.				
4. I work less than 50 hours a week.				
5. I have more time than I need to get things done.				

Productivity	Oops	Sometimes	Mostly	Always
6. I have an assistant to handle details ensuring I have time to focus *on* the business instead of just being *in* it.				
7. I exercise regularly and spend quality time with the people I care about.				
8. I am putting aside funds regularly with which to become financially independent.				
9. I have at least 10 daily well-being habits and I do them consistently.				
10. My days are well planned and I never run on adrenaline.				

SYSTEMS

Systems	Oops	Sometimes	Mostly	Always
1. Our systems are right for our business.				
2. Our systems are well documented and updated regularly.				
3. Important business performance information from all of our systems is readily available and easy to retrieve.				
4. Our business systems give me the information I need to make important decisions about our store.				
5. Our systems are reliable and there are minimal customer service issues as a result.				
6. Our critical computer data is properly backed up and safe and can be recovered quickly in the event of a disaster.				

Systems	Oops	Sometimes	Mostly	Always
7. Our systems are in place and our each member of our staff adheres to them.				
8. We have an ongoing system to regularly communicate our orders with our suppliers.				

OPERATIONS

Operations	Oops	Sometimes	Mostly	Always
1. No one area of our store is dependent upon a single supplier.				
2. Our suppliers and vendors are true partners to our business.				
3. Our internal financial statements are prepared without errors.				
4. Our financial statements help relationships with our lenders.				
5. I get accurate projections about my April 15th IRS bill.				
6. I look at our financial statements monthly, at the very minimum.				
7. Profit margins have increased over the last three years.				
8. Suppliers and service providers' invoices are routinely paid on time.				
9. Our profits are measured regularly. Profits will increase this year by no less than ___%.				
10. The ratio of the company's total debt to equity has decreased over the last year.				
11. We have the cash flow to achieve our objectives.				

FINANCIAL AND INVENTORY MANAGEMENT

Financial and Inventory Management	Oops	Sometimes	Mostly	Always
1. I have a good control over my inventory at all times.				
2. Each category of products we carry at our store are profitable.				
3. We systematically eliminate unprofitable inventory items from our store.				
4. Through reports and surveys, I have an accurate pulse on what is selling in my store at all times.				
5. I am aware of our best selling styles, colors, and sizes and purchase inventory accordingly.				
6. Inventory is closely monitored to ensure maximum turnover and minimal financial outlay.				
7. Terms are negotiated with all suppliers including early payment discounts.				
8. Debt service as a percentage of gross profit decreased last year.				
9. I have and utilize a budget when making inventory expenditures.				
10. I stay on top of our hottest styles and trends and make sure that these are in the store to sell.				

"The achievement of financial independence will require a tremendous number of small efforts on your part. To begin the process of accumulation, you must be disciplined and persistent. You must keep at it for a long, long time. Initially, you will see very little change or difference, but gradually, your efforts will begin to bear fruit. You will begin to pull ahead of your peers. Your finances will improve and your debts will disappear. Your bank account will grow and your whole life will improve."

—Brian Tracy, *The 100 Absolutely Unbreakable Laws of Business Success*, p. 180.

How to Score Your Business Checkup

	Oops	Sometimes	Mostly	Always
Scoring	0	1	2	3
Your Totals				

TOTAL SCORE: ___________

Total up points from each category

303 highest possible score

Now that you've taken this quiz, you've probably seen several areas you need to work on to improve. I would encourage you to take one category per month and work on that in your business so that you can focus on improving your skill in each one of these areas.

CHAPTER 1

CHART YOUR COURSE FOR SUCCESS

There are three types of responses to the current Great Recession that bridal store owners choose to embrace. First, many store owners have emotionally thrown in the towel. They have decided to wait it out thinking that it will only be a few more months before things turn around. They have stopped or significantly reduced their marketing and have accepted that things will just be bad for a while.

The second response is to continue to do the same thing that they have been doing. They either do *more* of the same thing or they do *less* of the same thing at their store. The problem with this response is that all of their activities are tied to doing the *same* thing as opposed to doing something *different* or *better*. On top of that, what used to work in our business no longer does. The mindset of brides has changed (partly due to their own fear about the economy and partly because your competitors are saturating the media that brides in your area are looking at with their own irresistible offers). By choosing to ignore the reality that the mindset of your target market has changed and not changing your own marketing approach to draw in the brides in your area, you likely have seen a reduction in the number of brides walking through your doors.

The third response comes from the understanding that the market has shifted and changed and these smart business owners have adapted to the change by hunting out and searching for *what works now* **and** *actively implementing* it in their business.

My question for you to think about is, "What response have you chosen to embrace at your store"? Have you emotionally thrown in the towel? Are you doing more or less of the same things you used to do with diminishing results? Or are you actively searching out and implementing the best ideas from other successful retailers and other industries? Your response to this question will in large part determine where your business will be when we eventually emerge from the recession into more prosperous times. Will you be in a position to capture more market share or will you be far behind your competitors watching as your market share erodes?

The very fact that you are reading this book is a very important indicator that you are on the right track. You are actively seeking ideas and strategies that are working now and that you can utilize in your business. One way to successfully overcome the recession is to look at what others in different industries are doing and then adapt them to use at your store. Other businesses the world over are also experiencing the same challenging effects of the recession that you are. Taking time to look around and observe what other smart and successful businesspeople are doing can be very helpful to you as well. I really like what Edward Eggleston once observed, "Persistent people begin their success where others end in failure." Another great statement by John Christian Bovee also illustrates this point. He said, "A failure establishes only this, that our determination to succeed was not strong enough."

It is my hope that you will always remember what author Napoleon Hill wrote: "Patience, persistence and perspiration make an unbeatable combination for success." When you embrace this attitude, constantly hunt out and look for the best ways to bring brides into your store, and actively implement these ideas and strategies, you'll find that you will come out on top because you are utilizing this unbeatable combination for success.

Here are six challenges with advertising today and how you can overcome them to flood your store with brides who are ready to buy now.

1. The marketplace is very noisy. Ads that scream "SALE, SALE, SALE!" have made brides deaf to you and your offer.

If you have walked through any mall lately, watched any ads on television, or listened to ads on the radio, it is amazing how many sales and discount offers are being promoted. The marketplace has gotten extremely loud and noisy because everyone is trying to grab the attention of their customers. How do you grab attention when everyone around you is shouting and the brides you are marketing to are becoming deaf to your message? The answer is that you have to grab attention in a creative way that pulls her into your store. The biggest part of grabbing attention is having a great headline.

Unfortunately, most bridal ads don't have a headline or if they do, it is not very effective. Instead, most bridal ads feature a picture, a logo, an address, the store's hours, and their web site. There will be a slogan that tells how long they have been serving brides in the such and such area and often will have a slogan that includes the phrase "unparalleled customer service". When everyone says something, it becomes an expectation and doesn't mean much to the brides. I am constantly amazed at bridal salons who tout that the reason why they are better than David's or Internet vendors is because they offer great customer service. Brides *expect* customer service from these retailers too. The brides that most bridal salons hear from that complain about the customer service of big box stores are the ones who didn't buy. The essence of what I'm trying to communicate here is that if you want to grab attention today, you have to do it in such a way that brides are drawn to you because of your uniqueness (what brides get from you that they can't get anywhere else), your point of difference (having exclusive lines that no one else has), and by becoming a celebrity authority figure in your market.

Simply promising great customer service and announcing that you are open for business doesn't motivate brides to come into your store. It may have worked in the past, but in today's hypercompetitive environment, stores who embrace this approach are finding that their traffic has dropped off significantly. It doesn't mean that there are fewer brides—it simply means that other stores are drawing the brides to their stores better than you are.

2. **Most ads indicate that bridal stores care more about their image than what brides perceive.**

The root cause of this problem is that most bridal stores use a great image in their marketing and then have their address, phone number, web site, and hours and stop there. There is no invitation for the bride to take action and do something specific nor any reason why she should act now as opposed to waiting it out. Having a pretty ad without great marketing copy that invites brides to do something may be noticed by *some* brides (but if everyone has access to those lines) you won't be very effective. The reality is that too many ads today are really creative without being persuasive. They have a pretty picture, but don't really cause the bride to want to take action.

It is much better to offer informative information that is believable, memorable and causes the bride to want to come into your store.

We recently started a marketing campaign where we are educating and marketing to our brides that waiting longer than a year before the wedding will cause them great stress and anxiety and at the same time we also offer a special benefit or bonus to the bride who buys her dress now instead of later.

Another big challenge with advertising today is that it tries to be clever or funny. Just being clever or funny doesn't mean that brides will connect your ad with your store. How many times have you heard or seen a funny ad, but then not remember who the ad is for or what it was trying to sell? This is unfortunate for the companies who have spent a lot of money on those ads. Instead, ask yourself the following eight questions before you send out your next ad. Then you can be sure that you have thought through the result you want when brides look at your ad.

1) Does your ad attract the brides who shop at your store? Does your headline grab the audience's attention?

2) Does your ad hold the bride's attention?

3) Does your marketing copy create desire?

4) Does your ad prove what it claims?

5) Does your ad establish confidence in your ability to help the bride find her perfect dress?

6) Does your ad build *your* store brand and authority or the manufacturer of the dress?

7) Does your ad make it easy for the bride to act?

8) Do you give your bride a reason to act now?

Once you have asked yourself these questions, take the time to ask yourself: "How can I improve this ad?" Write down your ideas and make your ad better. Be sure your ad is **selling**, and not just entertaining.

Jack Trout in his new book *In Search of the Obvious* made this observation about ineffective advertising. He said: "Most bad advertising is about entertainment, not selling." –p. 91.

If you want to be successful in advertising your bridal store today, you have to care more about *what* an ad *says* (and that it contains a persuasive message) than *how* it *looks*.

3. Most ads don't use persuasive words.

There is a power in well chosen persuasive words. Unfortunately, most bridal stores do not use persuasive words in their advertising at all. They rely entirely on an image to sell for them. One of the most important aspects of marketing and selling is the psychological one. In other words, getting into the heads of the brides you market to and understanding what they're thinking, how they're dealing with it, and what their concern(s) may be about planning their wedding and buying the perfect dress. In order to get into this mindset, you really have to set your biases and prejudices aside so that you can truly understand what it is like to be on the other side of the transaction.

It can be a nerve racking experience for some brides coming into a bridal store for the first time, since it is a large purchase, and most brides who buy from us have never purchased a wedding dress before and they aren't sure how to go about doing it. They may also be uncomfortable with their body and may not have worn a formal dress or gown in a long time.

Your job when marketing to each bride is to help neutralize her anxiety, help her, her mother and any other bridal attendants who might be with her feel comfortable around you and trust you, and sell her a one-of-a-kind experience where you literally help her fulfill her nearly life-long fantasy of a dream wedding. You won't be able to do this unless you can be more persuasive.

Brides today are more savvy and skeptical than ever before. They have more choices than have ever been available in more places and *they know it*. The best way to be persuasive and overcome their skepticism is to offer lots of social proof of other brides who have purchased from you and how you took away their fears, eliminated any and all risks they may be worried about and helped them have the most amazing experience finding their dress. Having written testimonials in your ads and video testimonials on your web site is an extremely effective way to do this.

Here are some questions for you to think about as you strive to create a memorable experience at your store and persuasively market to the brides in your area:

- What would delight them?
- What would be fun for brides?
- How could you surprise them?
- What would make them feel unique and special?
- What would make them feel good about themselves?
- What would reaffirm the way they see themselves and reinforce that identity?
- How could you customize the dresses you sell (or alterations) so they will identify it as being 'just for me'?
- How might you make it possible for them do to something out of the ordinary?
- How could you create the perception that doing business with your bridal store confirms or raises their status?
- How could you create feelings of validity and satisfaction about themselves?
- What could you do to make them feel safe and secure, give them peace of mind?
- How might you help them become the person they have always wanted to be?
- How might you give them the ability to do something they have always wanted to do?

Carefully thinking through and acting on the answers to these questions will help you be much more persuasive in your marketing and selling approach.

4. **Most ads don't contain elements that trigger response.**

As I mentioned, most bridal store ads have a picture of a dress they carry (similar to other lines that their competitors carry and that can be found online – which is a mistake in and of itself) and have their logo, address, hours, phone number and web site. The unfortunate reality is that in today's marketplace, this type of ad will rarely generate response. Most ads are ineffective because they don't invite brides to take any action and there is really not a compelling enough reason why they should put off the tendency to procrastinate and act now.

To help you generate better response in your ads, carefully consider these six ideas:

1) **Have something exciting, interesting, and compelling to say.**

2) **Target the media to the market.** Pick media that will help you get in front of brides.

   Don't waste money on ads where brides aren't looking (newspapers, printed yellow pages, etc.) Many bridal stores buy advertising because a salesperson comes into their store and tells them, "Hey, you need to do this." They put out an ad that isn't focused on their specific niche and probably won't be seen or heard by the brides they really want to see it.

3) **Have a great headline that grabs interest and attention.** Don't ever put out another ad without having a great headline.

4) **Have a compelling physical appearance that grabs attention.**

5) **Have a clear call to action.** Be sure your ad invites brides to do something (and that something should lead to a sale). Otherwise, what's the point?

6) **Have multiple approaches to get the ad out.** Use frequency and repetition to boost response.

5. Many ads today are where brides aren't looking. Be where your brides are.

Brides today are on the Internet. By only doing print advertising, many bridal store owners fail to grab the attention of brides in their area because they fail to advertise or market to brides in mediums that the bride is looking at. Social networking sites such as Facebook and Twitter have huge marketing aspects to them that many stores aren't aware of or utilizing. But the key to social networking (like any kind of good marketing) is that you have to have a list that you can market to first. This means that you have to actively build a great list that you can market to.

One great thing to observe about businesses is how they capture your name when you visit them. I was recently at a restaurant where the server invited me to get a free dessert with my meal in exchange for sharing my contact information so they could email us coupons for when we came back to their restaurant. This is a very smart approach. You may not have to offer something for free to get this information (although it didn't hurt – I sure enjoyed the dessert - and I've been back to the restaurant many times since and have received email invitations from them). The important thing is to ask.

Here are two things that you should be doing to build your list:

- Ask every bride coming into the store for her email address. Make this a part of your bridal registry. Ask the bride for her email if she hasn't given it to you on the registry form so that you can let her know about upcoming events and special offers to help her plan her wedding.

- Offer prizes, competitions and giveaways to get people to sign up on your web site. We have done this very effectively on both our prom and bridal web sites. Offer a free gift or the chance to win a free gift by getting people to sign up. We offer a free veil and tiara each month on our web site as a drawing. We offer a drawing for gift certificates for prom. You can use this idea for wedding gowns as well. The key is to get either a bride or prom girl's permission to send her future marketing by getting her to sign up for a contest. It doesn't matter what you decide to do, but you need to have a way to capture email names and addresses of brides in your target market.

New developments are being made all of the time with alternative media options such as text messaging, email, and social networking sites. Stay on top of how to use these mediums to get the word out about your store.

Social networking sites, podcasts, blogs, and texting services are the wave of the future to stay in touch with the brides in your area. You should get a foothold in these areas before your competitors do. Sign up for a Facebook account and Twitter account for your store. Follow retailers such as Starbucks, Alfred Angelo, and David's to get ideas for things you can be doing at your store.

6. **Most ads today don't use premiums or don't use them correctly.**

Premiums are great ways to get people to come in to your store or to encourage them to buy. They show appreciation to a bride for making a purchase and can also be used as a marketing tool to draw them into the store.

Successful premiums have at least one of the following combinations of appeal (and the more you can employ the better):

- ***A high value to the bride, and a low cost to you.*** Look for things that can draw brides in that don't cost you a lot, but have a high value to brides. Veils, earrings, necklaces for bridesmaids, a CD or book, or a Wedding Day Emergency Kit are examples of effective premiums we've used at our store.
- ***An appeal that interests the bride.*** The key thing about all of the premium ideas I just mentioned is that they all have interest or fill

a specific need that a bride has. If a bride really wants something and you offer it to her when she is ready, it can have an almost irresistible pull to help her make the buying decision now.

- ***Usability and reusability***. The best premiums are ones that the bride can use over and over again (earrings, etc.) You also want something that you are sure the bride will use. A cheap premium that has no perceived value and gets thrown away is worthless because it won't cause a bride to take action and come into your store. I have seen ads before offering a free garter with a wedding gown purchase. This is not an effective premium because it has very little perceived value and doesn't offer the appeal of something she can use again and again (like a pair of earrings).

- ***Uniqueness and originality***. Can you make it unique and original to the bride? If so, it will be valued and prized above other premiums (even costly ones).

- ***Prominence*** . You want something that they will display or use often so that it is visible to others (causes others to ask: where did you get that?) I came up with the idea for our Wedding Day Emergency Kit and our Wedding Memories Preservation Kit boxes as a result of thinking about what could be visible while the bride is getting ready on her wedding day that others would see and ask: "Where did you get that?" You can come up with a good idea for a prominent premium as well if you really think about it.

- ***Long term value***. This is pretty self-explanatory, but be sure that the timing of your premium works for the bride. For example, a free veil premium doesn't do much good if it is offered after the bride already has a veil.

Choose to adapt to the changes in the marketplace by hunting out and searching for *what works now* **and** *actively implementing* it in your business. The rewards of the future won't come to those who wait or those who are content to keep doing what they've always been doing.

Here are five fundamental areas of your business that you must pay attention to.

1. Where you are really going.

Because of the way the economy has shifted, many bridal stores have tried to hang on and hold on to what they have had in years past and have forgotten about *where* they are heading. Many stores are struggling to stay even with where they were last year. A few have seen their sales plummet in recent months and some have risen above what they did last year. Every area is a little different, but one constant truth remains. If in the midst of all of the turmoil around you, you forget where you are going, you *will* end up somewhere else.

Taking the time to determine where you are really going is a scary task for many. Most people feel as if it is too difficult to set goals or a vision for the future because there are too many unknown variables. Some have settled for just getting by and have inadvertently put off their goals and dreams because they have forgotten to take the time to plan where they are really going.

I recently read an excellent book by two-time heavyweight champion George Foreman entitled *Knockout Entrepreneur*. There are many great lessons in this book, but one I want to highlight here has everything to do with knowing where you are really going and wanting it bad enough to do what it takes to get there.

On October 29, 1974 in Kinshasa, Zaire, George faced Muhammad Ali in a fight that was called "The Rumble in the Jungle". During the fight, Foreman got knocked down by Muhammad Ali. Laying flat on the mat, he looked over to his manager Dick Sadler who had told him previously, "If you ever get knocked down, don't try to get up too quickly. Look around the ring. Find me, and let me do the counting."

Foreman said, "Rather than bounce back to my feet, I did just as we had always planned. I stayed on the mat for a few seconds, allowing my head to clear as I looked for Dick. I caught his eye and watched for his signal that it was time to get up. But something went horribly wrong. I was on the floor, but I was not listening to the count. I was watching Dick. By the time Dick signaled me to get up, the ref had rattled off a quick, 'Eight, nine, ten!' The fight was over and I had lost! I had been technically knocked out, even though I had the strength, the ability, and the will to get back up." –George Foreman, *Knockout Entrepreneur*, p. 186.

Foreman continues: "I was embarrassed and angry; angry at Dick for not getting me up in time, and most of all, angry at myself for not listening to the count. I hurt inside, not from physical pain, but from the embarrassment and revulsion I felt at losing that way. I was lower than low. The knowledge that I had not been beaten—but that I had actually beaten myself by not getting up in time—lurked constantly in the back of my mind. I said, "I will never allow that to happen to me again." –p. 186.

Have you been knocked down by a competitor? By a bridezilla who attacked you or your business personally on an online chat forum? Has the up and down roller coaster ride of the economy beaten you down?

I love Foreman's commitment and conviction in that last sentence: "I will never allow that to happen to me again."

Once a commitment is made, it will be tested. George Foreman's was tested 15 months later in a fight with Ron Lyle on January 28, 1976. Foreman was knocked down in the 4th round. He said:

"I knew that getting up meant that I was going to get clobbered again; I knew I couldn't stop him from coming at me, and this man's punches packed some wallop!"

He continues:

"Then I remembered how I felt that night in Africa when I should have gotten up, could have gotten up, but didn't. I said to myself, Today, I may die, but I must get up. I couldn't see very well, and I knew that Lyle would come at me with full force again, but I said to myself in those moments on the floor, I never again want to live with the knowledge that I could have gotten up and didn't. I don't want to look myself in the mirror and hear me saying, 'You didn't get back up.'

Foreman got up and hit Lyle "so hard that the blow dislodged his mouthpiece". When Lyle got back up, he came at Foreman even harder and stronger and knocked Foreman down again and the 4th round ended.

When Foreman went to his corner, his cornerman Gil Clancy said "George, the one that's gonna win is the one who wants it most."

Then Clancy asked him, "Do you want it most?"

Foreman came back out and knocked Lyle out in the 5th round. This story is a great example of what you should be thinking about as you plan your future in the bridal business. What do you really want? How badly do you want it? What are you willing to do to make it happen? Who will you get around and surround yourself with to get back on track? What will you do to keep your vision in front of you as you struggle through the difficulties to get there?

If you have stopped dreaming, now is the time to start again. Don't let the nightmares in your business closet stop you from getting out into the sun and thinking about what you want to accomplish. There was a reason you got in business for yourself. Adversity, heartbreak, despair, and discouragement have been holding you back from dreaming. Get out of the darkness and go towards the light – go toward what you want, not what you don't.

2. Losing sight of what matters most.

Former Lufthansa jet pilot Dieter Uchtdorf recently told this story about the importance of not losing sight of what matters most. He said:

"On a dark December night 36 years ago, a Lockheed 1011 jumbo jet crashed into the Florida Everglades, killing over 100 people. This terrible accident was one of the deadliest crashes in the history of the United States.

A curious thing about this accident is that all vital parts and systems of the airplane were functioning perfectly—the plane could have easily landed safely at its destination in Miami, only 20 miles (32 km) away.

During the final approach, however, the crew noticed that one green light had failed to illuminate—a light that indicates whether or not the nose landing gear has extended successfully. The pilots discontinued the approach, set the aircraft into a circling holding pattern over the pitch-black Everglades, and turned their attention toward investigating the problem.

They became so preoccupied with their search that they failed to realize the plane was gradually descending closer and closer toward the dark swamp below. By the time someone noticed what was happening, it was too late to avoid the disaster.

After the accident, investigators tried to determine the cause. The landing gear had indeed lowered properly. The plane was in perfect mechanical condition. Everything was working properly—all except one thing: a single burned-out lightbulb. That tiny bulb—worth about 20 cents—started the chain of events that ultimately led to the tragic deaths of over 100 people.

Of course, the malfunctioning lightbulb didn't cause the accident; it happened because the crew placed its focus on something that seemed to matter at the moment while losing sight of what mattered most."

Has this happened to you at your bridal store? Have you gotten caught up in the heat of the moment and lost sight of the fundamentals of your business?

It is so easy to get distracted by the new, new thing. Unfortunately, like the pilots of the disaster just mentioned, it is easy to lose your bearings when you focus on what seems to matter now at the exclusion of your business fundamentals.

Picking up a new line so that someone else doesn't get it first may be a good strategic move, but is it the wisest use of your financial resources? Will it help you be profitable? Spending your profits on picking up one new line without also eliminating unprofitable lines is an example of focusing on what seems to matter at the moment of market (preventing your competitors from having the line) with what matters most (your overall profitability and long-term business plan).

What happens in someone else's store isn't nearly as important as what is happening in *your* store. Be sure you focus on what matters most *to you* now. John Maxwell makes this point:

"I read a study of thirty-nine midsized companies stating that the characteristic that differentiated the successful companies from the unsuccessful was simplicity. The companies that sold fewer products to fewer customers, and who worked with fewer suppliers than other companies in the same industry were more profitable. Simple, focused operations brought greater results. As Warren Buffet observes, 'The business schools reward difficult, complex behavior more than simple behavior, but simple behavior is more effective.' By striving for simplicity, I [keep] my mind on the main thing." –*Leadership Gold*, pp. 97-98.

Don't get caught up doing so many things that you end up doing the wrong things. Find and focus on the main thing that will help your store be successful. The bottom line is that the things that matter most (getting brides in the door and closing the sale once they are there) should never be at the mercy of what matters least.

3. The limiting factors that are holding you back.

What are your limiting factors? A limiting factor is an area of your business that holds you back from accomplishing all that you could if it weren't present. For example, an inability to close sales is the limiting factor that holds you back from hitting your weekly and monthly sales goals.

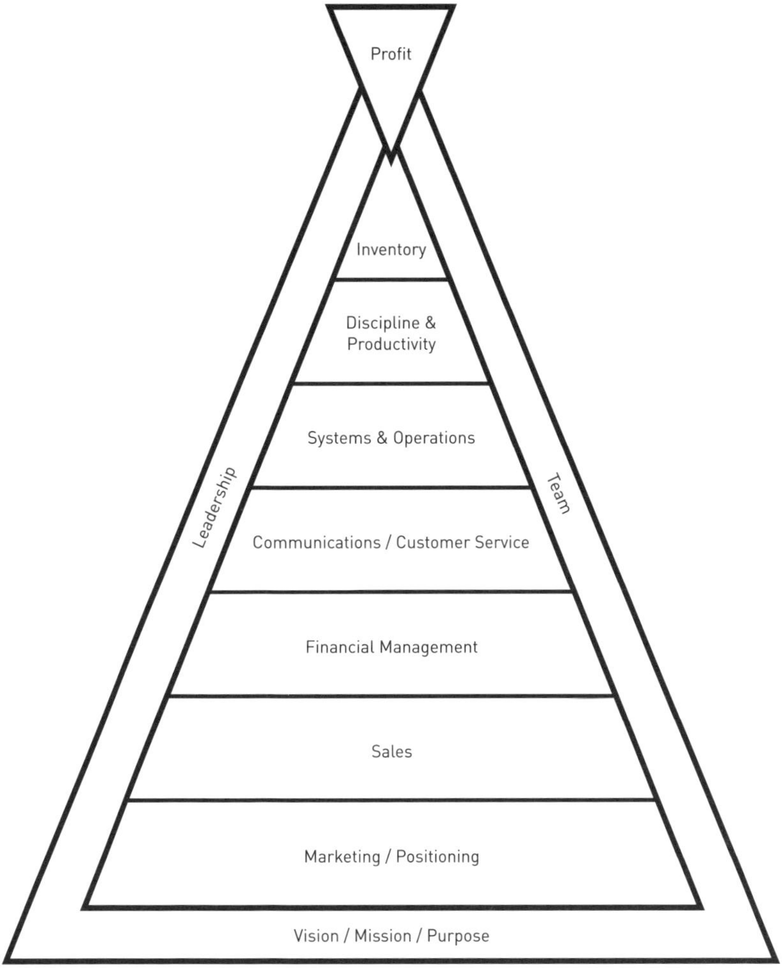

I've outlined above the Bridal Business Success Triangle (which I've adapted from Robert Kiyosaki's BI Triangle from his book, *Rich Dad's Guide to Investing)* to help you see the areas of your business and how they fit together. The outer aspects of the triangle that hold it together are 1) the base of your vision, mission and purpose, 2) your team – those you have around you to help you reach your goals, and 3) your leadership to help your team stay on task in the most important and critical areas of your business. The inner areas of the triangle are 1) marketing/positioning, 2) sales, 3) financial management, 4)

communications/customer service, 5) systems and operations, 6) your own discipline and productivity, and 7) your inventory. The keystone of the triangle or the part that keeps it all together and from falling apart is your profitability. I have this interconnected with your inventory since what you buy determines how profitable you will be in the context of all of the other areas.

There are parts of the Bridal Business Success Triangle that you may be ignoring or forgetting about that are the limiting step in why your business isn't growing like it could or should. You have to determine what these areas are and face them head on instead of pretending that they don't exist simply because you're not confident or competent in them.

In addition to these limiting factors, you may also be guilty of the ghoul of being afraid to make mistakes. In other words, you don't want to take on these areas of your business because you may make a mistake in them. Ignoring them doesn't make them go away.

You may have seen the sign in a high-pressure sales office that says, "Do you like to travel? Do you want to meet friends? Do you want to free up your future? All this can be yours if you make one more mistake."

Are you or your bridal consultants consumed with fear of making a mistake? Do your bridal consultants feel intimidated by you so that they are afraid to bring up warning signs because of how you might react? This fear of intimidation may be a limiting factor that prevents those around you from speaking up and telling you what you need to know.

Michael Abrashoff talks about this issue in his book, *It's Your Ship*. He says:

"The moment I heard about it [the tragic sinking of a Japanese fishing boat off Honolulu by the submarine USS Greeneville], I was reminded that, as is often the case with accidents, someone senses possible danger but doesn't necessarily speak up. As the Greenville investigation unfolded, I read in a *New York Times* article that the submarine's crew 'respected the commanding officer too much to question his judgment.'

If that's respect, then I want none of it. You need to have people in your organization that can tap you on the shoulder and say, 'Is this the best way?' or 'Slow down,' or 'Think about this,'....

History records countless incidents in which ship captains or organization managers permitted a climate of intimidation to pervade the workplace, silencing subordinates whose warnings could have prevented disaster. Even when the reluctance to speak up stems from admiration for the commanding officer's skill and experience, a climate to question decisions must be created in order to foster double-checking." –p. 33.

Be approachable. Let others know that you value their input and feedback on your team. Meet often to discuss the challenges and problems that are going on in your business. When you ask your bridal consultants and management team for help with issues that are going on, they will share wonderful ideas with you that can help you take your business to the next level.

Identify your limitations and surround yourself with others who can help you do what needs to be done in all of the areas of your business. Don't let your limitations hold you back from accomplishing more.

4. What your competition is doing.

One of the most frightening things that you may have been ignoring about your business is what your competition is doing. As economic times have been challenging, many competitors have become much more aggressive about their pricing and their marketing approach. The recession has likely changed your standing with your competitors in ways that you may not have considered. If any of your competitors have become a casualty of the recession, you may feel like you have lost a competitor. In reality, the recession has caused you to gain new ones. For example, higher end stores are now competing in lower price ranges as budgets have become tighter and as brides have been waiting longer to make their dress purchase. In our area, we have seen significant changes in the approach that David's and other competitors are employing to grab the attention of brides and get them into their stores. If business has been slower for you lately, it isn't just the "economy" that is the problem. It is that your competitors are being much more aggressive about bringing brides in with nearly unbelievable offers to get brides to buy from them instead of from you.

When marketing your business, focus on the total value brides get at your store, your contrast, and your differentiating point. Give the brides coming into your store a reason to choose you over your competitors. Having a distinct difference helps you build contrast in the eyes of the bride, and if the contrast is great enough, she will buy from you, since you have the best overall value. Also, pre-empt your competitors with a great pre-sales strategy and lots of testimonials from brides who have already purchased from you.

Here are six suggestions to help you stay on top of what your competition is doing:

1) ***Do a SWOT analysis.***

   Analyze your competitors in four areas:

   - Strengths: What are their strengths in your market?
   - Weaknesses: What are their weaknesses in your market?
   - Opportunities: What major opportunities exist to outsell them?
   - Threats: What major threats do they pose to our survival? What is their game plan?

   This is a good way to evaluate how to take on your competition.

2) ***Watch what your competitors are doing with their social networking sites and area advertising.***

Watch your competitors closely to see how they are marketing now. Study what they are doing. A great place to start is to watch what David's Bridal and Alfred Angelo are doing on Facebook and Twitter. This will give you a good indication of what brides in your area are hearing and can give you some good ideas for how to counteract what they are doing and have a competitive advantage.

3) ***Visit their web site often.***

When was the last time you went to the websites of all of your competitors? Most of them probably haven't updated their sites in a long time. If they update their sites often, go back to their sites frequently. They often will have coupons posted on their web site or announcements for upcoming bridal shows, trunk shows, or other events. When you know what they are doing to pull brides into their stores, look for ways you can pull attention away from them and towards your store.

4) ***Build a contrast diagram for what you offer in comparison with the other bridal shops in your area.***

Contrast is a powerful psychological trigger that helps people make the decision to buy. It is a good idea to put together a contrast diagram for how you are different from your competitors. If you haven't done this, I would strongly encourage you to take the time to do so. You don't have to show this to the brides who come into your store, but it can be a helpful way to build contrast in their minds if you do. It is a great exercise to do so you can discuss the benefits of buying at your store with your bridal consultants. I have put together a training CD on this psychological trigger and 29 other triggers that influence and persuade brides to buy. If you are interested in getting a copy of this training resource, please contact me at info@bridaltrainingsystems.com.

5) ***Listen carefully to what brides say about your competitors.***

   Ask them for the differences they experienced between your store and theirs. If a bride says something negative about one of your competitors, don't pass on that negative information to your brides. It will only make you look bad. Instead, use the information to more effectively position your store in the marketplace.

   Another important thing to do is to ask the brides who buy from you to share how your store compared with other stores she visited via a written or video testimonial that you can post on your web site.

6) ***Develop friendships with your competitors.***

   It is amazing what can happen when you get to know your competitors. Now, you may have some competitors that you could never envision being friends with in a million years because of some experience that you have had. Don't let that negative experience prevent you from getting to know your other competitors. When we first opened our store, I introduced myself to the managers of the David's store that was closest to us at a bridal show. I told her what we specialized in and where our business was. We got a lot of referrals from them because she told brides to come to our store when they didn't have exactly what the bride was looking for. Get to know your competitors. They are good people too. They may end up being a great source of referrals.

Final thought: Ignoring what your competition is doing is not a good idea. While you don't want this to dictate your long-term strategy it is very important to not only be aware of what is going on, but also to look for ways that you can pre-empt your competition and get brides to your business first.

5. What you are doing to stay up in a down economy.

In today's volatile economy, it is easy to allow yourself and your thinking to be swayed by the constant barrage of breaking news and the changing buying patterns of the brides coming into your store. If you don't learn to overcome the resistance you are experiencing in your business, your life, and from the brides who come into your store, your sales numbers will go up and down and cause you great anxiety and stress.

A great analogy that really helps me understand what it takes to stay up in a down economy is found in the difference between a thermomter and a thermostat. Consider this statement from John C. Maxwell in his book *Developing the Leaders Around You*:

"At first glance, a person could confuse these instruments. Both are capable of measuring heat. However, they are really quite different. A thermometer is passive. It records the temperature of its environment but can do nothing to change that environment. A thermostat is an active instrument. It determines what the environment will be. It effects change in order to create a climate."—pp. 17-18.

Great leaders are able to set the temperature and create an environment where growth and results continue even in difficult and challenging circumstances. Difficult moments reveal our true character. Are we easily swayed by the swirling winds around us or do we hold a steady course and do what it takes to persist in the face of tremendous adversity and difficulty?

What type of leader are you at your store?

Do you simply record the sales that are made at the end of each day or do you create the environment necessary to have your sales rise?

Having the courage to remain persistent and exerting the effort it takes to create consistent accomplishment and results is what generates momentum. It takes a lot of work and discipline to stay steady while continually analyzing performance in order to increase closing percentages **and** increase sales month after month.

Edgar A. Guest (one of my favorite poets) said this:

> "When things go wrong as they sometimes will,
> When the road you're trudging seems all uphill,
> When the funds are low and the debts are high,
> And you want to smile, but you have to sigh,
> When care is pressing you down a bit,
> Rest if you must, but don't you quit.
> Success is failure turned inside out,
> The silver tint in the clouds of doubt,
> And you never can tell how close you are,
> It may be near when it seems afar.
> So stick to the fight when you're hardest hit,
> It's when things go wrong that you mustn't quit."

As the poem says, persistence and steadiness are what keep the thermostat leader up in a down economy.

There is a big distinction in the results that come from being a thermostat leader versus a thermometer one. Make the commitment and choose to be a thermostat leader.

I recently read a book about the birth of Federal Express and the great thermostat leader, Fred Smith. The story of how Fed Ex got started is a great example of understanding the power of commitment, teamwork, and vision and the power of being a thermostat leader.

When Fred Smith created FedEx, he surrounded himself with a few committed people. Not many others believed his concept would work—it was so different than anything that had ever been done before. His concept was that all packages would fly from their city to a central hub in Memphis, Tennessee, to be sorted and loaded on planes returning to the city of the package's home destination.

Another way of looking at it – he believed that the best way to deliver a package from Sacramento to Los Angeles was through Memphis, Tennessee. You can see why he received some skepticism that his idea would work. When Fred Smith was at Yale and explained his idea in a paper, his professor gave him a C. The investment community thought his concept wasn't logical.

Fred believed in his mission and gathered a group of committed individuals around him. In April 1973, FedEx was born.

"You can imagine the excitement that first night of operation! Fourteen FedEx planes in fourteen cities made their first midnight trip to Memphis. The packages were sorted and then reloaded on planes that would take them to their destination. The entire FedEx team was waiting to count their packages and celebrate their success.

One by one they unloaded the planes. When all of the packages were counted, there were twelve packages on the fourteen planes. Two more planes than packages! Obviously, that's not a good business model. How discouraging the first night's results must have been!

Yes, everyone was disappointed, but Fred Smith had created [a leadership culture and his people] were committed to pay the price to make the business succeed.

In fact, when money was tight in the early days, several pilots used their personal credit cards to fuel their planes. Those people were committed and, as they say, the rest is history.

Tonight, FedEx will sort and deliver millions of packages. Revenues are over $50 billion. More than 300,000 employees are on the payroll, thanks to those first committed employees and the leadership of Fred Smith." —David Cottrell, *Monday Morning Choices*, pp. 18-19.

Now, it would be nice if our bridal stores could grow to *that* kind of level, but the key here is the environment of leadership that Fred Smith fostered even when they were small. He believed in his concept, cast his vision, and developed his key personnel to help make this vision possible. This is our challenge at our stores as well.

There is no question that all of us have been going through difficult times in this recession. What makes the difference is rising to the occasion in the difficult moments and showing others what to do by your actions and your attitude.

Jeff King, a sled dog racer who has won the Iditarod (an 1,100 mile race from Anchorage to Nome, Alaska) three times in 1993, 1996, and 1998 recently shared an experience about how he chooses the lead dog in his races that I think is very instructive. This story is shared by Kent Millard in John Maxwell's book *Leadership Gold*. Millard says:

"Jeff told us that when he starts the Iditarod race he starts with sixteen dogs and rotates the lead dog frequently to give all the dogs a chance to lead since every one of them wants to be the lead dog. Eventually, he finds the dog that is the real leader because it is a dog that is energetic and persistent in leading, and that dog becomes the leader of the pack. It is chosen as the leader because it leads; it is able to motivate the other dogs to follow by its own energy and enthusiasm. Jeff told us that in 1996, the lead dog was a two-and-a-half-year-old female, which is very unusual since there were only two females in the pack and she was so young and smaller than the other male dogs. But, he said with emotion in his voice, 'She was our leader; when a blizzard came, she didn't give up. She kept barking and running even when the snow was over her head and inspired us all to keep going. Even at her young age, she has the mental maturity of a leader.' When Jeff was congratulated for winning the 1998 Iditarod, he lifted up his lead dog and said, 'Here is the leader who won the race for us.'" —*Leadership Gold*, p. 139.

Which leaders do you have at your store that help you win your race each week by having high sales and consistent results no matter what is happening on Wall Street?

As Rudy Giuliani said, "When the right person is the leader, he does even better during tough times."

I hope this chapter has helped you think about some of the fundamental areas of your business that you may have forgotten or ignored. Study the Bridal Business Success Triangle and think about the aspects of your business that you have been trying to forget instead of face head on. Your business will only get better when you get better. When you focus on these areas, your confidence and your competence will grow and you'll be able to weather the storms to become a great success in the bridal business.

Chapter 2

Avoid Mistakes

The economic recession that we are currently experiencing has caused many retailers and bridal retailers to think much more critically about how they are operating their businesses. In many cases, fundamental weaknesses in business models are being exposed as a result of this situation. It isn't hard to succeed in most businesses in a flourishing economy with customers who are happily spending money they don't have with easily acquired credit. Now, that that this credit isn't as readily available, fundamental weaknesses in many business models are being exposed for what they are since a good economy often tends to cover up the fundamental weaknesses any business may have. In order to make it through these challenging times, we all need to focus on sound business fundamentals since those businesses with the strongest fundamentals across the board will be the ones who survive and thrive in the emerging new economy.

Most people don't like to confront their weaknesses. But simply ignoring them doesn't make them go away. In fact, it often accelerates the problem until the pending crash becomes even greater. Here are seven mistakes that many bridal retailers have had exposed as a result of the recession and what to do about them.

1. Mistake #1: Not understanding what your true costs really are.

Profit on wedding gowns is not *just* MSRP minus manufacturer's cost. As Shari Waters recently pointed out in an excellent article about retailing pricing strategies: "Two key elements in factoring product cost is the cost of goods and the amount of operating expense. The cost of goods includes the amount paid for the product, plus any shipping or handling expenses. The cost of operating the business, or operating expense, includes overhead, payroll, marketing and office supplies. Regardless of the pricing strategy used, the retail price of the products should more than cover the cost of obtaining the goods plus the expenses related to operating the business. **A retailer simply cannot succeed in business if they continue to sell their products below cost.**" The total cost is not just what you pay for the dress (and this is a hard truth that many retailers are coming to grips with in these challenging times). ***You also have to factor in your operating costs.*** Stores who try to operate without understanding their *true* costs jeopardize their long-term survival in the marketplace.

What you can do about this mistake: Invest in private lines that boost your profitability. Private lines have become very important to bridal retailers in recent years since they are often offered at lower prices than traditional manufacturers charge (because there is not high overhead and added advertising costs). In addition, they usually operate within a territorial framework (without any Internet sales) so that stores can mark the dresses up higher without fear of price cutting by close competitors.

In addition, you need to look carefully at your operating costs. Everything counts in this market and if there are operating costs that are unnecessary or things that can be done for less, make these changes as soon as you can. Knowing your costs and carefully cutting out unnecessary expenses will help you be more profitable as well.

2. Mistake #2: Charging less than your competitors.

Even though this has been proven to not be a good long-term strategy, retailers continue to slash prices in order to get sales. The only time this would be successful is if you have negotiated the best prices, reduced your operating costs and have a marketing strategy to focus on price specials. Wal-Mart is a good example of a business that has successfully done all three of these. Most independent bridal stores are not in a position to negotiate better prices because they don't buy the large amounts required for such prices. Stores who cut prices with special offers are cutting into their own profits to get the sale. Price cutting really is a self-inflicted wound.

What you can do about this mistake: Look for ways that you can build more value. When you scale back value in order to save money, you end up looking cheap to brides in your market. The best thing you can do is to raise value without adding expense. You can do this by offering additional information and resources to brides through monthly newsletters, wedding planning seminars (held at your store and put on by either you or wedding planners in your area) and by offering special incentives to brides only available when they purchase a gown at your store.

We have found that offering special incentives from local wedding vendors, promoting our referral program, and offering savings on accessories to decisive brides who buy the first time they come into the store have helped us to differentiate our store and build our value in the eyes of brides who come into our store. Look for cost effective ways you can raise your value in the eyes of the brides in your market. When you do so, you will differentiate yourself from your competitors in ways that will help you get the sale AND still be profitable.

3. Mistake #3: Not positioning your store properly.

As I mentioned, many retailers have resorted to lowering their prices because of their concerns about the economy. On the other hand, a few businesses have successfully raised prices (Colgate-Palmolive, Proctor and Gamble, and McDonald's very recently raised prices on many of their products). You may be wondering how any business could be looking at raising prices in our current economic climate.

Geoff Colvin in an article in *Fortune Magazine* (February 2009) entitled, "Yes, You Can Raise Prices" unveils a very interesting price / power matrix that helps to explain why some companies are profiting by raising their prices and why some are lowering their prices to get more customers (and consequently cutting into their profits). It is really an excellent explanation about positioning and how this should be done.

This matrix exposes a common problem that many bridal retailers have found themselves in as the recession has continued and deepened in some areas. This matrix explains a lot about why the companies that position their products as unique necessities can charge a premium price and get it even in slower economic times. The lesson here is one that all of us should carefully evaluate in our own bridal stores.

There are four categories in the matrix which is based on Colvin's illustration and observations in the article. You can see this illustrated below:

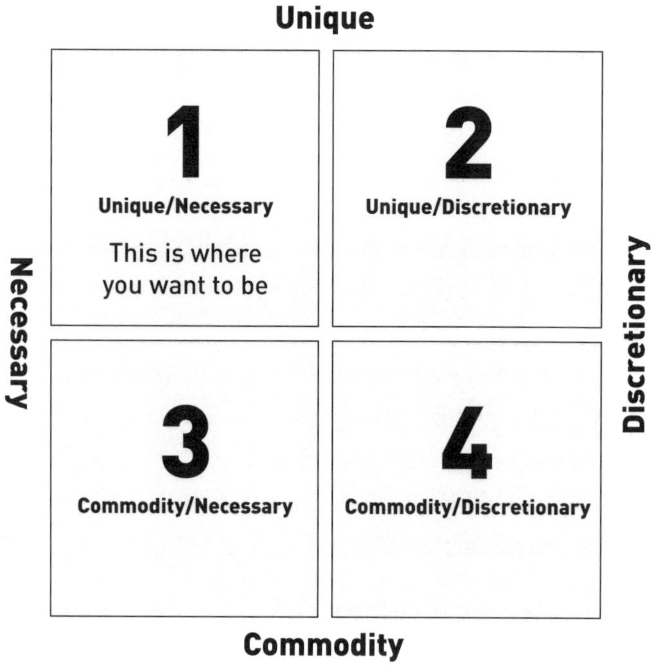

Category 4 (Commodity/Discretionary): This is where the greatest price suppression occurs and the marketer has the least power. Examples of businesses that are in this category are the airlines and the automobile industry. Many travelers don't *need* to travel now (it is discretionary) since they can postpone their vacation or drive instead. Businesspeople are using video-conferencing and online meeting resources such as Go-To-Meeting instead of traveling now. Cutting prices to **get** people to travel (when airline competitors are doing so) isn't necessarily effective either because this doesn't mean that people will anyway just because of that. The airline industry has become commoditized to the point that if you are flying now, the only reason to choose one commercial airline over another (mostly) is the route, time (when and how long), and who has the lowest price.

However, sales of private jets and time shares of private jets are way up because they have repositioned private air travel as unique and necessary (Category 1 – which will be explained shortly) to the market segment they specialize and focus on. It costs more but to their customers it is worth it because of the security, time-saving, hassle-free experience they'll have **and** as an added benefit it's hard to lose your luggage on your own plane.

The automobile industry is facing the same challenge. Car owners can wait another year before they get a new car. They don't have to have it now. In addition, there is an incredible number of choices and little to no differentiation between brands. To top it all off, the overcrowded marketplace is going through a phase of vicious price cutting to get sales that will eventually weed out the weakest competitors. The car companies that emerge from this recession will be those who have successfully cut their costs and focused on new, unique product offerings that are specialized and perceived as being an absolute necessity to the markets they serve.

Category 3 (Commodity/Necessary): This is where groceries and basic necessity items fall such as gasoline, light bulbs, soap, etc. As mentioned earlier, this is where some companies are able to raise prices because they dominate the market and what they sell is an absolute necessity. For example, when gasoline prices go up, overall sales don't necessarily go down since people **need** their transportation. The problem with being in this category is that most market categories are dominated by giant big box stores who have huge buying power and the financial ability to shrink their margins and still be successful. Most products and services that are in this category have very little differentiation and this is why they are commodities. David's Bridal and the Internet sites are in this category. They have larger buying power so they can afford to offer dresses for less (or package dresses with a free pair of shoes or accessory and offer free shipping).

Category 2 (Unique/Discretionary): This category includes Rolls-Royce, Ferrari, Hermes or Louis Vuitton handbags, dining out at an expensive restaurant, and high tech gadgets such as the iPhone. These are unique offerings in the marketplace, but no one **needs** any of these things *now* rather than *later*. Most items in this category are prestige items that buyers purchase because it reinforces or helps them establish their own image. Businesses that discount in this category are not very successful as discounting does not usually do much to increase sales here. This is because a discount doesn't do much to alter how someone feels about having a prestige item (there's a reason it is supposed to be expensive).

Category 1 (Unique/Necessary): This is the category where you want to be. When you are in this category, your dresses and services are *perceived* by brides in your area to be a necessity. Others in the market may not feel it is a necessity, but for your customers it is—a good example of this is celebrity authority figures such as Monique Lhuillier or Vera Wang (although she has diminished her brand as of late by trying to be all things to all people). You can also be perceived as being a unique provider or offering unique advantages by how you pre-sell brides coming into your store. You can also offer unique advantages to buying at your store that no one else does (wedding vendor coupons, referral program, etc.) In some cases, you can even move products from one category to another. For example, the iPhone has moved from being a unique/discretionary item to a unique/necessary item as more and more people have adopted it and people feel peer-pressure to have one because it elevates their status and because "everyone has one".

I really like Colvin's conclusion to this article. He says:

"Smart companies use tools like this to analyze customers. The matrix is based entirely on customer perceptions, which vary widely, so for any product or service it's useful to plot the perceptions of each customer segment. That way you can create different value propositions in which price will play greater or lesser roles. McKinsey, for example, reports that a beverage company found price sensitivity varied by a factor of three just across zip codes within Jacksonville. Offering all of them the same price wouldn't make much sense; varying prices in the obvious way would be a simple way to increase total profit."

He concludes with this observation:

"Pricing is always important, but in booms you don't have to get it exactly right. Now you do. Decide carefully, because you'll be living with the consequences for a long time."

If you want to make the recession irrelevant to your bridal business, you need to be *perceived* as being a unique necessity. This gives you the most power as a marketer and conversely the ability to charge a price that allows you to be the most profitable.

4. Mistake #4: Not improving your marketing materials or relying on outdated marketing that no longer brings in brides.

Today's marketplace is very crowded. There is more competition than there has ever been. Ads that brought brides into the store in the past no longer do so. Most ads have no call to action (or reason for the bride to act now) and most of the ads for stores today look like one another (except with a different picture). The root cause of this problem is that most bridal stores have relied on image marketing in the past (a picture with their logo, address, phone number, web site, and hours) and stop there. Many bridal retailers look at what their competitors are doing and then do the same thing (thinking, "It must be working for them.") The unfortunate reality is that these ads no longer work effectively because there is no invitation for the bride to take action and do something. Having a pretty ad without great marketing copy that invites brides to do something may be noticed by *some* brides, but if everyone has access to those lines, you won't be very effective. Too many ads today are really creative without being persuasive. They have a pretty picture, but don't really cause the bride to want to take action.

What you can do about this mistake: Revisit your marketing and hone in on your unique competitive advantages. Your marketing should be more than just a print ad. You should also be offering informative information that is believable, memorable and *causes* the bride to ***want*** to come into your store. You can do this through a monthly newsletter, on your website, or via email. The unfortunate reality is that many web sites of bridal retailers are doing more damage than good. Make sure your site is updated and helps brides understand exactly *why* you are the best choice for her to get her dress from you.

5. Mistake #5: Being passive about your marketing.

Marketing is the lifeblood of your store. If you stop doing it, you will eventually see the decline in traffic and corresponding decrease in sales. Unfortunately, many retailers don't market when they are busy thinking that things are fine and that there is no need to spend money when they are busy with brides. Marketing needs to be a proactive process. Waking up to the reality that your traffic has dropped off is an indicator that you are guilty of this mistake. You have to be proactive (especially when it is busy) to ensure that you have a flow of brides coming into your business. Having your marketing calendar in place a year in advance helps to ensure that you always have marketing promotions and campaigns in place to help you keep your traffic steady, but implementation of that calendar is the key to success.

What you can do about this mistake: If you don't already have a marketing calendar, make one now. It can be for the next three months to start, but you shouldn't stop there. You really should get together a marketing campaign that details all of the strategies you will use to get brides into your marketing funnel and into your store for an entire year. My "Marketing Your Bridal Store" CD set is packed with ideas on how you can do this and for more advanced help and strategies you may want to look into being a part of my Quantum Leap Program. This program includes made-for-you postcards and marketing collateral that stores are using to generate traffic and get results. If you are interested in receiving more information about being involved in this program, email me at info@bridaltrainingsystems.com.

6. Mistake #6: Not improving your sales process.

If you're like many bridal retailers, you've seen a dramatic drop in sales during the recession as prom sales have slowed and bridal sales seem few and far between. Coasting along with how you used to sell is no longer effective. Brides today are scared about parting with their money. They've been listening to the doom and gloom in the news and they don't have much confidence in buying anything at all.

There are two types of brides in today's economy: 1) Those that don't have the ability to buy, and 2) Those who have the willingness to buy. Unfortunately, some brides today find themselves in the first category because of lost jobs, foreclosures, and dried up credit. These brides may need lower priced options or may have to wait until they get back on their feet again. Fortunately, the majority of consumers in any market (especially the wedding market) have money but they are **not willing** to spend it **now** unless they are *persuaded* that now is the right time to buy by a confident, professional seller.

What you can do about this mistake: In order to overcome this challenge and sell now, you have to focus all of your energy into ***moving*** brides from a *completely unmotivated position where they are not willing to buy at all* to *one where they are willing to buy and they will.* To explain this, let's say that the threshold to buy a wedding gown is plotted on a scale from 1 to 100 (1 being completely non-motivated to buy anything to 100 being completely ready to buy a dress now). In more economically prosperous times, the majority of brides entering bridal salons may have been at a 50 (they would be willing and able to buy a dress now if they found the right one). The bridal consultant would have to raise her from 50 to 100 to make the sale.

Today, **the gap** between the attitude the bride has when she enters the store and the threshold to make the decision to buy **has widened**. Many brides now enter the bridal salon at a 10, 15, or 25 as opposed to the 50 that they may have been at a few months or years ago. This means that the bridal consultant working with each bride must expend *more* energy, enthusiasm, and excitement in order to move the bride up the scale to cross the threshold and make the decision to buy.

Since selling is really just a transfer of enthusiasm, many bridal consultants and store owners have found that it requires much more patience and finely honed sales skills in order to bring brides from the depths of apathy to the crest of the threshold to buy now. Unfortunately, many bridal consultants give up too soon or don't have the selling skills necessary to overcome the numerous objections that an apathetic buyer has. As a result, they have seen their sales plummet. Blaming this on the economy is a quick and easy excuse when the reality is that brides today have to be coddled with much more confidence, covert sales strategies, and enthusiasm in order to get the sale. It is easy to get discouraged in sales. There are so many ups and downs. As leaders at our stores, we have to constantly offer positive feedback to our consultants and look for ways to help brides move from an apathetic to excited state more rapidly. Those who do this will be much more successful in selling than those who emotionally throw in the towel because the nature of the sale has changed.

7. Mistake #7: Relying on manufacturers to promote their stores and do their marketing for them.

In years past, many retailers have relied on the marketing budgets of manufacturers to promote their lines to brides through numerous methods. Unfortunately, these same manufacturers also list all of the stores where their lines can be purchased. Brides find a dress they love and then call through this published list to find the store who will sell it to them for the best price. Even though most stores are supposed to sell a dress at a MSRP (manufacturer's suggested retail price), brides can play against stores until they get one of them to succumb to a lower price or buy online (since there is no sales tax and in many cases a free accessory offer as well). In the end, if everyone carries the same product (and it is available from multiple sources especially over the Internet where overhead is lower), brides will *always* differentiate on price.

What you can do about this mistake: The only way to successfully overcome the commoditization that is happening with many bridal lines today is to **focus on branding *your* store** instead of relying on others to do it for you. Over 10 years ago marketing and branding experts Al Ries and his daughter Laura Ries wrote an excellent book about the laws of branding. They make this statement in the introduction:

"From a business point of view, branding in the marketplace is very similar to branding on the ranch. A branding program should be designed to differentiate your product from all the other cattle on the range. Even if all the other cattle on the range look pretty much alike. A successful branding program is based on the concept of singularity. It creates in the mind of the prospect the perception that there is no product (or store) on the market quite like your product (or your store)." —*The 22 Immutable Laws of Branding*, p. 7.

When you brand your store, you can create brides that are loyal to your store and the different experience they will have at your store as compared to anywhere else. Because the bride knows about what you offer at your store, you can promote your difference and provide variety in a way that your competitors can't. I'll go into a lot more detail about how to brand your store successfully in chapter 10.

If you will take the time to overcome these common mistakes and really take the time to define *why you are unique and different* from your competitors, along with utilizing more effective marketing and sales strategies, you will be able to weather the recession and beat your competitors. If you don't, your competitors likely will and you will be defined by default. Look closely at the systems that make up your business and resolve to fix the leaks and weaknesses that may have sprung up or been exposed by the recession. There is a lot of good that can come from fixing these systems while improving your overall sales and profitability.

Chapter 3

Focus on What You Can Control to Produce Results

One of the biggest traps we fall into as small business owners is that we focus on what is happening to us and external problems in our industry that we don't have a lot of control over. Individually, we don't have a lot of control over what is happening in the stock market or the day to day fluctuations in our economy. Instead, we should do as achievers do—focus on what we want to produce and cause to happen.

Ask yourself: Where is your focus throughout the day?

Do you spend time thinking, talking, and focusing on things you have little to no control over?

or

Do you spend time thinking, talking, and focusing on things you can control?

Instead of listing and talking about the myriad of things we could focus on that we may not be able to control, I'd like to point out five things that we should spend more time on that we *can* control:

1. Productivity

This is everything in the bridal business. The most important areas that we can control are the areas of selling and marketing. A key shift to make in what you control is to shift your thinking from skills to systems. A system is defined as a set of things, actions, ideas and information that interact with each other, and in so doing, alter other systems. For example, ***if* you do not have a system for selling, you are at the mercy of the bride's system for not buying.**

Do you have a selling and marketing system at your store?

Do each of your bridal consultants handle objections the same way?

Do you each handle all of the situations that come up in the same way?

If you don't already have an effective sales and marketing system, I would encourage you to get one. The sales training DVDs I offer on www.bridaltrainingsystems.com have proven to be an effective selling system for stores across the country and can help you get better results as well.

Another key productivity area you can focus on is how well you are closing sales. The key is to evaluate both the successful ones and those that didn't happen. Find out the commonalities that are causing the sale to happen and the objections or obstacles to why they aren't. Then, train your staff members to sell better based on your evaluation. Our sales training program and the sales flash cards that we train our staff with were created out of such evaluations. You can't get better at closing if you aren't evaluating why you're not.

One of the most important things to focus on and manage is our bridal consultant's sales performance. Part of this is setting a standard of performance for the job. It is so important to create an expectation and hold bridal consultants accountable to reaching their daily goal. As the old saying goes, "If you can't measure it, you can't manage it."

Here are some questions we use to think through how well our interaction with the brides who come into our store went. Asking these questions or others like them has made a world of difference in improving our closing ratios.

1) How long did I work with the bride? Could I have been more effective?

2) Did I deliver the most compelling message about why our store is the best one to buy from? How could I have done this better?

3) Did the bride trust me? Did she feel comfortable enough to tell me what she really thought of the gowns she was trying on?

4) Would I have bought the dress I was selling from myself?

5) What did the bride do at the end of our time together? Did I create urgency for her to buy her dress now, rather than later?

6) If the bride bought her dress from me, could I have sold her accessories?

7) What do I think this bride would say about me, our store, and the time we spent together?

Then, as you evaluate these questions (or your own) give your consultants feedback that helps them improve, especially if they didn't close the sale.

We actually have our bridal consultants fill out a form each day that is titled "What I could have done to make the sale..." This helps me know what we should train on and gives me the chance to offer specific coaching and feedback to help them get better at selling, especially if I wasn't there to help them evaluate how well they did or help them close the sale. Our end goal should always be to help them improve and be the kind of leader they want to follow because they see us succeeding at selling.

The last productivity area I will mention here is your marketing focus. Here are two questions to ask yourself as you think about your marketing focus:

1. Which of my marketing or sales efforts brought in the bulk of my sales? What percentage of my business comes from this particular effort now?

2. Do I test various aspects of my marketing and selling activities to make sure they're producing the best and most profitable results?

If a marketing approach isn't working, stop doing it and look for productive ones that will bring in brides. You have to inspect what you expect. Always be looking for ways to get more back for what you spend.

Remember, efficiency is doing things right. Effectiveness is doing the right things. Sales and marketing are productivity areas that we should always be focused on.

2. Customer Satisfaction

With all of this talk about the economy and what we should be focusing on, sometimes we forget that the most important thing we do is personally interact with and focus on the brides coming into our stores. Remember, nothing good comes out of trying to think or do too many things at once.

Steve Chandler in his book *100 Ways to Motivate People* makes this observation:

"It's important that I don't race around thinking that I've got too much to do. Because I don't have too much to do. The truth is, there is only one thing to do, and that is the one thing I have chosen to do right now."

He adds:

"Doing more than one thing at a time produces fear, adrenaline, and anxiety in the human system and people pick up on that. People are not drawn to that. They keep away from that."

Think about this in context with the brides coming into your store. The only way you can create a great experience is to focus on the bride in front of you, not the mountains of work you have waiting for you in your office.

Focus on the bride in front of you. Isn't she the only thing that really matters at the moment you are working with her?

Most of the time when we lose the sale, it is because we are not *really* focusing on the bride.

Here are three questions to focus on in this area:

1) What are brides and prom girls saying about your store?

2) Are they talking about their great experiences at your store?

3) How can you encourage that better?

3. Profitability

One of the biggest mistakes businesses can make during challenging times is focusing more on sales than on profits. This may be a quick short-term solution to cash flow shortages, but long-term it can dramatically affect your long-term staying power in the bridal business.

Many bridal store owners today are re-evaluating the entire way they have been doing business and looking at carrying more private lines in their stores. Such lines can be promoted in your store by motivating your bridal consultants with results based bonuses when they sell those more profitable lines. Carefully analyze your P&L statements to help you make decisions about where you can cut back and how you can increase your profitability in future months.

Here are three questions to ask yourself as you focus on your store's profitability:

1) What are our most profitable products and services? Which lines are most profitable?

2) Are we focusing on selling those over other products?

3) What are the things that contribute most to our bottom line?

4. Quality of Experience Your Brides and Prom Customers Have at Your Store

The goal to delight each of the prospective brides who walk through our doors is a noble and challenging goal. It is something we can all strive for. We can all be better at going beyond just aiming to satisfy our customers.

The first six words of the business classic *Good to Great* state, "The enemy of great is good." We should never be satisfied with just *good* customer service. We should all strive to be *exceptional* throughout our entire interaction with each bride and prom customer.

Because in the end, if we only do what average bridal stores do, we'll never be better than they are. We have to aim higher.

At our bridal store, we want to partner with brides to provide exquisite and beautiful gowns that will help them look and feel absolutely gorgeous on their wedding day. We want every bride to leave our store feeling more beautiful than when she walked in. We want to give responsive service and personalized advice, be seen as a trusted advisor for each bride's wedding and to be known in our market area as the store that cares.

Here are some questions to focus on as you consider the experience your customers are having at your store:

1) How does the customer service in your store measure up? Does it beat the pants off your competitors? As the old saying goes: "When there is not much difference between your product and that of your competitors, there had better be a big difference in the way you deal with your customers."

2) Do you delight and dazzle the brides and prom girls coming into your store, or are they disappointed and discouraged when they leave or when they come to you with legitimate concerns and problems?

3) How are your brides treated when they deal with you?

4) Where do you rate in the marketplace in terms of quality?

5. Innovation

When you consider any type of innovation, consider the Law of Three – in order to be innovative, you need to be better in at least three areas. For example, 7-Eleven or Walgreen's competitive advantage is convenience. They build stores that are close to you so you don't have to drive very far to get medicine or basic needs items. Domino's and McDonald's have built their businesses around the competitive advantage of speed. Domino's became popular by offering pizzas in less than 30 minutes or they were free.

Here are some questions for you to consider as you focus on being more innovative in your bridal market:

1) Ask: What is your competitive advantage in your area in the bridal and prom markets? What makes you better? Are there things that you could change to be even better?

2) In what ways are you superior to your competition?

3) In what way does your store excel? You can't say you give

quality and service because everyone says that. When everyone says something, it doesn't mean very much at all. An important part of concentrating on what you do best is to specialize. The natural tendency is to generalize and try to be good at everything. Unfortunately, when this happens you end up being good at nothing.

4) Ask yourself: What products or lines do I carry today? What will it be tomorrow the way things are going? What could it be? What should it be? Stay on top of what is going on in the marketplace – ask yourself – What is selling and why?

Ralph Waldo Emerson once said: "Shallow people believe in luck. Wise and strong people believe in cause and effect." Focus on the causes that will create the effects you want. You are in control. You determine what happens. Work on the areas that you can control. Focus on the critical success factors that will lead to the results you desire and you will be successful even in these uncertain and complicated times.

Chapter 4

Create Perceptions You Want Others to Have About You and Your Store

I recently read a book by Bob Rice entitled *Three Moves Ahead* that articulated what I have believed for years about the key to successful marketing: the importance of becoming a specialist and dominating a niche instead of trying to be all things for all people. In the book he compares business to a game of chess.

The best part of this book is where he makes the distinction between the way beginners and experts look at a chessboard. He says:

"What novices see is a tangle of Knights and Bishops, pawns, and Rooks. They try to figure out what's about to take what. From their point of view, all the 'action' is at the piece level.

When Grandmasters look at a chessboard, they see something completely different: the squares themselves. Maybe there are pieces on them, maybe not, but they see the fight as one to control squares: lines of them in any direction (diagonals, files, and ranks), color complexes (light or dark), or even, as we'll see in this chapter, just one single square. The pieces are means of controlling space, not ends in themselves."

Then he makes this observation:

"Businesspeople exhibit a similar dichotomy. Average executives see products to push, attack, and defend; great executives see markets to control.

At the typical company, meetings about increasing revenue focus on attacking a competitor's product (his pieces) or pushing the existing product (our pieces) into a new market. This works infrequently because such thinking is all about the 'pieces', the products themselves, and not about creating the sorts of answers for underlying customer needs that would yield market control. Peter Drucker would call this selling (attacking or pushing products) rather than marketing (targeting market space by developing products to satisfy consumer demands)." —Bob Rice, *Three Moves Ahead*, pp. 120-121.

So, the marketing principle he is trying to teach and that I want to expand on in this book is this:

Dominate market squares, instead of focusing on selling individual pieces of a particular dress or designer.

I love this example in Rice's book:

"We can see the difference clearly by comparing Apple and Sony, an interesting pair because they both have long histories of creating cool electronics, and they have two of the great brands of the world. Their parallels, and currently very different trajectories, speak volumes about the right way to look at a business chessboard.

First, let's reflect on Sony's unprecedented 30-year run at innovating products that became runaway hits (a record that Apple is now chasing). What was behind the first transistor radio, the first portable television, early videocassette players, the Walkman, and the 3.5-inch floppy disk? More than anything else, it was that Sony's amazing founder, Akio Morita, along with a close team of advisors, spent huge amounts of time simply trying to understand what consumers were trying to do with electronics. Their goal was to use their expertise to deliver simple-to-use products that met unaddressed customer needs. They succeeded spectacularly, over and over again (if that sounds like the modern Apple, there's a reason). He was an incredible player, a guy who could see market squares and conquer them.

That incredible run more or less ended in the early eighties when Morita let go of the product innovation and launch process. Since then, Sony's product development process has become dominated by internal competition among scores of development teams. Each is pushing a design based on outflanking a competitive product's feature set or 'productizing' an engineering brainstorm. It is, essentially, an invention contest largely judged by marketing experts and financial types, who then look to push the winning pieces toward becoming products.

Sony's recent problems reflect the change in its board vision. It used to see market squares; now it sees product pieces. The result is many fantastic novelties, like the Aibo robotic dog, that have absolutely no natural market....When Steve Jobs taught himself business chess, you can imagine he studied 'Morita's greatest games'. He plays precisely the same style, applying his company's expertise to provide consumers elegant, easy-to-use products that do things consumers actually want done. He is completely focused on finding the squares and then controlling them, not just pushing his company's pieces around.

In fact, he has improved on the great master's play by extending the 'understand-the-customer' mantra to an entirely new level. It seems that every single employee at Apple knows who its customer is and what the customer wants. They design products to take control of a file or diagonal, a specific set of connected market squares; young users, graphics professionals, people who want computers to be simple and easy.

When Apple thinks about how cool a product would be, they're thinking about how it would satisfy market needs, not how novel or sleek it is (sure, that the product looks good helps, but that's secondary; their competitors make tons of attractive disasters). Apple understands the squares it's after and then finds a 'piece' to control them, whether that's a brand new appliance, like the iPhone, or just an intuitive application that makes common tasks easier, like iMovie. Apple focuses on the squares.

Perhaps the most amazing single aspect of this approach through, is how Apple has been able to extend it to the retail space. Here again, the comparison with Sony is telling.

Apple was pushed to open the Apple stores by the realization that the Best Buys of the world would never be able to display and explain Apple's products as anything other than just another computer; it was effectively forced into it to keep the basic value proposition intact. It started with a mock-up in a warehouse near the Apple campus but recognized that the first try was all wrong: The merchandise was laid out by product category (all the laptops were stacked together, as is typical in stores), not by customer needs (how the products could be used to solve different problems: video capture and editing, for example). So it tore down its first try and reorganized so that products were grouped together by what problems they solved for the consumer, a retail space manifestation of its design principles. And the coup de grace in user-friendliness was the 'genius bar' in the back, where customers could get all the advice—and repair services—they need.

Compare this approach with Sony's 'style stores': attractive, sleek, sort of a fashion house for their products. Indeed, that's what they were designed to be: a showcase. But showcases don't solve problems: they push product pieces. Indeed, it is difficult to get quality advice from the Sony personnel about how to hook up its premium equipment (an unthinkable occurrence at an Apple store), although they certainly do look good in that all-black.

The results are in, and Apple is now the world champion of retailing. Its stores generate by far the most dollars per square foot of retail space in the country, outstripping Tiffany by more than 50 percent and other electronics outlets by 400 percent and more, according to one report by Sanford Bernstein. Sony is a blip too small to measure." —Bob Rice, *Three Moves Ahead*, pp. 121-124.

When we had a temporary prom store in the mall during a recent prom season, I was amazed to learn about Apple's success. The VP of leasing at the mall told me that when stores come to find out their sales per square foot, they now have to separate Apple's sales from all of the rest of the stores at the mall because it skews the numbers *that* much.

Where is your focus? Do you try to succeed in the bridal business by solely attacking your competitor's products (such and such a line isn't very good or our price is better) or introducing your own new lines (and becoming the only store that carries such and such a line) or are you focusing on dominating a market square?

Bob Rice identifies the importance of having a business strong square. He says:

"Business strong squares are tightly defined market niches in which a company *is the best there is*. This is not a 'core competency,' which is merely what the company happens to be best at. The difference is absolutely fundamental. Strong-square strategy demands that you control some niche, no matter how narrow. If you don't have one, get one." —Bob Rice, *Three Moves Ahead*, p. 125.

What is your market niche in the bridal industry?

What are you the best in the world at?

What could you be?

When you look at the market in your area, what opportunities do you see?

What squares could you dominate and control in your market?

Some serious reflection on this issue is critical to the future success of your store. Specialization will help you become more successful, more profitable, and better known in your market. Generalization, or being a me-too store, will limit you to mediocre results, profits and obscurity.

Which one do you *really* want?

In order to help you in your quest to dominate the bridal market in your region, here are ten of the best marketing principles and numerous marketing tactics you can use to increase sales and beat your competitors.

1. Be first or create the perception of being first in the mind of your brides.

Several years ago in 1993, marketing gurus Jack Trout and Al Ries wrote a best-selling book entitled, *The 22 Immutable Laws of Marketing*. This is one of the best books ever written on marketing and positioning. You need to get, read and study this important book. The first five laws in this book are so important that I want to highlight them here because they embody the principle of being first in the minds of the brides in your area. Ries & Trout's first five laws are:

1) The Law of Leadership: It's better to be first than it is to be better.

Trout and Ries explain:

"You can demonstrate the law of leadership by asking yourself two questions:

1) What's the name of the first person to fly the Atlantic Ocean solo? Charles Lindbergh, right?

2) What's the name of the second person to fly the Atlantic Ocean solo? Not so easy to answer, is it?

> The second person to fly the Atlantic Ocean solo was Bert Hinkler. Bert was a better pilot than Charlie—he flew faster, he consumed less fuel. Yet who has ever heard of Bert Hinkler?" —Al Ries and Jack Trout, *The 22 Immutable Laws of Marketing*, p. 3.

There are numerous examples in the book of companies and institutions who were first that we all know and recognize, yet can't tell you who is second. Harvard, Hertz, IBM, Coca-Cola, *Time* magazine, *People* magazine, Gillette, Hewlett Packard (first desktop laser printer), Kleenex, Xerox, Advil, and Tylenol.

All of us know of these examples, yet it is amazing how many businesses try to offer a better product strategy instead of trying to be first in a category.

As Ries and Trout say:

"If the secret of success is getting into the prospect's mind first, what strategy are most companies committed to? The better-product strategy." —Al Ries and Jack Trout, *The 22 Immutable Laws of Marketing*, p. 8.

How many bridal store owners do you know who have gotten into this business because they had a bad experience at a bridal store when they got married and decided they could do it better?

The answer: A lot (and you may be one of them). Fortunately, even if you had that philosophy when you began, you can follow other marketing principles to help you rise to the top and dominate your market region.

As Ries and Trout ask:

"Neil Armstrong was the first person to walk on the moon. Who was second?

Roger Bannister was the first person to run a four-minute mile. Who was second?

George Washington was the first president of the United States? Who was second?

Thomas' was the first brand of English muffin. What was second?

Gatorade was the first sports drink. What was second?

If you're second in the prospect's mind, are you doomed to languish forever with Buzz Aldrin, John Landy, John Adams, some unknown English muffin, and some unknown sports drink? Not necessarily. Fortunately, there are other laws." —Al Ries and Jack Trout, *The 22 Immutable Laws of Marketing*, pp. 8-9.

So, in summary: The basic issue in marketing is creating a category (i.e. a given type of product or service) you can be first in. It's the law of leadership. It's better to be first than it is to be better. It's much easier to get into the mind first than it is to try to convince a bride you have a better product than the store that did get there first.

2) The Law of the Category: If you can't be first in a category, set up a new category you can be first in.

In the book, they give the example of how this can be done.

> Ries and Trout ask:
>
> "What's the name of the third person to fly the Atlantic Ocean solo? If you didn't know that Bert Hinkler was the second person to fly the Atlantic, you might figure you had no chance at all to know the name of the third person. But you do. It's Amelia Earhart. Now, is Amelia known as the third person to fly the Atlantic Ocean solo, or as the first woman to do so?" —Al Ries and Jack Trout, *The 22 Immutable Laws of Marketing*, p. 11.

What category in your market could you be first in?

The problem with this law is that it is counter-intuitive. Most bridal stores would rather promote the brand name of the designers they carry instead of a new category in the bride's mind that sets them apart from their competitors.

As Ries and Trout point out:

> "This is counter to classic marketing thinking, which is brand oriented: How do I get people to prefer my brand? Forget the brand. Think categories. Prospects are on the defensive when it comes to brands. Everyone talks about why their brand is better. But prospects have an open mind when it comes to categories. Everyone is interested in what's new. Few people are interested in what's better. When you're the first in a new category, promote the category. In essence, you have no competition." —Al Ries and Jack Trout, *The 22 Immutable Laws of Marketing*, p. 3.

What category could you create in your region?

Could you promote how you are the first store to....?

Or the only store to...?

Or you region's preferred choice to...?

There are nine differentiating factors you can use to promote yourself in comparison with your competitors. I go into detail on how you can use these factors on a CD entitled *Marketing Ideas that Work*. Email me at info@bridaltrainingsystems.com if you are interested in getting a copy.

3) The Law of the Mind: It's better to be first in the mind than to be first in the marketplace.

As Ries and Trout proclaim:

> "Is something wrong with the law of leadership? No, but the law of the mind modifies it. It is better to be first in the prospect's mind than first into the marketplace....Being first in the mind is everything in marketing. Being first into the marketplace is important only to the extent that it allows you to get into the

mind first." —Al Ries and Jack Trout, *The 22 Immutable Laws of Marketing*, p. 15.

4) **The Law of Perception: Marketing is Not a Battle of Products, it's a Battle of Perceptions.** I'll talk more about this principle in depth in the rest of this chapter.

5) **The Law of Focus: The Most Powerful Concept in Marketing is Owning a Word in the Bride's Mind** (the way that Coke 'owns' the word 'cola', or Xerox owns 'copier'). What word or category do you want to own in the bride's mind? Is it available? If not, what category can you create?

There is a lot you can learn about marketing by studying the laws in this book. Study and implement these marketing strategies to strengthen your brand and perception in the marketplace.

2. Use testimonials in all of your advertising and marketing.

Testimonials are so powerful because what others say about you is 10 times more believable than what you say about yourself. Think about how you interact with others on a daily basis. If one of your neighbors or best friends told you about a movie you had to see or a new restaurant you had to try, how much more willing would you be to see the movie or go to the restaurant as opposed to going as the result of just seeing an ad for the film or the restaurant? Of course, we would go to the movie or the restaurant at a much higher percentage if one of our best friends recommended it.

This is why capturing and using testimonials is such a key way to beat your competitors, since testimonials add credibility. When your store is more credible, you have automatically reduced and essentially overcome the biggest fear that most brides have.

Here are three ways you can capture more testimonials so you can use them in your marketing efforts:

1) *Ask.* You will never have testimonials if you don't ask for them. When a bride comes in and tells you what a wonderful experience she has had or how you saved her wedding in a dramatic way, ask her if she would be willing to write it down. On occasion, I have given out gift certificates for dinner at a local restaurant for a great testimonial. Usually we give the bride a free garter or necklace in exchange for her testimonial. This motivates each bride to put it on paper and also ensures that they will write the testimonials in persuasive language (since there is something in it for her). It is even better if you can capture a short video of each bride relating her experience at your store with a Flip video camera.

2) *Make it easy.* Have them fill out a testimonial form at the moment when they are most excited about their purchase – right after they have bought their gown. Most people don't like to write much and even if they do, it is usually not very emotional, compelling, or something that will be great to use in future marketing. The best way to get great testimonials is to use a form like this to elicit better testimonials from the brides who buy from you:

Your Experience at Our Store

Name: ____

Address: ____

City: __________________ State: ________ Zip: ___________

Occupation: _______________________________________

What is your overall feeling about _________________________
(your store name) and your bridal consultant?

Describe in detail what part of finding your wedding gown made you the happiest:

Describe one or two of the most important benefits you've received from buying your dress at our store...Please explain specifically what *you've* gained from the experience:

Thank you so much for your time and your honest answers. As payment for utilizing your comments in any or all future promotional materials for our store, I accept this (_____ garter, necklace, etc.).

Signature: ____________________ Date: ____________

It is easy to get brides to fill out this form since it is short, tells them what specific areas to talk about and offers them a FREE bonus in exchange for using their comments in the future. We have used this method to gather literally hundreds of testimonials in the past several months.

Then, post the testimonials on your web site and use them in your advertising. We have a box in our office at the store where the bridal consultants put each testimonial once they have gathered them. Then, I give each bridal consultant $1 for every testimonial they turn in. It isn't a lot, but it is something (and it adds up) and it is worth every penny to you since it gives you a wealth of bridal testimonials that you can then share with future prospective brides.

Something we have just started doing is to add the bride's profession and the city and state they are from at the bottom of the testimonial. This adds even more credibility to your store since it tells future brides what types of people are buying dresses from you.

Example:

In all the stores that I have been to, this has been the BEST experience, I will continue to come back." — Christina Platt, Registered Nurse, Mesa, Arizona

3) *Take your best testimonials and put them on your phone hold.* I am currently looking to put my best testimonials on hold instead of the music that we currently have on our phone system. This is a great way to let the brides who are waiting to talk with you know about the great experiences that other brides have had at your store. You can record these on an audio tape, or you can plug a microphone into your computer and capture the testimonials this way. You can even offer something more than just a garter or a veil if they will allow you to capture and utilize their audio testimonial.

Be sure to capture the testimonials in such a way that they don't sound rehearsed, but that they sound like real, honest-to-goodness comments.

You can capture these by asking questions such as:

- What is your name and where are you from?
- How did our store compare with the other bridal salons you went to?
- What was your favorite part about your interaction with your bridal consultant?
- Did you feel pressured in any way to make a decision to get the dress that you love?
- What did you love most about your experience at our store?

Here are four examples of real testimonials from our store's web site:

"Nycollette was great. Very helpful! She found out all the right dresses and of course the perfect one! She has a very sweet personality, made me feel comfortable, and she is professional and clean cut. My dress is exactly what I was looking for! Arizona's Bridal & Formal just makes me feel like a princess! Thanks!" —Deja Hancock

"I had a great experience today! Tami met me at the door and told me and my friend the four different styles of dresses, took us to the area that had my size dress. She then started a dressing room with at least six dresses, and she laced me up and helped zip me. She gave me her opinion which was very helpful. She was happy and smiley and helped me choose a beautiful veil and explained the packages. I went to other places that weren't nearly this helpful. Thank you!" —Karina Keithly

"Our experience today was wonderful. We have been shopping at several stores and felt like we were at home coming here. Carly was so helpful and wonderful & we could not have asked for better service from her. We are so grateful we had her helpful cheerful personality and patience to help us make our final decision! Your store is definitely the best in the valley and we are grateful that you have a selection of modest dresses! Thank you!" —Stephanie Bates

"As soon as I came in Sarah greeted my family and I with a smile. The dress selection was great and Sarah went out of her way to pull brand new dresses for me! One of those new ones was actually the one I got! I love it! Arizona's Bridal made getting my dress as stress free as possible! Thank you so much!" —Tonya Booth

Once you've captured these great statements, you can also categorize them by issue and then bind them in a notebook, so you can refer back to them to help you overcome objections.

4) *Keep in touch, stay in touch.* Create a blog for your web site at a free site like www.blogger.com or www.wordpress.com. This site guides you through the process and is very easy. You can then link to the blog site you've created from your home site. You can then capture great testimonials from brides and hear their thoughts about their experience at your store. You can also create marketing ideas to help promote your store to the friends of the brides who visit your blog. This will create a sense of community and brides can refer back to this area again and again.

3. Market better to the brides who almost bought or almost came in.

Brides are fearful. In today's uncertain economy, many of them are hesitant. They are afraid of being sold something they don't want or paying more than they think they have to.

Many brides understand that they have a low sales resistance and don't want to get in front of a talented and trained bridal consultant for fear of buying something. They will make up smokescreen objections to get out of buying anything.

Many times, brides may have seen your invitation to come into the store, but because they were busy that weekend, they may not have responded to your marketing invitation.

Having a good follow up sequence can help you get brides to respond to an offer that they may have neglected previously. Here are four ways you can do this:

- Mail a secondary offer.
- Use www.voiceblast.com to transmit a message to them (inviting them in for a special sale during a weekend).
- Use bounce back coupons to encourage brides to come back into your store more frequently.

- Have four bounce back coupons over the course of one month (one per week) For example:
- 1st Coupon – Buy one, get one free (bridesmaid)
- 2nd Coupon – Free bridesmaid necklace with the purchase of jewelry set
- 3rd Coupon – 50% off bridal shoes with the purchase of Cinderella package
- 4th Coupon – 40% off any accessory with larger purchase (tiara with purchase of MOB dress or tuxedo rental)
- Use lottery cards, contests, or other promotions to encourage brides to come back in.

4. Ignite your brides and help them spread the fire to their friends.

Greg Stilestra, author of *Pyromarketing*, lists a four step process for igniting customer evangelists (those who spread the word about your store). On his blog, he recently detailed how musician John Mellencamp is a marketing innovator. This story was related by a fan named Clark who recently attended one of Mellencamp's concerts in California. Here's how Clark described his experience:

"Just returned from a John Mellencamp concert here in Santa Barbara. During the last song—Jack and Diane—he stopped for a moment while the band played softly in the background and asked everyone to take out their cell phones and call a friend. Once our friends were on the line he said hello to them and then launched into perhaps the most memorable lines John Mellencamp ever crooned. "Two American kids doin' the best they can...."

Here we were, a few thousand people who had paid $50 or more each to see Mellencamp in concert. Pretty dry tinder indeed. And we're now on the phone allowing our friends to experience a little bit of the concert too. Our being there and our calling the friend is even an endorsement of the product."

Greg Stielstra then makes this observation: "It's a great example involving three of the four *PyroMarketing* steps.

1. **Gather the driest tinder:** John was speaking to fans at a concert. These were his passionate customer evangelists.

2. **Touch it with the match.** John gave people an experience by letting friends of his fans experience part of the concert.

3. **Fan the flames.** John was leveraging his current customers to spread his message to their social network. He even used their technology (cell phones).

The only thing Mellencamp didn't do was **save the coals**. Perhaps next time he'll use a service like TextMarks and, following the song, ask everyone to text a keyword to a short code to receive a coupon sent to their cell phone good for a discount on his music. Something like that would close the loop and create a complete PyroMarketing plan.

How could you take the testimonial aspect one step further? Textmarks.com is a service that allows you to text information to individuals who request it. You can also have T-shirts printed right from this site. Imagine going to a wedding and seeing someone wearing a T-shirt that details where the bride got her dress simply by texting 41411 with your keyword (which you can create for free at www.textmarks.com). Utilizing these new technologies will be a huge aspect of future marketing to promote our bridal businesses.

Here are six ideas you can use to create a sense of community and create excitement among the brides shopping at your store:

1) ***Have a love poem contest or wedding vows contest.*** You can essentially do this at any time, but I have put the timelines based on starting in December and ending on Valentine's Day. Of

course, you could also start this every few months and have four preliminary contests throughout the year, and then allow brides visiting your web site to vote for their favorite one.

Here is how it works.

Brides and grooms can submit a poem that they've written about their fiancé and submit it to win a prize on our web site (whether they've bought their dress at your store or not). In our case, we're going to be offering a FREE cruise to the winner.

They can also submit their wedding vows. The goal is to get them to interact with one another on your web site and to get brides checking back often to see what other entries have been submitted. Have a list of rules and an end date for the contest. Then, post three of the top entries, and send out an email to all of the brides and grooms who have entered. Then, you can have them vote within a 24 hour time period and the winning bride will get a gift card to your bridal store and the winning guy will get a $200 gift card to Lowe's, Home Depot, or Best Buy.

Here are a couple of other reminders:

- Post entries online
- Also, be sure to have each bride register her name, email address, and mailing address in order to vote.
- Give out the web site link to every bride at your store and promote the event through the news media
- Announce the winner on February 14th

2) ***Start a wedding shopping spree.***

In this marketing promotion, you (along with other local wedding vendors) can put together a program where you have a bridal show or a promotional event at your store. Brides have to register at your store, or at any of the other participating vendors' stores, and then come to an event at your store. There will be several prizes awarded at the event:

1st Prize - $200

2nd Prize - $100 (2 prizes)

3rd Prize - $50 (5 prizes)

Each vendor should give away one of the prizes. If you have fewer vendors, have fewer prizes. You contribute the advertising for the program. Make a poster to hang at your store announcing the promotion and maybe do a co-op mailing with the other stores to get brides to come into the various businesses to win.

You could even have their likelihood of winning increased by allowing the bride to enter multiple times at the different businesses.

3) ***Have brides submit funny pictures from their weddings and have a "Wedding Picture of the Day or Week Caption Contest".*** Other brides and grooms will log onto your site each day or week and compete to see who can write the best caption. The winner each week will receive a $50 gift card to use at your store. This is a great way to create a sense of community and to get brides and past brides coming back to your site.

4) ***Free Date to see a movie (for bride and groom)*** – Every year there is usually a wedding themed movie that comes out such as *Made of Honor* or *Bride Wars*. We recently had a group in our area buy out a theatre for the movie *Made of Honor* and then give away the tickets for brides and their fiancés.

When one of these movies comes out, plan ahead and you could have a pre-screening event (on a weekend or Friday night showing) and then charge vendors to come and promote their businesses to the brides and grooms before the show. You can also give away free prizes at the event to encourage people to come.

All the brides and grooms have to do is register on your web site or have your bridal consultants confirm that they will be there. Then, you can buy the tickets and have them waiting for the couples once they've entered the theatre.

You can also call brides who have committed to come and then ask:

"Do you know anyone else who would be interested in free tickets to see... the new wedding themed movie coming out...?"

5) ***Roll the Dice Weekend Sale*** – invite homecoming or prom customers to come into the store for a weekend event right before school starts. Then, have the girl roll the die to see how much of a discount she will get off the dress (a one gets $10 off, a six gets $60 off).

   I don't really recommend giving discounts like this, but this may be a good way to help you move some of your previous year's or discontinued prom merchandise.

   Send out an email or postcard explaining the promotion and you can really create an air of excitement and unpredictability in your store as the prom and homecoming customers come in.

6) ***Bingo Card*** – this is a fun way you can encourage brides to come back into the store.

   Have a bingo card featuring 16 items at your store (4 in a row).

   Each time a bride tries on one of the featured items, you can have one of your bridal consultants stamp it out on the card. Every 'bingo' that the bride gets (horizontally, vertically, or diagonally) can have a pre-determined gift certificate.

The bingo card should have an expiration date of 30 days from the time she purchased the dress or first came into the store.

5. Pre-sell your brides in all of your marketing.

The essential idea here is to develop a marketing campaign where everything the bride receives from you pre-sells them on why they should buy a dress at your store. Here are several ways you can do this.

1) ***Change your business cards.*** Detail on your card why your store is different. Use the principle of contrast to show why you are better than the competition. Use both sides of the card to promote all of the compelling reasons and specific benefits as to why brides should buy from you. You can even make a special business card for your top bridal consultants that has a bridal consultant of the year designation on it. The bridal consultants will work harder to get this designation (if there is a prize attached) and the brides will know that they are working with the best of the best.

2) ***Overwhelm the bride with testimonials and contrast statements and marketing collateral that pre-sell her to the point that she can't imagine doing business with anyone else.*** We send out a "What to Expect at Your First Visit to Our Store" brochure via email to each bride who schedules an appointment with us that has over twenty testimonials. This has numerous perspectives from the bride's peers that are very persuasive.

3) ***Utilize scarcity in your marketing.*** Scarcity creates demand. People want something that others can't have.

    - Remember, lines create demand. People want something that others want. Louis Vuitton does a brilliant job of this when they open a new store. I saw one not too long ago. They had a huge line and what was most interesting was the reaction of people to the line as they walked by

> (they were looking in to see what was going on – the store was packed with people and they were only letting a few people in at a time". They had a big sign that said:
>
> "Due to the crowd in the store, please kindly wait a moment. We apologize for any inconvenience caused."
>
> Scarcity also creates word of mouth, because people talk about lines, shortages and hot products.

This backfired on Apple recently with the launch of their G3 phone because they made getting the phones really difficult. They wouldn't accept cash, people had to wait in line, only to not even get a phone, etc.

Marketing expert Seth Godin made this observation and these recommendations in a recent blog posting about Apple's release of their new iPhone that is good advice for our stores in promoting event launches or trunk shows.

> *"Principle 1:* Use the internet to form a queue. If you have a scarce product, you almost certainly know it's scarce in advance. Instead of taxing customers by wasting their time, reward the early shoppers by taking orders online. A month before sale date, for example, tell them it's coming. If you sell out before ship date, that's great, because next time people will be even quicker to order when they hear about what you've got. (And you can do this in the real world, too—postcards with numbers work just fine.)
>
> A hot band that regularly sells out on the road, for example, could put a VIP serial number inside every CD or t-shirt they sell. Use that to pre-order your tix.
>
> *Principle 2:* Give the early adopters a reward. In the case of Apple, I would have made the first 100,000 phones a different color. Then, instead of the buyer being a hero for ten seconds, he gets to be a hero for a year.

> *Principle 3:* Treat different customers differently. Apple, for example, knows how to contact every single existing customer. Why not offer VIP status to big spenders? Or to those that make a lot of calls? Let them cut the line. It's not fair? What's fair mean? I can't think of anything more fair than treating the people who treat you well, better.
>
> *Principle 4:* When things happen in real time, you're way more likely to screw up. One of the giant advantages of the Net is that you can fix things before the whole world notices. Try to do your rollout in small sections, so you can fix mistakes before you hurt the very people you're trying to embrace.
>
> *Principle 5:* Give your early adopters a forum to celebrate. A place to brag or demonstrate or show off or share insights and ideas. Amplify the heroes, which is far better than amplifying the pain of standing in line.
>
> Imagine what the Apple and AT&T stores would have been like this weekend if they were filled with happy customers who had pre-paid, pre-registered and were just dropping in for three minutes to pick up their (very coveted) phones, walking up the VIP line, past all the others just waiting for a chance to buy one..." —Seth Godin

And finally, scarcity drives your product to the true believers, the ones most likely to spread the word and ignite the ideavirus. Because they expended effort to acquire your product or service, they're not only more likely to talk about it, but they've self-selected as the sort of person likely to talk about it.

6. Stop making marketing mistakes. Study and learn from the lessons and mistakes of others.

Sam Levenson once observed:

"You must learn from the mistakes of others. You can't possibly live long enough to make them all yourself."

So, here are nine of the most common marketing mistakes and how you can avoid them as outlined in Jack Trout's book, *Big Brands, Big Trouble*:

1. The "Me-Too" Mistake

This mistake is made by bridal retailers who see another bridal retailer do something, assume it works, and then try it too.

When we are all doing the same thing, eventually each store becomes like everyone else's store and there is no differentiation. The bride ends up differentiating on price because that appears to be the only difference.

When you answer the phone, most "Me-Too" bridal stores have conversations like this:

> Bride: "Do you carry _______ (designer)?"
>
> Store: "Yes, we do." (We're like every other store.)
>
> Bride: "Great, what is your price on ________ (style number)?"
>
> Store: "Our price is $____."
>
> Bride: "Oh. I found it online for $____."

2. The "What Are You Selling?" Mistake

Are you selling *your* brand <u>or</u> the *manufacturer's brand*?

If you are trying to let brands carry you (in other words relying upon manufacturer's advertising dollars) instead of building your own brand and building your store around that, you are guilty of this marketing mistake.

This branding problem is very evident with companies like Xerox *(who tried to start a computer line, but failed because people don't see Xerox as being anything other than a copier company).* **Once you are known for something, it is very hard to change those perceptions to be**

something else. That is why it is so important to take time to think about your overall store branding strategy.

We see what we want to see. Promoting your store brand and creating perceptions in the minds of the brides in your area is critical to the future success of your store.

- It is your responsibility as a marketer to create the perceptions you want your brides to believe.
- If you don't, someone else will. And you will lose the marketing battle while losing sales.

3. The "Truth Will Get Out" Mistake

This mistake is made by retailers who assume brides will find out the truth about big box retailers and why their dresses are better. Brides will never learn the truth about your store if your competitor creates a different perception of you in the marketplace. You have the responsibility to get out and create the perceptions you want brides to believe first.

Jack Trout in his book, *Big Brands, Big Trouble* observes:

"The failure to understand the simple truth that marketing is a battle of perceptions trips up thousands of would-be entrepreneurs every year. Marketing people are preoccupied with doing research and 'getting the facts'. They analyze the situation to make sure the truth is on their side. Then they sail confidently into the marketing arena, secure in the knowledge that they have the best product and that ultimately the best product will win.

It's an illusion. There is no objective reality. There are no facts. There are no best products. All that exists in the world of marketing are perceptions in the minds of customers or prospects. The perception is the reality. Everything else is an illusion." —*Big Brands, Big Trouble*, p. 7.

4. The "Other Guy's Idea" Mistake

This is where one store tries to copy a word or perception that is already ingrained into the consciousness of the brides in your market area.

Jack Trout says this:

"Marketing is a battle of ideas. So if you are to succeed, you must focus your efforts around an idea or an attribute of your own. Without one, you had better have a low price. A very low price." —*Big Brands, Big Trouble,* p. 8.

Why? Because undifferentiated products become commodities and the value of commodities is always determined by price.

So, the lesson here is that you can't own the same word or position that your competitor owns. You must find another word to own – you have to find another attribute that brides will believe about you.

5. The "We're Very Successful" Mistake

In their book, *The 22 Immutable Laws of Marketing*, Ries and Trout identify Law #18 as "The Law of Success: Success Often Leads to Arrogance, and Arrogance to Failure."

Trout explains in *Big Brands, Big Trouble*:

"Success often leads to arrogance and arrogance to failure. When people become successful, they tend to become less objective. They often substitute their own judgment for what the market wants."

One of the classic examples of the arrogance that can come with success involves Digital Equipment Corporation. They brought us the microcomputer and built a $14 billion business.

Then the founder Kenneth Olson became arrogant and believed his ideas of what the market wanted were better and more accurate of what the market actually wanted. He once famously said in 1977: "There is no reason anyone would want a computer in their home."

One great thing about being small business owners is that we are humble. We know how hard it is to be successful in our businesses. Last month's sales don't pay this month's bills. We have to continually improve and get better in order to succeed.

Jack Trout makes this point in his book *Big Brands, Big Trouble*:

"Small companies are mentally closer to the front than big companies. That may be one reason for their rapid growth in the past decades. They haven't been tainted by success." —*Big Brands, Big Trouble*, p. 10.

This is such an important point for us to never lose sight of. We are only as good as our last season.

We *either* have a handle on what is going on in our market or we don't. We can't become arrogant like DEC or we may cease to exist like they have.

6. The "All Things for All People"Mistake

You can't be all things to all people. Manufacturer's today recommend that we become generalists (be all things to all people and offer everything for everybody at the wedding).

Why?

Because that is what they sell.

If you want to be a success in this business, you have to specialize.

7. The "Live by the Numbers" Mistake

This mistake causes businesses to lose focus on a specialist approach and become a generalist in hopes that the business can sell more and make more money. This is called line extension. Businesses try to do everything for everybody in order to try to make their sales numbers hit their projected targets. If one store asks another "How many wedding gowns did you sell or how many prom dresses did you sell last season?, it is easy to compare yourself to another store without understanding the complete dynamics of how those numbers happened.

If you've ever heard someone mention numbers that are vastly better than your numbers, it is easy to find yourself in this marketing trap.

When you hear of the sucess of others it is easy to try to be somone that we are not. You become everything for everybody in order to bring sales in, instead of focusing on your niche and what you do better than anyone else in the world.

Rather than staying focused on being strong *somewhere* to drive numbers up, you really opt for being weak everywhere.

8. The "Not Attacking Yourself" Mistake

Oftentimes, the best way to stay on top in any business is to attack your own core business with something unique that makes what you used to sell obsolete. Gillette and Intel are great examples of companies who do this well. They introduce a new razor or computer chip to market before their competitors. This makes it very difficult to successfully compete against them because they are always moving.

9. The "Not Being in Charge" Mistake

Don't leave your marketing or your branding to someone else. You can delegate, but you have to always set the direction and be in charge.

Why?

The bottom line is that they will never care about it as much as you will, but more importantly you are responsible for bringing brides and prom customers into your door <u>every day</u> and coming up with creative ways to differentiate or brand your store in your crowded market.

7. Detail your marketing strategy in writing.

Here are several questions to ask about your marketing plans in 14 distinct areas as adapted from *Market Smarter, Not Harder* by Monique Myron Reece and Pamela Truax.

Competitive Strategies

1. Do you compete with many similar sized bridal shops in your region, or are you facing the threat of a large national competitor like David's in your marketplace?

2. Are you experiencing slow, eroding market share or a sudden loss of customers because of a new competitor? If so,

   - Be clear to differentiate your dresses, accessories, or services (alterations, etc.) according to what brides want.

   - Be clear about the problem(s) you solve or benefit(s) you have to offer.

Target Market Strategies

1. How will you differentiate your marketing to your primary (brides and prom girls) and secondary (bridesmaids, MOB, etc.) target markets?

2. What is different about your competitor's target market as compared to yours?

3. Is there potential in other target markets not currently being served by you?

Product/Service Strategies

1. How will you market new lines that you decide to carry – do you promote your store or are you relying solely on the marketing done by the dress manufacturer?

2. Which products will you focus on more than others in the next one to three years?

3. How can you increase the number of purchases a bride makes at your store?

4. Can you bundle your accessories to sell together?

5. Are there global or marketplace factors (economic conditions, political matters, environmental concerns) which will affect the styles and price points of the gowns in your store?

Pricing Strategies

1. How does your pricing rank with that of your competitors?

2. Is it too high or too low?

3. Does it need to change to be more competitive?

4. If it is higher, do you give your brides a reason to pay more, with intangible, personal and unique value?

5. What are you doing to protect yourself from online shoppers?

6. Can you put more exclusive dress or product lines in your store that other competitors don't have access to?

Positioning Strategies

1. Does your message clearly communicate your differentiating point and the benefits you offer brides who shop at your store?

2. Is it effective for the target brides you are trying to reach?

3. Is your positioning consistent with your price? Should your price be higher?

4. Is your positioning different from that of your competitors? What does the bride perceive?

5. Is your positioning reflected in all printed and online advertising?

Promotion Strategies

1. How many marketing promotions do you use to bring brides into your store?

2. Do you track the results of each promotion?
3. What promotions do your competitors use that are successful? Which ones can you adapt and use? What successful promotions from other industries can you use?
4. How can you create a joint promotion with other wedding vendors to reduce your costs yet provide you with additional coverage?
5. Do you have your marketing promotions figured out a year in advance?

Public Relations Strategies

1. Do you have a public relations plan?
2. How much time do you allocate to developing public relations?
3. What is unique about what you do at your store that would interest the media?
4. Through what media can brides in your market be reached? Is there an opportunity to promote your store through these mediums?
5. How can public relations benefit your advertising and marketing strategies?

Advertising/Media Strategies

1. How is your advertising strategy different from that of your competitors?
2. Does it adequately reflect your positioning?
3. How does your spending compare with that of your competitors?
4. Is there a medium that your competitor uses but you do not?
5. What are the strengths and weaknesses of your advertising?
6. Do your ads effectively communicate your difference to brides?

7. Do your ads exploit your competitive advantages?

8. Do your ads add extra value to the advantages of shopping at your store?

9. Do your ads create a brand image that sets you apart from your competition? Do brides respond to your brand? Why or why not?

10. Do you measure and test the effectiveness of your advertising in some way?

Merchandising Strategies

1. What value-added incentives might increase sales?

2. How often do you chage up displays to better market your merchandise?

3. How can you improve point of purchase displays to make them communicate to your brides and prom customers and inspire impulse purchases?

4. How can you display your merchandise to enhance a s bridal show event or sales process in your store?

Customer Service Strategies

1. Amongst your competitors, who has the strongest customer service policies?

2. What are your policies?

3. What can you do to improve customer service?

4. Do you regularly communicate with your brides to get feedback and look for ways to improve?

5. How do you ensure your bridal consultants implement your customer service plan?

Selling Strategies

1. How does your market share compare with that of your competitors?
2. Are competitors growing or declining in market share? How do you know?
3. Is your sales effort efficient? Effective? What is your sales closing ratio?
4. Do you have a sales plan to follow up with brides who have purchased from you and those who haven't?
5. Are you using your sales process to give you immediate feedback about the wants and needs of brides in your area?
6. Are you assessing this information and making buying decisions at market based on this feedback?

Distribution Strategies

1. How does your distribution channel differ from that of your competitors?
2. Are there opportunities for different distribution channels that you are not currently using?
3. What are the strengths and weaknesses of your competitor's distribution methods?

R&D/Marketing Research Strategies

1. Are you looking at and testing new lines for your store?
2. What one area of your business can you focus on this year?
3. What should you look at and research on an ongoing basis?
4. Should you test sales and marketing efforts to a new target market this year?

5. How can you best test a new market niche?

6. What new social networking platforms or other technological breakthroughs should you research and test?

Packaging Strategies

1. Does the way you currently package your wedding gowns and other products as they leave your store meet your objectives and build your store brand?

2. Is your packaging consistent with your company image and positioning?

3. Is it attractive and effective with your target market(s)? What are brides or prom girls saying about them?

4. Have you tested any packaging changes with your brides, prom girls, or other market niches?

5. Is it modern enough or does it need freshening?

6. Can new packaging add value either functionally or perceptibly for the bride?

Be sure to take the time to think through and reflect on the answers to these fourteen areas of your business. Doing so will help you detail your marketing strategy in writing.

8. Employ the principle of reciprocity by offering a gift with a purchase at your store.

Reciprocity, which is giving a gift to someone else, is a powerful tool.

Russell Granger makes this statement in his book, *7 Triggers to Yes*:

"Every time you provide a gift or service you create a debt that must be repaid....You do something for me and I am morally, ethically, and psychologically required to provide some sort of payback. The concept is built into our limbic system and is triggered as invariably as the fight-

or-flight syndrome; it's hardwired in the brain." —Russell Granger, *7 Triggers to Yes*, p. 139.

Here are two examples of how reciprocity is used:

- At a home shopping party, the host gives each person a gift. The indebtedness begins there, after which almost everyone buys something. The time share business provides the gift of a free resort weekend to get you to listen to a sales pitch.
- A gift with purchase is used by virtually every cosmetic company. In fact, Estee Lauder created the "gift with purchase" idea where a separate gift was offered as a bonus for specific purchases. The gift was often valued higher than the required purchase and because of the "debt" created by the gift, the buyer usually bought more than intended.

How can you use this principle at your store?

- Gift card – give the bride a $50 or $100 gift card that can be used towards the purchase of anything in the store when she comes in again.
- Referral card – give the bride a $25 coupon she can give to her friends and an opportunity to get the money back for her dress minus sales tax.
- Give the bride a lottery ticket where she has a chance to win something or double its value during non-peak hours at your store.
- Offer praise more generously to the brides you work with, the bridal consultants in your store and your vendors.
- Offer bonuses, lunch, involvement, or traveling with you to certain events, time off, etc. as a way to express appreciation.
- Smile more. Og Mandino, author of numerous books including *The Greatest Salesman in the World* once observed: "I will smile at friend and foe alike and make every effort to find in him or her,

a quality to praise, now that I realize that the deepest yearning of human nature is the craving to be appreciated."

9. Focus. True marketing success comes from specialization and sacrifice.

In their best-selling marketing book, *The 22 Immutable Laws of Marketing*, Al Ries and Jack Trout identify Law #13 as the Law of Sacrifice. They say:

"If you want to be successful today, you should give something up. There are three things to sacrifice: product line, target market, and constant change.

First, the product line. Where is it written that the more you have to sell, the more you sell? The full line is a luxury for a loser. If you want to be successful, you have to reduce your product line, not expand it.

...The generalist is weak. Take Kraft, for example. Everybody thinks Kraft has a strong brand name. In jellies and jams, Kraft has 9 percent of the market. But Smucker's has 35 percent. Kraft means everything, but with a name like Smucker's it has to be jelly or jam because that's all Smucker's makes. In mayonnaise, Kraft has 18 percent of the market. But Hellman's has 42 percent. (Kraft does have a leading brand in terms of market share. However, its name isn't Kraft, it's Philadelphia. Philadelphia brand cream cheese has 70 percent of the cream cheese market.)"

They continue:

"Take the retail industry. Which retailers are in trouble today? The department stores. And what's a department store? A place that sells everything. That's a recipe for disaster." —Al Ries and Jack Trout, *The 22 Immutable Laws of Marketing*, pp. 78-79.

Why do so many bridal retailers try to be all things to all people? Why do they feel they have to carry every line? This brings us to what Ries and Trout call the second sacrifice.

"Let's discuss the second sacrifice, target market. Where is it written that you have to appeal to everybody?"

"Finally, the third sacrifice: constant change. Where is it written that you have to change your strategy every year at budget review time? If you try to follow the twists and turns of the market, you are bound to wind up off the road. The best way to maintain a consistent position is not to change it in the first place." —Al Ries and Jack Trout, *The 22 Immutable Laws of Marketing*, pp. 82-83.

The law of sacrifice is not a complicated law but it is a costly one. It is one of the simplest to understand, and one of the most difficult to put into practice. The bottom line is your desire and willingness. Here are three things to consider as you make sacrifices in your product line, your target market, and the constant change that our business (and all businesses) face.

1. ***You must be willing to let go of what you have for the potential to do something greater.***

It is said that all you need to catch a monkey in Africa is a glass jar and some fruit and nuts. The jar is filled half way with fruit and nuts and buried in the ground so that it cannot be pulled up without being dug up. The opening of the jar is near the surface of the ground. The monkey must open its hand to grasp the food, but when a fist is made in order to pull the food out, it cannot get its hand back out of the jar. The hunter can literally walk right up to the monkey and capture it in a cage or with a tranquilizer dart because the monkey is not willing to let go of the food. Some people are not willing to let go of what they have even if the consequences are great.

What are you holding onto that may keep you where you are?

The Law of Sacrifice demands that leaders let go. Like a trapeze artist, if you do not let go of the bar, you will never perform to your potential. Many store owners will go to market year after year and continue to pick up a line because they are afraid that someone else will get it or have it, regardless of whether the line really makes them money or not. As I mentioned, sacrifice is simple to understand, but very difficult to put into practice because it requires change.

2. ***You must be willing to risk everything for the cause you believe in.***

Martin Luther King, Jr. is a greate example of this principle. The majority of his adult life was lived with some sort of sacrifice. He was stoned, stabbed and physically attacked. His house was bombed and his family threatened. He gave his life, the ultimate sacrifice, for the cause of freedom. Over 30 years later, our hearts are still stirred by his famous "I Have a Dream" speech. Even more importantly, we have a little less hate and prejudice in this country because of his sacrifice.

3. ***You must truly believe in what you sacrifice for or you are likely to quit and lose.***

It is easy to doubt your resolve to sacrifice. It can be very difficult to stay true to this commitment to contract your focus.

One of the best ways to sacrifice is to focus on targeting a specific niche.

Niche marketing is targeting a specific group like certain neighborhoods or a specific demographic of brides. As I've mentioned, it is much smarter to target certain niches than it is to target everyone. People feel important when they feel like you specialize in helping them.

Think about this for a minute. Who would you rather use: a general CPA *or* an accountant that specializes in retailers and in particular retailers in the bridal industry? If you had someone you could work with who understands your unique needs, you will stay with that person or entity (even if they charge more) because of the benefit you get.

Specializing is critical, yet it is often not the strategy most retailers follow as they are doing everything they can to make any sale they can.

In my market, we have several retailers who have a certain focus. As you read these, think about how their sacrifice helps them stand out to brides.

- Bridal retailer who focuses on the affluent (only sells wedding gowns for $5,000 and up)
- Bridal retailer who specializes in servicing the Hispanic community (weddings and quincineras)
- Bridal retailer who focuses solely on selling dresses in a certain price range (none higher than $____)
- Bridal retailer who only sells and carries their own line
- Bridal retailer who only sells bridesmaid dresses
- A bridal retailer who sells everything but the wedding dress
- A bridal retailer who focuses and sells only modest wedding attire
- A bridal retailer who has a consignment shop
- A bridal retailer who sells only to 2nd, 3rd, or 4th time brides

In addition, we have numerous bridal shops who try to be all things to all people. They carry numerous lines and just like in your market, we have a bridal retailer who price matches and sells every gown below MSRP.

If you want to be successful in marketing, you have to understand and use what author Dan Kennedy calls the Results Triangle.

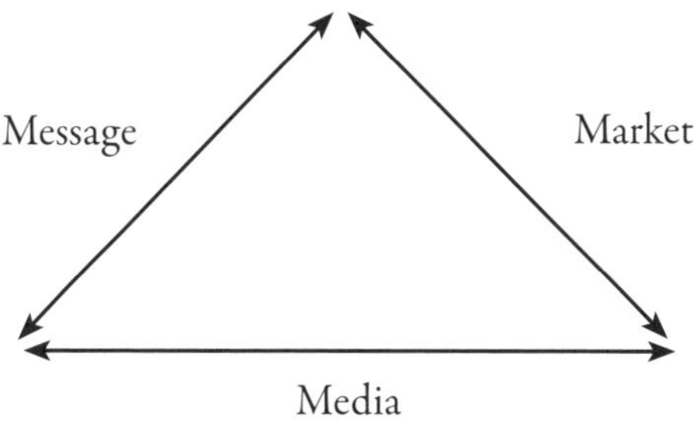

There are plenty of ways to mess this combination up.

Right Message—Wrong Market—Right Media
Right Message—Right Market—Wrong Media
Right Messsage—Wrong Market—Wrong Media
Wrong Message—Right Market—Right Media
Wrong Message—Wrong Market—Right Media
Wrong Message—Right Market—Wrong Media
Wrong Message—Wrong Market—Wrong Media

There is only ONE way to get it right:
Right Message
Right Market
Right Media

So, how do you specialize in your niche?

1) ***Pick an area of expertise.*** Determine which area will be the most profitable and successful for you.

2) ***Start targeting this group.*** Identify how you are a specialist for her group and share with her testimonials that indicate how you've helped other brides in a similar situation to hers.

3) ***If you have a well-known bride in a certain demographic, offer her free merchandise from your store in exchange for having her write a testimonial letter*** that you can mail from her office on her stationary with her business card, etc. You can pay for the mailing yourself. Another way to do this is to offer a free gift (such as a gift card to a restaurant or a branded product such as a hand bag with your logo on it) to any bride who refers four people to you. Here is an example of how you could do that:

   Write:

   If you would like a beautiful handbag that you can use to carry a change of clothes with you on your honeymoon, simply take the time to write four personal recommendations via personal letter, fax, or email to friends of yours who know and respect you, recommending they buy their next formal, or if they are engaged their wedding gown, from our store. Then, send a copy of the four letters, along with your own experience about shopping at our store and we will send you your choice of either a beautiful handbag or a $___ gift card to use at your favorite restaurant.

Then, include sample text that the bride can use in her letter:

From: _______________

Dear: ________________

I just got my wedding gown from _______________________ (store name) and it was one of THE best shopping experiences I have ever had and I thought you would want to know about it. I worked with ____ and she was so helpful and knowledgeable about the wedding dresses and made finding my perfect dress such a wonderful experience. It was stress-free and I am so excited about my wedding in my beautiful dress!

I am including a $25 coupon that the store gave me to pass onto you. You can use it to purchase any of their exquisite formal fashions or if you know anyone who is getting married, they can use it towards the purchase of their wedding dress.

Also, just for coming into the store, they have a special lottery ticket you can scratch off that has a winning ticket each day. All you have to do is come in and pick it up. If you come in between 12 and 3 each weekday, you can get double the value of the prize won.

You can thank me later. Hurry into the store now!

_________________ (bride's name)

10. Expect your competitors to make their best moves to counter what you do and act accordingly.

In their book, *The 22 Immutable Laws of Marketing*, Ries and Trout identify Law #17 as "The Law of Unpredictability: Unless You Write your Competitor's Plans, You Can't Predict the Future."

One of the biggest mistakes we can make in the bridal business is to think that we act in a vacuum. I really like this statement that Bob Rice makes in his book *Three Moves Ahead* (comparing business to the game of chess):

"Always, always expect your opponent to make his best move. One of the silliest things beginners do is make moves that are fundamentally unsound in the hope that their opponents won't see something. Hey, this is the information age: Everybody sees everything. You absolutely must make decisions based on the market, your competitors, and your customers seeing the consequence of your move and being very smart and self-interested in the way they react." —Bob Rice, *Three Moves Ahead*, p. 180.

He also says that this is one of the challenges with business books today:

"Readers of recipe-for-success books often fail to produce a cake for a simple reason. In the kitchen, there are rarely opponents who fight you tooth and nail for access to the springform pan. Most business advice books do not account for this fact. Instead, they preach that internal factors are primarily responsible for an entity's success. But in real life, someone's over there playing the Black pieces, and she gets just as many moves as you do." —Bob Rice, *Three Moves Ahead*, p. 12.

Remember, the key to marketing is to seek to dominate market squares instead of focusing on selling individual products. When you do this and do it well, you will increase sales and obliterate your competition.

Chapter 5

Sell Like Your Life Depends on It
(Because it Does)

I recently had the chance to hear from and meet two-time heavyweight champion of the world George Foreman. Not only has he had significant achievements in the sporting arena, he is also a very successful businessman. His lean, mean grilling machine is owned by more than 1 in every 3 Americans. He said two things in his talk that inspired me to write this chapter. The first thing he said was that "The most important product that you sell is yourself. If you sell yourself, people don't buy what's in your hand, they buy you." That is great advice that all of us need to remember more often. It's not just about the dress. The second thing he said that greatly impressed me was: "Learn to sell and you will never starve." George came from a background of poverty. While he was very successful in the boxing ring, he is extremely successful at his many entrepreneurial ventures today because he learned to sell. The future of your bridal business depends on this same critical skill: how well you can sell. It is imperative that you and everyone at your store learn to sell and that you sell like your life depends on it (because it *really* does). The challenge today is that the process of how a bride goes about shopping and looking for a dress has shifted...brides are making more decisions before coming into bridal stores and they have much more resistance to buying now than ever before. If you've been frustrated lately because what you used to do to sell doesn't seem to be working anymore, this chapter is for you. In it, I'll show you how and why the process of selling has shifted and where you should be placing your emphasis in order to sell today. You have to make these shifts now because your livelihood and the success of your store depend on it.

Most stores recognize that something is different, but they aren't sure what it is. Not only can they not seem to put their finger on what is happening, more importantly, they haven't adapted to this change. Even worse, they don't understand how this process shift is influencing the bride much more than it ever did in times past.

There are seven steps to the marketing and sales process that all brides must go through before they will buy. This process has never changed, but the order and the speed with which a bride goes through this process has shifted and the biggest shift has been in what occurs *before* the bride comes into the store.

Here is the seven step process to buying from the perspective of the bride:

1. **The Search** *(I'm engaged – where should I go to get my dress?)*

2. **Getting Educated** *(Checking out pictures, web sites, shopping with friends)*

3. **Assessing Budget vs. Value** *(My budget is this much, the dress I love is how much?)*

4. **Validating Decision** *(Do I like this dress I saw online or at another store? If I have seen it at multiple locations, what is the best price?)*

5. **Justification** *(I haven't seen this dress anywhere else and this seems to be a good value and price)* **or** *(I like this dress but I saw it online for $-- or I want to see if I can get it for less.)*

6. **Decision** *(looking at pictures, searching for lowest price and/or lowest risk provider)*

7. **Buy the Dress** *(online or at the store where she saw it)*

Here is the seven step process to selling from your perspective at your store:

1. **Marketing** *(Engaged? We have the perfect dress...)*

2. **Approaching the Bride** *(Welcome to our store, educating the bride)*

3. **Building Rapport and Trust** *(Finding out what the bride is looking for, here's who we are...other brides who have bought from us...building trust with each member of the wedding party so they feel that we're here to help them find the perfect dress...)*

4. **Needs Assessment** *(What do you like, what don't you like...Have you considered?)*

5. **Building Value / Presenting Gowns** *(11 questions)*

6. **Answering Objections**

7. **Finalizing the Transaction / Closing the Sale**

I have placed these two processes side by side along with when and where these steps happen from both your perspective and the perspective of the bride. Take a minute to look at this chart (on the next page).

	Process for Deciding on the Dress *(Perspective of The Bride)*			Process for Selling the Dress *(Perspective of Your Bridal Store)*	
	Process / Sequence	**Where/When**		**Process / Sequence**	**Where/When**
Before bride comes into store.	**The Search** *(I'm engaged – where should I go to get my dress?)*	Online	Before bride comes into store.	**Marketing** *(Engaged? We have the perfect dress...)*	Your Marketing Funnel
	Getting Educated *(Checking out pictures, web sites, shopping with friends)*	Online, Magazines, Friends, Stores		*Should be educating online through pre-sale process*	
	Assessing Budget vs. Value *(My budget is this much, the dress I love is how much?)*	Online			
After bride comes into your store.	**Validating Decision** *(Do I like this dress I saw online or at another store? If I have seen it at multiple locations, what is the best price?)*	Store	After bride comes into your store.	**- Approaching the Bride** **- Building Rapport & Trust** **- Needs Assessment** **- Building Value / Presenting Gowns**	Store
	Justification *(I haven't seen this dress anywhere else and this seems to be a good value and price)* **or** *(I like this dress but I saw it online for $-- or I want to see if I can get it for less.)*	Home, Online, Your Store or Other Stores			
	Decision *(looking at pictures, searching for lowest price and/or lowest risk provider)*	Home, Online, Your Store or Other Stores		**Answering Objections**	Store, Home, Online
	Buy the Dress *(online or at the store where she saw it)*	Online, Store		**Finalizing Transaction**	Store

When you understand how a bride thinks and decides and contrast that with what you are doing to sell to her, you'll notice some very important distinctions.

You probably noticed several things about this process by comparing them side by side. I want to point out three shifts that have occurred that are affecting how well you are selling at your store.

1. **Brides are getting more information online and from a myriad of other sources on their own BEFORE they are coming into your store.** It used to be that the education step and the entire search process happened in the store. Now, the store has become a place to validate what she has seen online in pictures to find "her look" for the wedding. If she has already seen the dress online, she will likely use the bridal salon as a try-on store and then differentiate on price if she can't see any other difference. More than ever, you have to have a differentiating point and overcome her skepticism through an overwhelming number of testimonials (preferably video testimonials).

2. **Brides are coming in with much firmer budgets than they have in the past.** They or their parents have reigned in their spending (depending on who is buying the dress) and there is no question that initially she is assessing your overall value based on her budgetary number much more so than she ever has before. Understanding this shift and helping her match her budget with your price is very important in how she perceives you and the overall trust she has in you and your store. It is also critical that you help her see what makes up a price by educating her so you can build value in her mind.

3. **For the most part, brides are in control of the process.** Because of the explosion of choice and the information available online, brides can be much more aloof in how they present themselves at your store. In the bride's mind, she has plenty of time to decide what and when to buy and she is quietly assessing how you and your store will fit into

her wedding plans. Your challenge is that she is rarely making this decision alone. She is also bringing and involving many more people in the search and experience of shopping than ever before.

How do you counter these shifts? Here are seven ways you can do so.

1. Get better at pre-selling the bride.

With technology today and the Internet, brides literally have instant access to shop around for better pricing on a gown, see what your store reputation is and see what other brides are saying about your store BEFORE they even come into your store. If you don't actively present information that pre-sells *why* you are the best store for her to visit and to buy from, one of your competitors likely will.

Pre-selling the bride is all about building trust and how quickly and deeply you can build it so that any concern, objection, or obstacle that would otherwise stand in the way of you making the sale is completely eliminated.

The big reason why you need to pre-sell brides today before they come into your store is to pre-empt your competitors so that everyone else the bride sees *after you* is seen within a frame of reference that highlights your differentiating strength.

We now email a free report to brides when they schedule an appointment at our store and invite them to read it before they come into the store. The essence of this strategy is to persuade the bride of our experience and expertise so she wants to do business with us before she even comes into the store. It is a great way to build credibility and expertise and has been a very effective way of shifting the control of the sale back to us as the seller.

In its current state, it is 13 pages long and is graphically laid out in a way that showcases our store in the following ways. The report is entitled: "What to Expect at Your First Appointment"

It includes:

- A message from the owner/designer. This brief intro letter includes a picture of my wife Heather which helps create authority and celebrity and uses multiple psychological triggers that build desire and create authority and trust.

- A detailed explanation of what will happen when the bride arrives at our store. It is titled "When You Arrive". Here is what it says:

  - "You will be greeted warmly by one of our professional and courteous bridal consultants and assisted in completing a simple bridal registry form. This will help your bridal consultant get a sense for your personal style and the ideas you've already put together for your wedding plans. Your bridal consultant will also show you the four silhouettes of gowns and briefly explain some of the different fabrics and construction of the wedding gowns you will try on.

  - Your Entire Appointment will take from one hour to no more than 90 minutes."

- An article that details 10 things brides need to know before they buy their wedding gown (which covertly sells them on why they should buy at our store)

- An article that explains why shopping online won't save them money and a specific and horrific story of a bride who did and her letter to brides explaining why they shouldn't

- 24 testimonials from brides about their experiences at our store

- 16 reasons why brides from all over Arizona buy their dress at our store

Having a pre-sale brochure will help you set up the sale. Don't neglect this important step.

2. Accelerate the speed at which you build trust for the bride and her entourage.

With the popularity and example of the TLC television show, *Say Yes to the Dress*, many brides today are choosing to bring a big entourage along with them as part of their experience.

Unfortunately, larger groups can be harder to build trust with and it can be easier to lose control of the sale. Remember, if you lose control of the sale, you can recover it quickly by asking questions. Your goal is to accelerate the speed with which you build trust with everyone in the party. You can best do this by being resourceful.

Many times when we lose control of a sale, it is because we haven't shown true value to the mother or the person who is trying to take over. They feel like they can do it better. Look for some way to re-connect with each person who is with the bride as well as the bride herself. If you approach the bride with information about you, she'll consider you a salesperson. If you approach the bride with ideas and answers, she'll consider you a resource. Which one are you? Choose to be helpful and resourceful. Ask great questions. Listen carefully. Offer ideas and present gowns that fit the description she is giving you and mom will allow you to come in, help and control the sale again. If not, you may want to share a story about a possessive mom who came into the store and how the bride left crying because her mom wouldn't let her pick out what she wanted. You have to be sensitive about this, but most of the time when a mother takes over, it is because you haven't really created trust. People sometimes ask for a specific technique or phrase to say when dealing with this situation, but the reality is this: *intent counts more than technique.* If a mom perceives that you are a resource and really care about her and her daughter she will open up and let you offer your help.

If someone puts you off and takes control, do whatever you need to do to get control back. Don't give up and walk away (giving them even more power over you). A great example of this happening would be when a mother goes to the racks and starts grabbing tons of gowns and bringing them back to the dressing room area. Recommend that they start out with the four cuts and then you can go from there. Encourage the mother or friend to have a seat and enjoy the different gowns that their daughter will try on and look and listen to what *she* likes best. Take the initiative in this by asking questions as the bride comes out of the dressing room. Remember, the old saying: "The person asking questions is in control of the conversation." No matter what happens, you are only one great question away from being back in control and re-establishing yourself as an expert and resource.

Finally, if a mother, maid/matron of honor, or other friend is really pushy and demands to take over, offer help in ways that will be remembered long after they have left the store. Your goal is to build trust, eliminate risk and help the bride *and* the other members of her party feel that you are offering something that no one else in your area can—the experience of buying a dress from you. I can't tell you how many times brides and their mothers have come back to buy their dress because we were a great resource and friend to them. Be memorable and stand out.

So, the next time a mother or a member of the entourage starts to take over the sale and tells the bride she doesn't like what the bride likes—how should you handle this? The best way to handle this is to focus on befriending that person better. If you feel resistance or antagonism from her on this, this is an indicator that you need to focus more on building a connecting point with her that will help her relax and enjoy the experience more. Help that person relax and let her know that you are there to help the bride, her friends, and her family have a wonderful and memorable wedding experience that they will always treasure and never forget.

If you have a large entourage that is preventing the bride from getting the dress she loves, consider this observation by Kevin Hogan on page 94 of his book *Covert Persuasion*. He says:

"Peer pressure doesn't end in high school. We are often very concerned with what other people think about our purchases or choices.

Sometimes after your [brides] have made the decision you wanted them to make, it doesn't stick, and they end up changing their minds."-- *Covert Persuasion*, p. 94.

You can avoid this by inoculating the bride similar to how a viral medication inoculates against contact with future diseases.

If the bride is by herself, you can ask her:

"You and I both know that you've made the right decision today to get this dress *because* we know all of the facts. But what will you say to those who wonder why you're buying this dress and try to change your mind?

This turns the emotional decision into a fact-based decision and you will be much more successful with this approach as you anticipate objections and then overcome them.

If there are others who are trying to persuade the bride not to buy, consider asking those in the party what Yvonne Spinelli of Bridal Gallery by Yvonne in Latham, New York does:

"I know some of you may have had different ideas of what the bride was going to wear on her wedding day....would *anyone* be disappointed (a little emphasis on that word) if she were to pick this gown?"

What happens with this great question is that those in the bridal party who may have been objecting to the dress, will typically say, "No, of course not, it's her dress, she can wear what she wants!" This is a great way to point out that the decision is the bride's without offending her friends who have accompanied her to find the dress of her dreams.

Another way to accelerate trust is through online videos that point out your differentiating point and that highlight testimonials of brides that eliminate skepticism and build your overall value.

3. **Always be educating and building value. The more you can do this before the bride comes into your store, the more successful you will be.**

Very few bridal stores actually educate brides about their store other than promoting what lines they carry in their store. As a result, brides don't know what unique value is really being offered. To be more successful at selling, you need to prepare the brides who are coming into your store by educating them. You can do this by writing articles or creating videos that promote your uniqueness and advantage in the marketplace. These articles should include all of the interesting details regarding the construction of gowns, how you select them, and what influences your decision to bring them into your store (when you view them in comparison with all of the other dresses you see at market). This doesn't have to be complicated. You could keep brides up to date with what is happening in your store by posting this information on your blog or on your FaceBook or Twitter pages.

One of the biggest marketing mistakes you can make is to fail to educate the brides and prom customers in your area about the unique advantages your store offers to them. If you aren't educating your brides, you can be sure they are gaining the information – but it is probably from a competitor—who is likely promoting their differentiating strength and more importantly is probably not as flattering to you as you would like.

Don't make the mistake of not communicating with and educating the brides in your area about what you are doing to provide the best wedding gowns in the world. For example, if you went to two bridal markets last year and reviewed over 1,000 different dresses from numerous lines to pick the very best styles to bring into your store, tell them how you made that choice. It will impress the brides you share this info with that you've screened out dresses that don't have the quality, construction, beauty, fashion, style, endurance and dependability you know they want. Your brides won't know these facts unless you tactfully point them out.

When you educate your brides, you will see your sales and profits soar.

Doubt this is true? Think about yourself. When you buy (or consider buying) an item or service for you or for your store, you may realize that you don't know as much as you would like about the item. If you have unanswered questions about the item, you're less likely to spend money to buy it.

When someone (a sales professional) takes the time and initiative to objectively educate you on all of the product offerings available in the area in which you are contemplating a purchase, you really appreciate it. It helps you have more trust and favor in the sales representative and in the company he or she represents.

Education is an extremely powerful marketing strategy. Educate your brides about everything (including a few of the bad or less positive aspects of dresses, accessories, alterations, the risks of ordering online, etc.), and you'll sell to many more brides than you are now because of the rising trust and expertise you will gain from positioning yourself this way. Educating your brides will help you gain an inordinate advantage over your competitors because most bridal retailers don't take the time to do this.

The other benefit of educating the bride is that you will lead her to action. People need to be explicitly told how to act in order to take advantage of the dresses you have now. Every marketing communication that you send out to brides should tell them what to do next. Give them a brief education, then take them by the hand (figuratively speaking) and tell them what specific action they need to take next. Create urgency so they will act now.

Be sure that your educational marketing message gets in front of *your* brides (the ones that you sell to). Are they really the brides who will respond to what you sell? The goal is to focus on selling to an audience that is hungry or thirsty for what you sell. If they aren't, you won't be successful in this type of approach for building value. If they are your market, and they are hungry or thirsty, you want to focus on selling them a second helping or a second glass (or upselling them on additional offerings that will be helpful to them in preparing for the perfect wedding).

4. Appeal to how she validates and/or justifies her decision. Sell in the context of how she builds value.

In the sales comparison chart illustrated earlier in this chapter, I detailed what brides are thinking about as they validate the dresses they like and justify their decision. When she is in your store, she is thinking about the price she'll pay and the overall value she'll receive. The important thing to remember is that just because *you* value something doesn't mean that *she* values it in the same way. Remember, you have to appeal to how *she* validates and justifies her decisions, not how you do. Here is what she is thinking about:

- *PRICE - Do I like this dress? Have I seen it online or at another store? If I have seen it at multiple locations, what is the best price? Can I get it for less?* If you want to avoid being shopped on price, carry lines that your competitors don't. Protect yourself and build your value. Promote what is unique about you, not what is the same.

- *VALUE – What else do I get when I get my dress here? Help the bride to see that it is more than just a transaction to you—that it is really about the relationship, your service, and what else she gets in addition to the dress.* Everyone assesses value differently. You should make a list of all of the benefits that brides have told you over the years that you offer *that they have valued.* Incorporate these into your pre-sale materials and into what you say when you are selling the dress. If you aren't pointing this out, she will likely say to herself: "I don't see any difference between your store and one of your competitors. Since I can't see a difference, I am going to buy the lower priced dress." Building value is a skill that you can't ignore. Remember, it is not about how much it costs, it is about how much it is worth. What is it worth to the bride to buy from your store, have your expertise, and have your follow-up service? When you promote these three things that she can't get anywhere else, you will sell value and not just price.

Don't forget that what the bride says matters so much more than anything you may say. Be sure you understand how she perceives value. A great formula to help you understand this is found in Ron Karr's book *Lead, Sell, or Get Out of the Way*. He says that perceived value equals the cost of no change minus the cost of change (which includes the amount of time, money, and effort it takes to acquire, learn about and buy a dress from your store). If the cost of no change (not buying now and continuing to look around) is less than the cost to change (buy the dress now), her perceived value of making a decision now will always be too low to persuade her to buy now.

This is one of the reasons why we offer incentive accessory packages the first time she comes into the store. If she leaves without buying, her cost of no change (not buying) is a lot higher than the cost to change (buy now) since she will have to pay more money for the accessories when she returns. The greater the value you can create in the bride's mind, the more successful you will be in making the sale.

5. Have a unique marketing offer with a deadline that creates urgency, interrupts what she is doing, and helps her to make a decision.

Many brides today have a difficult time making a decision because they think they need to keep looking when they've found the dress. Even more importantly, she will not be moved to action unless the value of what you are offering exceeds the amount of money she will spend at your store. This is a simple concept to explain, but a much harder concept to quantify since everybody perceives value differently.

It is easy to believe that you offer the best dresses in the world and that all brides should buy from you. However, until the bride in front of you believes that, you won't make a sale. Your sales results hinge on the bride's belief that the dress she is wearing is the perfect one for her.

Until she believes this, she will always hesitate and wait.

Having the right dress in the store is only part of the equation. The other part is having an offer with a deadline that creates urgency. Great marketing interrupts what you are thinking about and shifts your thinking to the marketing message and the offer you should consider. All of us are busy and caught up in the details of our own lives. When the offer to buy from you at your store outweighs the cost of waiting, the bride will make the decision to move forward. Most importantly, when *she* sees tremendous value and knows she has to act now, the speed at which she moves through the steps of validation and justification accelerate.

6. Get better at selling.

Most bridal consultants do not spend enough time working on improving their sales skills and techniques and they actually think they have more skills than they *really* do. In good economic times, you don't have to possess as many selling skills to be successful at selling. However, in tough economic times, only the best trained and developed bridal consultants will consistently close and help brides find their dream dress. This means that you have to get better at selling.

Bridal consultants who really understand *why* brides buy are those that rise to the top. They are continually learning and developing themselves. They have an organized system they use to study, practice, and implement what they are learning so they can stay on top of their game.

If you haven't read or studied anything on selling in the past month or six months, the reality is that your skills aren't as sharp as you think they are. Don't wait until you've lost a sale to work on overcoming the objections that are holding you back. You know what your most common objections are. Objections in selling are predictable, so be ready for the objections you fear most when they come up through diligent study and focus.

If you are not personally closing as many sales as you know you can, consider these seven suggestions:

Get back to the basics. When we stop selling, usually what's wrong is not something super complicated. In fact, you probably know what's wrong. Often, our biggest problem is that we have turned inwardly and think our problems are all someone else's or a competitor's fault. Wrong. Nothing could be further from the truth. Take out a list of the top nine skills necessary to succeed in sales and list two or three of the things you need to start changing right now. If you will do the same and be determined to take action, you will see immediate improvement.

Have a game plan. Study sales training materials at for at least thirty minutes each day. Come in a little earlier every day and revisit what you are going to do to turn things around. Make two to three phone calls to brides every day.

Study and practice how to present gowns and create more urgency when you sell so that the bride will want to buy now.

Think more from the bride's perspective. Ask, "What would I need to see or hear as a bride that would convince me that this store is the lowest risk and that they have my wedding plans and dreams at the forefront of their attention?" This new approach can give you new ideas to sell better.

Spend time watching and learning from the best. Watch and learn from fantastic salespeople, especially the top salesperson at your store or at a fantastic store where you shop. Find out what she is saying and doing that allows her to make sales. If you are really brave, ask for her feedback on what you can do to improve.

Involve the bride more. People love to buy. As bridal consultants, we don't have to force brides to buy; we just have to allow them to participate in the sale and feel good about the choice they have made. Brides want to buy; but before they do, they want to feel that they are in competent hands: yours. Brides want a bridal consultant who shows leadership and is willing to guide them in the right direction.

Ask questions in the right sequence. You make sales by building momentum through the proper sequence of questions that help you find out exactly what the bride is looking for. Questions help you uncover the needs and desires of the bride. If you go out of order or skip steps, you will lose the sale. Pushing to close the sale too soon by asking "Is this the one?" before she has narrowed it down to the last two dresses (and you are sure which one she likes better) is a sure way to kill the sale.

When your skills improve you will be more confident at selling. You will also know better where the bride is in the sales process at all times. This will help you know what the bride is thinking so you can help her build buying desire to take action now.

Stay sharp by constantly improving your skills. If you don't, they will stagnate by default.

7. Utilize psychological triggers more often.

One of the most fascinating parts about selling is understanding how the human brain thinks, reasons, and makes decisions. According to Patrick Renvoise and Christophe Morin in their book *Neuromarketing: Understanding the "Buy Button" in Your Customer's Brain*, there are three distinct parts of our brain that communicate with each other. These areas are "the new brain, the middle brain and the old brain." Each has a separate function (The *new brain* **thinks** - it processes rational data, the *middle brain* **feels** - it processes emotions and gut feelings, but it is the old brain that actually **decides. It is the actual trigger of decision.**"—*Neuromarketing*, p. 6.

Why is this important? The reason is that the old brain triggers decision based on six very specific stimuli. When you understand these, you can influence how the brides you work with each day go about making decisions.

These Six Stimuli are:

1. **Self-centered** - We all think mostly of ourselves. To counter this tendency, you have to be careful to focus solely on the bride in front of you because the old brain is only responsive to things that pertain to her.

2. **Contrast** - "The old brain is sensitive to clear contrast, such as before/after, risky/safe, with/without, or fast/slow. Contrast allows the old brain to make quick, risk free decisions. **Without it, the old brain enters into a state of confusion leading to a delayed decision or no decision at all."** What this means is that "you must create contrast to get the old brain's attention." Help brides see the contrast and your sales will go up because you will trigger the decision making part of the bride's brain.

3. **Tangible Input** - This refers to word patterns and combinations the brides can wrap their head around. To do this effectively, speak in simple language that is familiar and friendly and most of all recognizable. Don't confuse the bride by using unfamiliar words without teaching these new words to her first. Remember, how you felt when you first learned descriptive terms of wedding dresses. Educate brides and they will like and trust you even more.

   The word combinations that have the most meaning to brides are: save money, we'll take care of all the details, no hassle, painless process of getting alterations completed, etc. Be sure the input you give to brides triggers decision and not confusion.

4. **The Beginning and the End** - The old brain enjoys openings and finales and often overlooks what is in between. Such a short attention span has huge implications on how you as a seller should *construct* and *deliver* your messages. Placing the most important content at the **beginning** is a must, as is **repeating** it at the end. Anything in the middle of your message will be mostly overlooked. When selling, heighten the degree of anticipation that your bride will feel as she walks down the aisle wearing the dress she

loves. Always be comparing and contrasting two dresses (the one she likes most and the one she has on) and keep comparing and contrasting them until she finds the dress. Many times, the first dress the bride puts on is the dress she loves most – so keep coming back to it over and over again, until the end of the sale and this act will help trigger the old brain to buy.

5. **Visual Stimuli** - Selling wedding gowns or prom dresses is a visual sale. Never forget that the bride is analyzing how she looks in the dress from multiple angles. It is best to find out how she is reacting to the dress and then repeat the things that she likes or that she finds attractive about the dress when closing to drive them into the old brain and trigger the buying decision.

6. **Emotion** - Highlight the bride's buying experience with emotion. Ask implication questions to help build emotion in the sale. When emotions run high, the old brain is triggered into making a buying decision. Great questions can help brides picture themselves in the wedding dress they are wearing on *their* wedding day. Helping them picture the dream they want in their mind introduces emotion and excitement as well. If you want to be more successful at helping a bride visualize herself wearing the dress she has on (and it is the one), use word phrases and pictures that will help her visualize the outcome of her wedding day.

There are more than 100 psychological triggers you can use to trigger decision. I outline many of them and teach you how to use them when selling in my three CD sales training program, *Psychological Triggers You Can Use to Create Buying Frenzies at Your Store.*

If you will utilize these seven strategies I've outlined in this chapter, you will shift the power and control from the bride back to you at the store and you will make more sales. You have to focus on selling as though your life depends on it, because it does. Improve the areas of your business that will help you become more valuable in the eyes of the brides in your area and most importantly be sure to communicate this by teaching and educating the bride. Give brides a *reason* to believe that your store is the best choice and *accelerate the process of building and earning trust.* When you do this effectively, you can develop a relationship and help each bride find her dream dress now.

Chapter 6

Know How to Buy and Sell Your Inventory to Make a Profit

Understanding what is going on with your inventory and making decisions around that is one of the most important keys to succeeding in the bridal business. It can also be one of the most complex since there are so many factors to analyze to make sure you have the right merchandise in your store in the right colors and sizes at the right times.

If you don't know what you have or what is selling, you will likely make big mistakes when it comes to what you will buy at the next market. Most stores have a very organized system they use to manage and control their inventory and to specifically determine what they need and will buy when they go to market.

To help you know how to buy and sell your inventory to make a profit, here are some insights into how to make the difficult decisions around inventory. I won't mention any particular brands or manufacturers when talking about how these choices should be made. Instead, I'll ask and answer ten questions so you can better understand how to do the buying in your business. I won't share a list of who you should buy from. You can determine this on your own.

1. How do you determine what to buy when you go to market? What's your overall buying strategy?

I determine what we will buy for our store with three criteria:

1. What's selling now and where do trends seem to be heading?

    - What fabrics are selling most in your store?
      - Silk? Taffeta? Tulle? Organza? Chiffon?

2. What line will give me the greatest exclusivity and margin? In the case of prom, which line will give my store the most visibility, the most sales and the greatest margin?

3. What season is approaching and what is needed to meet the demands of our marketplace?

It is a good idea to divide your inventory into departments and classify it accordingly. You can assign members of your staff to be in charge of certain classifications of inventory (prom, bridal, accessories, mother of the bride, shoes, etc.) If you have it broken down into divisions, and delegate this successfully, it can give you a much more accurate analysis of what is selling, why it is selling, and how often you need to reorder or stock a certain dress or item. It can also help you predict where the market is moving so you can move there as well.

When I go to market, here is my overall buying strategy:

- I walk the market first to get a general feel for who is there, who is not there, and what new vendors may be of interest.

- Then, I see our vendors that represent our top selling bridal and prom lines first. I look at their new lines and consider my top picks. I wait to place my order until after I've seen everything at market and feel I have made the best decision.

- Then, I consider accessories (veils, tiaras, etc.) and buy things that may be low in stock or bring in new items that will fill holes.

- Next, I consider new vendor possibilities. In particular, I look for private lines and high margin lines not sold online by Internet vendors.

- I also seek to network with friends and industry peers who I can learn from. I strongly believe that market is all about ROI – relationships, outcomes, and improvements.

2. **How do you monitor your inventory? What types of reports do you do to evaluate what is selling and what isn't? How often do you look at these reports and how do you use them for your next buy?**

Here are the reports I look at:

- Inventory by Category (tells you YTD sales for each item and how many remain in inventory) – can find best sellers from this report
- Sales by size
- Sales by color
- Sales by vendor (should be checked every week)
- How many gowns sold in each category

You should look at certain reports weekly and others monthly depending on the volume and type of sales you do.

Put together an inventory control form like the one illustrated on page 135 that you can use to put all of your data on each week (this will help you make great decisions and will provide a guide and road map to see trends over time).

3. Is it necessary to increase inventory to increase sales? Why or why not?

The short answer is yes. If you specialize in a certain niche where engagement times are short, and there isn't time to order a dress, the answer is definitely yes. More and more brides expect to buy off the rack because that is what the big box retailers do. The convenience of having gowns in stock can be a factor to help you get more sales of brides who are getting married sooner than later.

4. Do you stock or special order? Why have you chosen to emphasize one over the other?

85-90% of our gowns are sold out of stock and the remaining 10-15% are sold via special order.

We are a stock store because it is a point of difference for us and because we have figured out how to make the numbers work for us this way. Most of the brides we sell to are fine with us selling off the rack because that is how we sell and because we treat the dresses with great care and respect (since it will be worn by a bride on her wedding day).

We have done special orders for prom and we have also stocked for prom.

You will have to determine what will work best for you for each area of focus of your store. There are pros and cons to both options. If you do decide to become an off-the-rack store, talk with others who have done it first, so you can learn from their mistakes *before* you make your own. Making mistakes with inventory can be very costly and can take a long time to recover from (if the mistakes don't cause you to go out of business first).

During prom season, you have to be particularly sensitive to what is selling and what is not moving since you have such a limited time frame to sell gowns.

My philosophy is that if a dress doesn't sell at least once within 30-45 days of

Inventory Control Form:

Week of: ______________________________

Gown Statistics:

of Bridal Gowns Sold: ________
# of Bridesmaids Sold: ________
# of MOB Sold: ___________
# of Accessories Sold: __________

Trends Breakdown:

Silhouettes
# of Ball gowns sold ________

- Asymmetrical
- Dropped waist
- Basque waist
- Natural waist

# of Empires sold ________

# of Princess cuts sold ________

# of sheaths sold ________

Sizes Sold

Colors Sold

What fabrics are selling best?

Sales by Vendor:

Vendor	# of Dresses Sold This Week	Overall % of Dresses Sold This Week

Best Selling Styles:

Pricing:

Are there any gowns that need to be adjusted in price (up or down)?

Styles to Reorder (for stock):

Vendor	Style #	Cut	Size / Color

Trends to Watch:

What is the average size of wedding gowns we're selling? Is this different than what it has been historically?

What are brides asking for that we don't have?

What are brides loving that we are just getting in?

What pictures are brides bringing in that you don't have styles like?

Are there any styles that our competitors have that we don't have and that brides are asking for?

putting it out for sale, you should sell the sample off the rack, recover your investment cost and then invest it in something that will sell.

If you sell multiples of a dress off a sample, order more of that dress and have it in stock to offer to brides (or sell off of the sample for as long as you can).

5. What is the biggest mistake you've ever made with your inventory and what did you learn from it?

The biggest mistakes I've ever made happened when I allowed myself to be swayed by the persuasiveness or charm of the seller and the "attractiveness" of a line.

At a market in the infancy of our bridal store, I purchased several dresses from a new line of quincinera dresses that were "unbelievably hot" and "were selling like crazy" in my market. Our store is in a predominantly Hispanic community and we wanted to get into this market. Without doing any research (other than taking the salesperson's word for it—as he was very persuasive and seemed to want to help), I went ahead and bought the dresses. He told me that he knew our market well and what was selling and would recommend the dresses that we should buy that would sell.

When the dresses came in, we had absolutely no interest from any of our quincinera prospects to buy or even try on the dresses. Later, when the sales representative approached me again at market, he asked me how the dresses were doing for the store. I told him that we hadn't sold a single one and that they weren't working for us. He said, "Well, that's too bad. I guess your store isn't a quincinera store. Your customer is white and blonde. Why don't you come and check out some of these dresses?"

I couldn't believe his audacity and I chose not to buy from him again. I learned from this experience that you should never invest in a line unless you have a specific plan and budget for that line and you have carefully thought through how the margin, exclusivity, and your market fits into the equation.

I also learned from this experience to be cautious as many sales representatives are primarily interested in making their commissions regardless of how well the dresses will sell in your store.

6. When you look at a new line, how do you evaluate it?

Here are four great questions to ask when evaluating a new line:

- Can you develop a working relationship with the vendor?
- Will they respect and protect your territory?
- Will the line fill needed gaps in silhouettes or styles and give you a good profit margin?
- What line will I replace with this line?

As you look at a line, have some method for grading gowns such as stars or numbers next to your favorite gowns – then go back and carefully analyze how the buy will fit into the rest of what you are doing.

Finally, remember your numbers and your budget. Have a plan and stick to it.

Robin Saltzman of Jon's Bridal in Tampa, Florida once told me and a group of store owners at a Better Bridal Group seminar:

"Don't talk yourself into a dress. Ask instead: Is it a silhouette you need? Will it show well?"

That is great advice. Also, you should look at a line twice at market before committing to it.

Here are three other big mistakes I've made when buying for our store:

1) **Getting caught up in the emotion of the moment.** The emotion of seeing others order a dress and feeling that I didn't

want to be left out has caused me to make poor judgments about how well a line will sell in our store. Remember, investing in a line of dresses is just like investing in stocks or in real estate. ***The real money is made when you buy, not when you sell.***

2) **Being unprepared.** Not knowing exactly what I had in my store when I came to market and exactly what I needed (sizes, colors, styles, etc.) One of the biggest mistakes you can make is to guess what you think will sell based on your gut feeling. We made this mistake early on in our business and found after one prom season that we had nearly thirty size 6 dresses in calypso.

   Now, we carefully count and evaluate each color in each size before placing an order so we don't have too many of one color and not enough of another in each size.

3) **Not having patience to see everything and the discipline to make decisions based on what the store *really* needs as opposed to an emotional gut reaction.** The worst mistakes I have ever made have been when I haven't been patient enough to see everything through because I was tired and just wanted to be done.

Have you ever made any of these mistakes? If so, it was likely because you came to market less prepared than you should have. Do your homework *before* going to market and stick to your plan.

7. How many lines do you carry and what influenced your decision to carry that many?

I think one of the biggest mistakes made in the bridal business is made here. If you have too many lines that you feel you need to be competitive in your market many times you end up **tying up money that will not yield the best profit margin or competitive advantage (exclusivity).**

This often happens because the seller promotes it as the "hottest" and "best" line at market (they all say this and tell you which dresses to buy by saying such things as: "This dress booked in our top ten at the last market." "Everyone loves this dress." "Here is another money dress." "This dress is doing very well." – oftentimes, the sellers will be promoting inventory that they have in stock or that they have coming in because they want to get rid of it.)

Beware of dresses that look attractive but have no proven market for you. The temptation is to have an invest a little and see approach. This may work but it ties up your capital and everyone wants you to do this. After a few seasons, you find that you have more lines than you need and you don't have any capital left to invest in lines that *can* make you money until you sell off what you already have.

The most successful stores I know limit how many lines they have and the majority of what they sell goes through one, two, or at the most three profitable lines.

Be careful to focus on your area of exclusivity instead of trying to be all things to all people.

8. How do you determine if you should keep a line?

Here are several questions to consider when evaluating a line that you should know the answers to *before* you attend market (and you are swayed by the seller to buy the line again):

- Does it sell?
- How well does it sell?
- Are you really making money with the line?
- How profitable is the line in comparison with other lines you carry? Would putting more money into more profitable lines be a better use of your funds?
- Do I have exclusivity with the line? How close is the closest competitor who also has access to the line?

- Is the stress factor of working with the vendor too high because of late deliveries, rush shipping fees, etc.?

9. What do you do with discontinued dresses?

When a dress has been discontinued, immediately sell the samples.

If a lot of the merchandise that you have ordered is being discontinued, **call the manufacturer and find out why.**

If you are primarily a special order store, look to i**nvest in lines that don't discontinue very often** so you can get a good shelf life out of the samples you order.

One of the best ways that you can **create urgency** in the sales process is to talk about how you never know when a dress may be discontinued and that if they love the dress they should get it now while it is still available.

"If you want to buy this dress, you had better buy it now. If you wait, it will be gone. We never know when a dress is going to be discontinued or when it won't be available any more. I would hate for you to come back and find out that this dress is no longer available to order."

Many bridal stores have many discontinued gowns that take up a lot of room at their stores. If you find yourself in this situation, have a limited time sale for one week which you can promote to brides in your area.

Put all of the discontinued gowns and damaged gowns on a rack and put a sign up that says – ONE WEEK SALE – Today ALL gowns on this rack ___ % OFF (Then, lower the price of the dresses down 10% every day until the end of the week.)

You can promote this to brides by telling them about the one week sale and inviting them to come in during that week to get the gown of their choice (best gowns will go fast) at a deeply discounted rate and that all brides who come in will be entered in a drawing to win the dress of their choice of whatever is left absolutely FREE.

Then, you can tie the premium offer to it by saying:

"Free gift for the first ____ people beginning at 11am, Thursday, ______ 19th."

Start the sale on a Thursday and have it go to a Wednesday. That way you will have your biggest discounts on a slower day – which will help you bring your sales up that day and only have to discount your dresses 30-40% off on Saturday or Sunday.

10. What one piece of advice would you give to a new store owner who is deciding whether to carry a line or not and how heavily they should stock it in their store (samples vs. stock)?

Ask yourself these questions:

Do you really need it?
If your competitor had it, would your business go on?
How much can you really commit to a line?

I like what I heard Robin Saltzman of Jon's Bridal say once: "It is better to be a big fish to a few companies than a little fish to lots of companies."

Find a line or manufacturer that you can invest in that will support you and **do more business with them**.

Final thought: Who you buy from is nearly as important as what you buy. Strengthen relationships with your key vendors.

CHAPTER 7

ALWAYS KEEP THE BRIDE'S EXPERIENCE IN MIND

After every interaction / transaction at your store, a bride is one of three things:

1. Disappointed – she got less than she expected
2. Satisfied – she got only what she expected
3. Delighted – she got more than she expected

Which one of the three are the majority of your brides?

The goal to delight each of the prospective customers who walk through our doors is a noble and a challenging goal. It is something we can all strive for. We can all be better at going beyond just aiming to satisfy our customers.

As I mentioned before, the first six words of the business classic *Good to Great* state, "The enemy of great is good." We should never be satisfied with just *good* customer service. We should all strive to be *exceptional* throughout our entire interaction with each bride and prom customer.

Author and speaker Mark Sanborn makes this distinction between marketing, sales, and customer service:

"Marketing creates demand. Selling creates transactions. Service creates customers."

The goal of this chapter is to help you ***move*** from average or good customer service ***to exceptional and great customer service that delights your customers***.

In the end, if we only do what average bridal stores do, we'll never be better than they are. We have to aim higher. We have to always keep the bride's experience in mind.

One way to do this is to establish your store's vision of customer service. Here are our store's goals with each bride we work with:

- To partner with brides to provide exquisite and beautiful gowns that will help them look and feel absolutely gorgeous on their wedding day.

- To give responsive service and personalized advice.

- To been seen as a trusted advisor for their wedding.

- To be known as the store that cares.

How does the customer service in your store measure up to your competitors?

Does it beat the pants off any and all competition? As the old saying goes: "When there is not much difference between your product and that of your competitors, there had better be a big difference in the way you deal with your customers."

Evaluating How You Are Doing:

Do you delight and dazzle the brides and prom girls coming into your store, or are they disappointed and discouraged when they come to you with legitimate concerns and problems?

We all need to better assess how we are doing with our customer service. Here are 9 ways to evaluate how well you are doing in meeting the needs of your brides. Evaluate how your store is doing in each area by circling the number that best reflets where you are on a scale of 1-10 (10 being the highest):

1. Vision and Philosophy

1 2 3 4 5 6 7 8 9 10

Do you have an ambitious and inspiring customer service statement or philosophy that makes a bold declaration about how much you value the brides and prom customers coming into your store?

Do your employees know what that vision and philosophy is?

Have they embraced it?

Do you see this vision in their actions with customers each day?

One way to look at this is in your approach:

Do you have a caring or a conquering approach?

In selling as in medicine, prescription before diagnosis is malpractice. Selling requires caring.

In the end, every bride wants to feel important, appreciated and valued.

Most customer service problems originate from forgetting others and thinking only of ourselves. Instead, we should always strive to keep the bride's experience in mind.

Help your team to think of others first and care about the concerns that they bring up.

2. Example

1 2 3 4 5 6 7 8 9 10

Do you live your customer service creed?

It is impossible to avoid leading by example. Somebody is always watching.

Do your bridal consultants and other employees catch you offering great customer service? Or do they catch you grumbling about how mad it makes you when...."

Jim Cathcart says, "We judge ourselves by our intentions, but others judge us by our actions."

Does your walk match your talk about customer service issues?

Is it consistent with the vision or philosophy you have in your store?

Do you support employees who go out of their way to take care of problems that come up or do you lash out in frustration or anger?

Do you give your staff the resources they need to excel?

3. Selection of Employees

1 2 3 4 5 6 7 8 9 10

Are the members of your staff emotionally, culturally, and intellectually prepared to provide the quality of service that your brides expect and deserve?

Do you treat your employees well?

I really like this statement from Herb Kelleher, former CEO of Southwest Airlines:

"If you don't treat your own people well, they won't treat other people well."

Staff members who are treated with thoughtfulness, respect and compassion are more likely to treat your customers with the same type of respect.

Stephen Covey in his book *The Seven Habits of Highly Effective People* uses the analogy of the Emotional Bank Account to really emphasize this point. He says:

"The Emotional Bank Account represents the quality of the relationship you have with others. It's like a financial bank account in that you can make 'deposits', by proactively doing things that build trust in the relationship, or you can make 'withdrawls', by reactively doing things that decrease the level of trust. And at any given time the balance of trust in the account determines how well you can communicate and solve problems with another person." —Stephen R. Covey, *The 7 Habits of Highly Effective Families*, p. 46.

Strive to help your team members take emotional ownership for the service goals you have for your store.

Hire the right type of people. Hire people who have the insatiable desire to serve people.

If you see a mistake being made by one of your employees, take them aside and privately teach them how it should have been done.

I like this statement by former NFL coach Dick Vermeil:

"To not confront poor execution and behaviors is to *endorse* it."

On the other hand, if you observe one of your employees doing a fantastic job, let her and *everyone* on the team know it.

Dick Vermeil also observed: **"To not reinforce good execution and behavior is to *extinguish* it."**

If the people you hire aren't excited about serving the brides who come into your store, you've made a hiring mistake.

Have you ever noticed how clean Disneyland is? It's no accident. Rather, it's a subtle way of building employee morale and telling the customer, 'We take pride in our work.'

It is obvious that they value cleanliness. But, they also work very hard to hire and train people who delight in cleaning and creating an amazing experience for their guests at their resorts and parks.

Think about this value in your store:

Do brides coming in see a clean store? Is a smile the first thing they see when they come in?

Carefully evaluate what you see around you – do the brides coming into your store see a clean, neat, professional operation, or one that looks poorly maintained?

Ask, 'What can I do to make our business look even better?'

Take some time to look at your business through the bride's eyes.

Eighty-five percent of what we remember comes through our eyes, eleven percent comes through our ears and the rest through our other senses.

Be sure to hire those who are motivated to serve. Remember, it is much easier to hire customer service oriented professionals than it is to train professionals to focus on the skill of customer service.

I really like this statement by Mark Sanborn in his book, *The Fred Factor*:

"There are no unimportant jobs, just people who feel unimportant doing their jobs."

What are you doing every day to let your bridal consultants and other staff members know that they are important to you and the success of your store?

As Mark Sanborn says: "The difference [in organizations] is in the people. Uninspired people rarely do inspired work.

Passionate people in an organization are different. They do ordinary things extraordinarily well....Customers don't have relationships with organizations; they form relationships with individuals. "—*The Fred Factor*, p. 74.

Add meaning to the lives of your employees everyday. If one of your bridal consultants doesn't see much *meaning* in what they do, they won't bring much *value* to what they do.

4. Performance Expectations

1 2 3 4 5 6 7 8 9 10

Do your employees know exactly how you expect them to behave in the various customer service situations they encounter? (ex.: answering the telephone, greeting people at the door, helping them try on gowns, answering questions, creating realistic expectations, etc.)

- Answering the Telephone – When brides call in, how are they treated? Remember, brides are thinking, 'Is this the kind of operation where I would like to spend my hard earned dollars or can I think of some other place that would treat me better?'

- Remember, you have to inspect what you expect. Train your front line staff on your expectation for how the phone should be answered, how a bride or prom customer should be properly greeted, etc. You create the expectation. If you don't create any expectation, don't be surprised when the result you want doesn't happen.

- Perceptions are realities. What perceptions do the brides in your area form when:

  - They call your store? If they are put on hold, how long are they on hold?
  - They receive a letter, catalog or invitation from you?
  - They ask a question?

- They see your store?
- They see your employees?
- They do business with you? Do they receive a thank you card or a personal call thanking them for their business?

The reality about our world today is that *an hour of brilliant service* that you personally offer **can be undone** *by a minute of indifference* by you or one of your employees.

Let's say that you have a bride who is absolutely livid about something. Whenever you deal with an upset bride, you are dealing with two issues:

1. Her feelings (she feels hurt, betrayed, or wronged in some way)
2. How to solve the problem that made her mad in the first place

If you try to solve the problem without soothing her angry feelings, she won't be back and she'll tell everyone she knows how insensitive you were.

You really have to satisfy both issues.

Here are 5 ways that Michael LeBoeuf in his book *How to Win Customers and Keep Them for Life* recommends that you create a performance expectation for the bridezillas you encounter:

1. Keep your cool.

He says: " If you are right, there's no reason to lose your temper. If you're wrong, you can't afford to lose it. Never allow a customer to put you on the defensive. It's only normal to want to defend yourself when a customer verbally assaults you, but it only makes things worse. Lashing back or saying, "Don't blame me. I didn't do it," or making excuses will only make [her] angrier."

He continues:

"One of the worst things you can do is argue with the customer.... Instead, go on the offensive with a positive approach. Get on the same physical level as the other person. Keep a comfortable distance and look [her] in the eyes with the expression of someone who is concerned about [her] problem. Respond to [her] comments with something like 'I'm sorry you're upset. Let's see what we can do to solve this problem and make things right for you.'"

The important thing is to let the bride blow off steam and calm down. If her tirade is distracting or obnoxious to other customers in your store, invite her to a more private place where you can hear her out.

Try not to take her remarks personally. When we are angry, we all say things we don't really mean. She is obviously frustrated and needs to vent her feelings.

Instead of getting frustrated yourself, listen closely for things that she says when she is critical. She will often give you important information that can help you solve the problem. Brides will teach you how to deal with them if you'll pay attention to the messages they are sending.

2. Listen with empathy and for the facts.

"An angry [bride] will usually respond well if [she] feels that you really care about [her] problem and are trying to feel what [she] is feeling. Treating [her] problem as if it is routine or asking [her] to fill out a form without first listening to [her] is just asking for more trouble. Angry people need to be heard and understood."

Try to look for areas of agreement and agree with the bride whenever you can.

Use statements like these to help the bride see that you empathize with her frustration:

- "I can understand why you're angry."
- "I agree that this was quite an inconvenience for you."
- "If I were you, I would be mad too."

These types of statements help to neutralize the anger so that you can come up with a reasonable solution together.

I love this statement by Dr. LeBoeuf:

"Most customers start to calm down after you listen to their initial outburst. Your next step is to be a problem-solver while continuing to be a hand-holder."

Ask questions at this point to get more clarity about what happened:

- "What went wrong?"
- "What did you do then?"
- "Who told you that?"
- "Can you tell me more about that?"

Take notes if it is appropriate. You may even want to feed back the most important points and then ask: "Did I get that right?"

3. Take action to solve the problem.

"Once you have a good grasp of the problem, do what you can to help the customer as much as you can. If possible, offer the customer several options and let [her] choose. If you can't solve the problem for [her], refer [her] to someone who can and do what you can to put [her] in contact with the problem-solver. And if your company is at fault, by all means, apologize profusely." —Michael LeBoeuf, *How to Win Customers and Keep Them for Life*, p. 96.

Be positive about what you can do, not what you can't.

Don't Say	*Instead Say*
We aren't open on Sundays.	We'll have the dress ready for you Saturday by 1:00pm.
I can't get this taken care of today.	I'll have this taken care of so you can pick it up first thing in the morning.

4. Bring the incident to a polite close.

After you have offered a solution and she has accepted it, say "Is there any other way I can be of service to you today?"

If the answer is no, thank her for sharing her concern with you and follow up with her after the resolution has been completed to make sure everything was handled to her satisfaction.

5. Don't expect to win them all.

"No matter how patient, helpful and understanding you are, there will be a small percentage of irate customers that it's impossible to satisfy. Unfortunately, some customers are just plain angry, and get their satisfaction from giving others a hard time."

"If you have someone who refuses to calm down or insists on being obnoxious despite your best efforts, calmly tell [her], 'If we are going to continue to do business, it has to be a good deal for both of us." Then calmly offer the solution again and move on. If a customer shows definite signs of becoming hostile or violent, don't try to handle it alone. Get help from higher management or the authorities." —Michael LeBoeuf, *How to Win Customers and Keep Them for Life*, p. 96.

Dealing with angry, upset brides takes a tremendous amount of self-control and is a tough job for anyone. If you have these situations occurring regularly, go back to your processes and determine how to eliminate potential stumbling blocks. Find an outlet to release your emotional tension from these types of situations as well.

I like what Dr. LeBoeuf says: "Don't expect to always be perfect in dealing with angry customers. You're human too."

5. Overcoming and recovering from customer complaints.

1 2 3 4 5 6 7 8 9 10

Make a list of the most common customer complaints that you

are experiencing. For example, a dress altered incorrectly, a dress didn't come in like they expected, a deadline missed for receiving a dress.

Complaints point out things that need improvement. We don't typically consider complaints to be good things, but if we use them to identify weak spots in our systems and take corrective action they can be a great help to us.

Most complaints happen because the expectations of our customers are being violated in some way.

Remember the old saying : "Frustration is the result of violated expectations." Before you get emotionally upset, try to look at things from the bride's point of view and analyze what expectations she might have had.

A good question to ask is, "How well do you train your staff on what to do in certain customer service situations?"

When you encounter a complaint from a bride or prom customer, look at it as an opportunity to better train your staff. This is especially important if one of your staff created an expectation that couldn't be met.

Are each of your staff members trained on what the rest of the staff does or cannot do? This will eliminate problems as well because they see the big picture of how everything works and how it works together.

As B.C. Forbes, the founder of *Forbes* magazine once said:

"Complaints offer opportunities to make friends or to make enemies...Isn't it worthwhile to exert every effort to turn complainers into boosters?"

Sometimes brides can be downright rude, demanding or wrong...but, the customer is always one thing...the customer. They pay our salary, they pay the salaries of our employees, and they keep our stores open.

There are some great crazy stories mentioned in the November/ December 2006 issue of *Vows* in an article entitled "Customer Harassment". Many of us have our own crazy stories of difficult bridezillas that we've dealt with to tell. The reality is that this is a free country and we can still *choose* who to do business with.

I really like this point that author Laurie Fisher makes on p. 28 of this article: "If you sense you can't make a person happy, politely invite them to shop elsewhere. They will say good things about you, and you can pass the problems on to someone else. Follow your gut and know when to cut losses. The quicker you do, the better off for everyone." —Laurie Fisher, Customer Harassment, *Vows*, Nov/Dec 2006, p. 28.

The article also gives some great advice on how to deal with customers who cross the line and go from being obnoxious to downright dangerous.

Even the best stores make mistakes, especially when it gets really, really busy.

The difference in average stores and great stores is how they ***recover***.

Remember, it's rarely ever too late to save a customer's business if you recover remarkably. The best way to do that is to satisfy the two things that every customer wants: ***solutions to their problem and good feelings.***

A sincere apology is the first step in dealing with a customer complaint. Then explain why something may or may not have happened and explain how you are going to take care of it. Don't make excuses. Do your best to take on the problem head on. Don't evade it. ***People today want action, not excuses.***

The best problem solving approach to moving brides from mad, sad, or scared to glad is to:

- Ask two questions calmly:
  - What is the situation now?
  - What would you like it to be?

- Once you know the answers to these two questions, you can decide how to solve her problem. Even if you can't solve her problem, letting her express it and taking the time to listen will make her feel better. Just knowing that you cared enough to listen and tried to help will leave her with a much better impression than if you had taken a 'that's not my problem' attitude.

On a scale of 1-10, how well do you and your team overcome customer complaints and focus on creating solutions to their problems and good feelings again?

6. Underpromise and Overdeliver

1 2 3 4 5 6 7 8 9 10

Most of the customer service issues that have come up in our store come from one individual overpromising something that created an unrealistic expectation.

Don't overpromise and create unrealistic expectations. You may make a sale by promising something, but you may also create a nightmare situation later on. Don't let your mouth write a check your store can't cash. The higher you build customer expectation, the harder it becomes to meet and exceed them.

The most important rule in customer service is this: **Underpromise and Overdeliver.** If you think you can finish the job in three weeks, promise it in four to six weeks.

Do you or members of your staff underpromise and overdeliver?

Do you exceed customer expectations at every opportunity by doing the little things that mean a lot?

Do you personalize and customize your service?

Do your brides believe that you meet their unique needs?

Keep in touch with customers and keep them informed. If we fail to keep in touch with our customers, they won't be aware of the great service we are giving them until something goes wrong and they don't get it. Stay in touch and let them know that their satisfaction is our priority in word and deed.

7. Add value to every transaction.

1 2 3 4 5 6 7 8 9 10

Author Guy Kawasaki, an early McIntosh evangelist for Apple Computers, tells this story:
"A young girl bought gumdrops from a small shop even though a more convenient supermarket opened nearby. Asked why, the girl said, "Nick [the store owner] always gives me more candy. The girl in the other store takes some away." Apparently, salesclerks in the supermarket put more than the weight, and then the clerks subtracted a few gumdrops to get the right amount. Nick, the owner of the small shop, put in too little and then added more. The children were convinced they got the better deal from Nick." —Guy Kawasaki, *How to Drive Your Competition Crazy*, pp. 125-126.

What things can you do to create value for the brides and prom customers coming into your store?

What can you do to differentiate yourself from your competition in the following areas:

- **Be nicer** (offer more courtesy during their interaction with you)
- **Offer more value** (especially in intangible, personal, and unique ways)
- **Sell better and higher quality products** (gowns, jewelry, etc.)
- **Be faster** (offer speed on getting a gown in or sell it out of stock instead of special ordering it)

- **Be different** (have styles that no one else has, or come up with creative ways to promote yourself to the bride)

- **Be easier and more fun to deal with** (allow the bride to have a blast at your store)

8. Nurturing the Bride

1 2 3 4 5 6 7 8 9 10

Remember that most brides have never made this type of purchase before. Help them to know what the next steps are. Help her feel confident and secure that you will be able to take care of her and make the experience of finding her wedding gown an extremely enjoyable and wonderful event.

Help the bride know that you are genuinely concerned about her well-being and helping make her search easy and fun.

Think about how you appear to others.

Do your best to treat brides:

- Warmly, friendly, sympathetically, courteously, attentively, sensitively, responsively, thoughtfully, and appreciatively

- Let them know that you treasure them by how you treat them.

"When the relationship is right, the details are negotiable. When tension is high, the details become the obstacles." —Jim Cathcart

9. Soliciting and responding to customer feedback.

1 2 3 4 5 6 7 8 9 10

Do you make it easy for customers to get in touch with you?

Do you listen to your customers in every way possible in order to understand what they expect from you and how well you're providing it?

Do you act on what you've heard to improve the experiences that brides have in your store?

The only way to get feedback from your brides is to ask them. Here is an example of our customer survey or comment card:

Customer Satisfaction Survey or Comment Card:

1. How do you feel about the styles of gowns and selection at our store?
2. How was the service you received at our store?
3. What made the difference between our store and other bridal shops?
4. What can we do to improve?

At the bottom, put a phrase like "We reserve the right to share your comments with others and use them in advertisements."

Now that we've talked about 9 ways that we can evaluate our customer service, let's talk about 12 specific situations where we can train our staff to move from the mundane to the majestic in our approach to customer service issues in the store.

1. Greeting a bride or customer who walks in the door

Avoid	*Instead Try*
"Hi" *(can appear unprofessional)* or "Yes?" *(can appear uncaring)*	"Hello," "Good morning," or "Good afternoon"
"May I help you?" *(disengages prospective customer and always invites the "I'm just looking response")*	Is this your first time in the store? • If yes, "What brought you in?" or "What special event brings you into our store today?" • If no, "Thank you for coming back; what brings you in this time?"

2. **Greeting a bride who walks in when you are really busy and you aren't able to help her immediately**

Avoid	*Instead Try*
Ignoring the bride or saying "You'll have to wait a minute."	"Welcome to our store. We'll be right with you. Please fill out our bridal registry and I'll go get someone who can help you."

3. **Bride asks if you can help at a time when you are able to give her attention**

Avoid	*Instead Try*
"OK" or "Sure." *(These are more unprofessional responses and while appreciated in some situations, can be improved on.)*	"I'll be happy to take care of that for you." or "I'll take care of that right away."

4. **You have to leave a bride to check on something.**

Avoid	*Instead Try*
Leaving without saying anything or saying, "I'll be right back."	"Can you wait a few minutes while I check on that for you? I'll be right back." Then be sure to thank them for their patience.

5. **You return after checking on something for a bride.**

Avoid	*Instead Try*
"Here's what I've learned."	"Thank you again for your patience. Here's what I've learned."

6. You need a bride to fill out a bridal registry form.

Avoid	*Instead Try*
"You need to fill out this form."	"Can you please fill out this bridal registry form for me. It will give me some very helpful information which will allow us to better serve you today." Then be sure to say, "Thanks. I really appreciate it." *(Make it a personal request and give a reason why.)*

7. You are asked why you are out of a particular size of a popular dress.

Avoid	*Instead Try*
"They (meaning management) didn't anticipate such a demand for that dress." (Never use the word 'they' when referring to your store).	"That's proven to be a very popular dress. We have a couple of other styles that can give you the same type of look, or if you are set on that dress, let me check on when we have more of that style coming in."

8. Bride asks you to do something that someone else at the store is assigned to do.

Avoid	*Instead Try*
"That's not my job" Or "I don't handle that."	"If you wait here, I'll find just the person who can help you." *(Then explain the customer's need to the person who handles that so the bride doesn't have to repeat herself.)*

9. Bride comes in and her dress or veil isn't steamed on schedule.

Avoid	*Instead Try*
"We didn't get it done. We're doing the best we can, but we're swamped right now."	"I am so sorry this isn't completed for you on schedule. I will take care of this personally and get this done for you right now. Is there something you can go do for __ minutes while you are waiting? I'll get this done right away." *(Then once it is finished apologize again and thank her for her patience.)*

10. You are having a hard time hearing what the bride is saying.

Avoid	*Instead Try*
"Can you speak more clearly?" Or "It's difficult to understand you." (Don't blame the bride even if that is where the problem lies.)	"I'm sorry, I didn't hear that. Can you please repeat what you just said?"

11. You complete the sale and are walking up to the register to complete the transaction.

Avoid	*Instead Try*
Saying nothing.	"Congratulations on finding your wedding dress!" "You've made a great decision today!" "It was so fun working with you today to find your dress."

12. The bride thanks you or compliments you on your service.

Avoid	*Instead Try*
"No problem." Or "It's my job."	"My pleasure." "You're welcome." "It has been such a pleasure to work with you." *(Add the brides name at the end of your statement, if possible.)*

Here are three reminders about always keeping the bride's experience in mind:

- Remember Tony Alessandra's Platinum Rule: "Do unto others as they would have you do unto them".
- The old saying is true: "People don't care what you know until they know that you care".
- There are no traffic jams in the extra mile.

What would happen if everyone at your store made it a point to delight at least one bride or prom girl every day?

The simple answer is that your store would grow to be legendary in your area.

Make the effort to do the little things that will make the biggest difference. I invite each of you to take some time to think about what I've discussed in this chapter, talk with your team about it, and sit down and write tangible goals for how you can improve. Your goal should be as Mark Sanborns says to: "Go beyond simply satisfying the customer. Aim to astound."

If this is your goal, you will take your customer experience up a notch and you will grow to new heights as brides experience what you are all about.

Chapter 8

Create and Use Systems to Run Your Business

The goal of this chapter is to help you as a business owner to shift from your store being entirely dependent upon your own personal skills to a business that is dependent upon a systematic process through which these skills can be transferred to anyone to whom you teach your system.

Why is this so important? Because the majority of small business owners and most bridal store owners I know feel that they can't take a break or go on vacation or ever leave their business because it is entirely dependent upon them and their skills.

If this is how you currently feel about your store, I hope this book will help you start the process of shifting your thinking from skills to systems.

A system is defined as a set of things, actions, ideas and information that interact with each other, and in so doing, alter other systems. For example, ***if* you do not have a system for selling, you are at the mercy of the bride's system for not buying.**

What I have found is that most bridal stores don't have a selling system. They wing it. They sell off the cuff. They react or respond to what the bride says. They sell one way this week and another way two or three weeks from now. The best sellers in the bridal business (or any successful business) have a system for how they sell. They have a scripted, practiced presentation which they have memorized.

They know what points to cover and when to cover them as they approach the bride, as they present wedding gowns and as they close the sale. In reality, it is an organized process that is set up so that the process of selling happens in the same way in the same order every single time.

Does this happen at your store?

Do each of your bridal consultants handle objections the same way?

Do you each handle all of the situations that come up in the same way?

The thing I've realized over the years is that sales is a pretty predictable process. You are not going to have brides come in tomorrow giving you objections to concerns you've never heard before. Since this is the case, I have felt that it is best to train our staff to anticipate objections that may come up (such as "Mom has to see the dress before I can buy" and that they have to "think about it".)

If you are in any way wondering whether a sales system might be helpful at your store, I invite you to ask yourself this question: "What would happen if all of my bridal consultants overcame every objection and had the tools and resources to help them close the sale virtually every time?"

If you can help your staff to overcome the most common objections, think about how much more powerful your sales team could be.

That is the power of an effective system.

In the bridal business, a system is a way of doing things to produce a marketing and a sales result. The system is the solution to get the results you want.

A great system has three characteristics:

1) *It leverages or magnifies people to the point at which they can produce extraordinary results consistently again and again* (like the sales example I just mentioned.)

2) *Every possible problem has been thought through and a solution is known and practiced by all who follow the system.* For example, you have thought through, identified and have a solution for every customer service issue that could come up at your store and how you will handle it.

3) *Every part of the system is organized, has order, and every process is defined in detail.* For example, when a bride buys a dress, everything that happens to that dress, how it is ordered, what happens when it arrives at your door, how it is altered, how it is prepared before the bride picks it up, how the bride is approached for referrals, etc. is all carefully defined and executed. The goal of a great system is to give each bride a consistent experience and value that meets and hopefully exceeds her expectations.

As a business owner in the bridal industry, I am constantly asking and thinking: how can I improve my store so that it is systems dependent rather than people dependent?

We all like order. Order is the basis of having and executing a great system. When brides come into your store, they can sense how orderly you are by how you act. When they sense that your store is orderly and organized, their sense of risk disappears, and they feel they can trust you.

This allows you to utilize your system of selling to help the bride find exactly what she is looking for and help her have an incredible experience in your store.

When you refine operations to improve how the systems in your store work, you are working *on* your business, not just *in* it.

We each see the world in different ways. We have different paradigms and mind sets that influence the way we think and the way we act. In order to achieve the highest levels of success and achievement, we must make mind shifts that take us from the status quo to new vistas and levels.

Most of us who got into the bridal business probably didn't have an entrepreneurial background before we started. If you went to and graduated from college like my wife and I did, we basically found that our educational training did more to prepare us to be an *employee* than to be an *employer*.

We all have different stories of how and why we got into this business, but I really like how Michael LeBoeuf points out the successful mindset of a business owner in his book, *The Perfect Business*:

He gives six mindshifts and mindsets that are critical to success as an entrepreneur:

1. ***"Focus on opportunity instead of security.*** This is one of the toughest mindsets to adopt because we instinctively seek security.... The problem with seeking security is that it doesn't exist. Security is a state of mind, not a reality. You may feel secure or insecure, but once again, perception creates reality. What you think you are is what you will become....The reality is that life is an insecure state."

   He continues:

   "When you mention the possibility of going out on your own, friends, relatives, and others may advise you to forget about it and cling to the security of a paycheck, paid health care, sick leave, a pension plan, and all the rest of it.

   If and when that happens (and it has probably happened to you like it did to my wife and I), ask yourself this: Are they financially independent from their work? Are they living their dreams and the kind of life you would like to lead? If your experience is anything like mine, the answers will always be no. They mean well, but like most people, they're caught in the security trap.

You beat the security trap by...focusing on learning the skills and seeking the opportunities that will make you set for life.... Real economic security is generated from within. It comes from knowing that you know how to spot, create, and capitalize on opportunities."—*The Perfect Business*, pp. 36-37.

2. ***Focus on what sells instead of what you know.***

   I like what Michael LeBoeuff says: "Knowledge + Credentials – Sales = Bankruptcy."

   Selling is the lifeblood of any business and the bridal business is no different. Becoming excellent at this skill is so important. The training we offer to our bridal consultants has become one of the proven systems that has been instrumental in the growth of our store.

3. ***Focus on getting results instead of following routines.*** As Michael LeBouef says: "[As an entrepreneur], putting in long hours means nothing. Being well organized means nothing. Knowing the right people means nothing. Following a daily regimen means nothing. Being efficient means nothing. You can do all those things and still go broke. Results are everything. You either close the sale or you don't. You either make a profit or you don't. You keep your overhead low or you don't. You get paid or you don't. Your customers come back or they don't....

   Am I against following rules, routines, and regimens? Absolutely not—as long as they contribute to getting results. Just don't let them become ends in themselves....

   Efficiency is doing a job right. Effectiveness is doing the right job. Effectiveness means results, and when you're an [entrepreneur], results are everything." –*The Perfect Business*, pp. 38-39.

John Maxwell tells of a sign he saw once that was posted in a small business. The sign read:

"The 57 Rules of Success:

#1 Deliver the goods.
#2 The other 56 don't matter." —*Today Matters*, p. 5.

Results are what matter in business and in life.

4. ***Focus on earning a profit instead of earning a paycheck.*** This is such a critical mindshift when you go into business for yourself. Profit is what allows you to pay yourself and your employees a paycheck. As Michael LeBoeuf says:

   "The profit mindset is simple: keep your sales high and your overhead as low as possible. Budget for taxes, health insurance, and the like. You have no control over the tax or insurance rates. And you don't have total control over your sales. However, you do have complete control over one very important item: Repeat after me: 'I have total control over how much I spend.' It's crucial that you be an absolute miser when it comes to overhead, particularly in the early years of your business. Work diligently to keep your fixed expenses as low as possible." —*The Perfect Business*, p. 41.

   Remember, your bridal business exists to make a profit and that is what is has to do. As business owners, we have to make our time count and make every business activity that we do a profitable one.

   A good rule of thumb when considering whether to add any other product lines or offerings to brides at your store is:

   "Is this something that's going to help make more profit for the business?"

   If it's not, don't do it, don't add it or sell it! Remember, you have complete control over how much you spend. The rule for successful investing has always been that you make money when you buy, not when you sell.

I have always loved the alliteration of the 3 Ps that lead to profitability coined by Jack Mitchell in his book, *Hug Your Customers*:

Plan, Prepare, and Practice lead to Profits.

5. ***Focus on trying new ideas instead of avoiding mistakes.***

Michael LeBoeuf makes this observation:

" 'Don't make mistakes.' That's a message we learn repeatedly from the time we're old enough to understand. In school, the person whose test has the fewest mistakes makes the best grade. In sports, the team that makes the fewest mistakes usually wins. And at work, we learn the fastest way to do a job is to do it right the first time. It's great advice—when the rules and procedures are clearly defined and the right answers are known. But that's not the environment of a...business. The problems you encounter cannot always be solved by following the rules. The options are many and the answers to important questions are unknown. The only way to truly find out if something will work is to try it.....If you wait for someone to give you the right answers, you'll wait forever, and waiting pays very poorly."

He continues:

"Every mistake and set back carries the seeds of future successes if you are smart enough to look for them and learn from them. IBM founder Tom Watson's formula for success was to double your rate of failures. George Bernard Shaw remarked, 'When I was a young man I found that nine out of ten things I tried didn't work. So I did ten times more work." ...Those who never make mistakes usually end up working for those who aren't afraid to." —*The Perfect Business*, pp. 41-43.

Many mistakes in this business are made when buying inventory as I mentioned in Chapter 6. The key to avoiding this mistake is to strive to have just enough product in your store. This is different for every store and there are many variables that go into making good buying decisions. If you don't already have good systems set up around how you evaluate, buy, and turn over your inventory, you need to do so right away. When you have good systems in place and know what you need and why you need it, you'll be so much farther ahead than a store that just wings it at market and buys on gut instinct.

Jack Mitchell in his book *Hug Your Customers* makes this point about inventory:

"Having too much inventory is very costly and can ruin your business fast. On the other hand, if you have too little inventory, you risk being out of stock when customers want something. If someone comes in looking for [a size 4 or 14 in a new dress], and you don't have it, no matter how great your service is, you're not going to make a sale, and more important, you risk losing a loyal customer. That's why an important aspect of our system is how it helps us manage our product."

Good systems will help you know how many of each size and color you have sold in a season and can help you make informed decisions before ordering more inventory.

Be on top of what is selling well and order more of those styles to come in. Since it takes a lot of time to order dresses in our business, you have to really stay on top of this to be successful.

Making mistakes is how we learn, but don't let the fear of making mistakes stop you from trying something new.

6. Focus on the vision instead of the short-term payoff.

Michael LeBoeuf makes this comment in his book *The Perfect Business* on page 43:

"Thinking long-term is a rarity in today's world, where instant gratification is the norm. Most people in the job world get up every day in return for a paycheck, interesting work, and the opportunity to interact with people they like. They give little thought to what their career and work life will be like in five, ten, or twenty years. They assume that whatever happens to them is something over which they have little or no control....We have an enormous amount of control over our future if we take charge of it and don't resign it to the winds of fate." —*The Perfect Business*, p. 43.

Michael Gerber makes this statement in his book on page 86:

"Your Primary Aim is the vision necessary to bring your business to life and your life to your business. It provides you with a purpose. It provides you with energy. It provides you with the grist for your day to day mill." —The E-Myth, p. 86.

He then offers these eight questions to help you determine your primary aim:

1. What do I want my life to look like?

2. How do I want my life to feel on a day-to-day basis?

3. What would I like to be able to say I truly know in my life, about my life?

4. How would I like to be with other people in my life—my family, my friends, my business associates, my customers, my community?

5. How would I like people to think about me?

6. What would I like to be doing two years from now? Ten years from now? Twenty years from now?

7. What specifically would I like to learn during my life—spiritually, physically, financially, technically, intellectually? About relationships?

8. How much money will I need to do the things I want to do? By when will I need it?

Take time to really think through the answers to these questions. Never forget that you create your future.

Michael E. Gerber says, "The difference between great people and everyone else is that great people create their lives actively, while everyone else is created *by* their lives, passively waiting to see where life takes them next." — *The E Myth*, p. 85.

How do you see yourself?

Do you consciously create your life?

Or do events of life create you?

A great story that illustrates the importance of vision is the story of Coca-Cola.

"In the first year (1886) of Coca-Cola's life, sales raised a measly $50 with marketing and advertising costs blowing out to $73.96. [The drink was not an instant hit...it sold for five cents a glass...the most glasses sold in a day was thirteen]. The inventor John Stith Pemberton knew he had a good product but he was no good at marketing and it was only being sold locally.

So he embarked on a very messy trail of deals to try to finance his business...One of the people who put up the money to fund the business was an ambitious pharmacist named Asa Griggs Candler. In early 1888, Candler acquired a share of Coca-Cola for $1,200. Later that year, Pemberton died and Candler bought out the rest of the company for a total of $2,300.

In 1892, Candler and a consortium formed the Coca-Cola Company. He registered the Coca-Cola logo in 1893, began offering free samples, and developed a range of branded products including clocks, calendars, and pharmacy scales with the signature Coca-Cola logo. He also invested heavily in advertising...His strategy worked and by 1895, Candler had Coca-Cola syrup plants in Chicago, Dallas, and Los Angeles and the drink was available in every U.S. state.

He sold the Coca-Cola syrup to drugstores, but was not excited about bottling the drink.

In 1899, Candler was approached by Benjamin Thomas and Joseph Whitehead, two lawyers from Chattanooga. They worked out a deal where they could buy Coca-Cola syrup for $1 per gallon and they would do the bottling.

This is what really led to the expansion of the Coca-Cola company, yet since Candler didn't have much vision about the potential of bottling, he gave away the bottling rights, thinking nothing would come of it. This actually turned out to be a terrible deal for the company and this caused much conflict and many lawsuits throughout the years."—*100 Great Businesses and the Minds Behind Them*, pp. 74-76.

Today Coca-Cola sells 12,600 drinks a second. There is tremendous power in vision and having an entrepreneurial mindset where you think about the future and the needs of customers in the future. This is one of the important lessons of *The E-Myth*.

The E-Myth by Michael Gerber has sold over 500,000 copies. He has helped re-engineer more than 15,000 small businesses to aid people in gaining control over and results from their businesses. He updated his book in *E-Myth Mastery* in 2005. There are critical lessons from both of these books that you need to take and apply to your store. You need to get and study the *The E-Myth*. It is an absolutely essential read to understand systems.

The essence of the E-Myth is this: understand that your business is a system rather than a place to go to work—a system designed to give the brides who come in to your store what they want in a way that successfully differentiates your bridal business from your competitors.

Michael Gerber explains the E-Myth as follows:

"To understand the E-Myth and the misunderstanding at its core, let's take a closer look at the person who goes into business. Not after he goes into business, but before.

What were you thinking before you started your business? If you're like 99 percent of the people I've known, you were working for someone else.

What were you doing? Probably technical work, like almost everybody who goes into business. You were a carpenter, a mechanic, or a machinist. You were a bookkeeper or a poodleclipper; a draftsperson or a hairdresser; a barber or a computer programmer; a doctor or a technical writer; a graphics artist or an accountant; an interior designer or a plumber or a salesperson. But whatever your profession, you were doing technical work. And you were probably [really] good at it. But you were doing it for somebody else.

Then one day, for no apparent reason, something happened....It could have been anything; it doesn't matter what. But one day, for apparently no reason, you were suddenly stricken with an Entrepreneurial Seizure. And from that day on your life was never to be the same....

In the throes of your Entrepreneurial Seizure, you fell victim to the most disastrous assumption anyone can make about going into business. It is an assumption made by all technicians who go into business for themselves... That Fatal Assumption is this: *if you understand the technical work of a business, you understand a business that does that technical work.*

...When the technician falls prey to the Fatal Assumption, the business that was supposed to free him from the limitations of working for somebody else actually enslaves him. Suddenly the job he knew how to do so well becomes one job he knows how to do *plus a dozen others he doesn't know how to do at all.*" —Michael Gerber, *The E-Myth*, pp. 8-11.

The reality is that the technical work of a business and a business that does technical work are two totally different things. To the technician, the business is not a business but a place to go to work.

Why is this important to understand?

Because, we all have a split personality in business. We are three people in one: the Entrepreneur, the Manager, and the Technician.

The problem comes because in Michael Gerber's words: "Each of these personalities wants to *be* the boss, but none of them wants to *have* a boss. So they start a business together in order to *get rid of* the boss." — Michael Gerber, *The E-Myth*, p. 12.

He gives a great analogy to how our multiple personalities interact with his analogy of the Skinny Guy vs. The Fat Guy.

He says:

"The Skinny Guy and The Fat Guy are two totally different personalities, with different needs, different interests, and different lifestyles. That's why they don't like each other. They each want totally different things.

...Anyone who has ever experienced the conflict between The Fat Guy and The Skinny Guy knows what I mean. You can't be both; one of them has to lose. And they both know it. Well, that's the kind of war going on inside the owner of every small business. But it's a three-way battle between the Entrepreneur, The Manager, and The Technician. Unfortunately, it's a battle no one can win." —*The E-Myth*, p. 15.

The three personalities can best be described by making three columns and showing what each one focuses on.

Entrepreneur	Manager	Technician
Visionary	Planner	Doer
Lives in the future	Lives in the past	Lives in the present
Looks for control	Looks for order	Does the work
Thrives on change	Clings to the status quo	Resents the entrepreneur for the changes
Sees opportunity	Sees problems	Sees activities
Dreams	Frets	Ruminates

Since most small business owners tend to gravitate back to being technicians, it's the technician who goes to work while the other two sort things out.

As Gerber says:

"To The Manager, then, The Technician becomes a problem to be managed. To The Technician, The Manager becomes a meddler to be avoided. To both of them, The Entrepreneur is the one who got them into trouble in the first place." —*The E-Myth*, p. 19.

In *E Myth Mastery* on page 6, Michael Gerber makes this point:

"The E-Myth says that all of these technicians, anyone who does technical work of any kind, make the same, fatal assumption: that because they understand how to do the technical work of the business—building a house, cutting hair, practicing law, cooking food [and I might add altering dresses]—they understand how to build a business that does that work.

Untrue, says the E-Myth.

Untrue, untrue, untrue.

The truth is that knowing how to do the work of a business has nothing to do with building a business that works.

Failing to understand and appreciate, deeply, the difference between entrepreneurial perspective and the perspective of a technician suffering from an entrepreneurial seizure is almost sure to be catastrophic for anyone starting her own business.

...Let's look at the difference between the two. Between the technician's point of view and the entrepreneur's.

"The technician builds a business that depends on him, around his skills, his talent, his interest, and his predispositions. He devotes his time, his energy and his life working for a living, albeit self-employed. In the end, there is a little equity to show for the investment of his time. At the beginning, he bought a job. In the end, if he's lucky, he sells the job to a person who acquires it for little more than break-even, but most often at a net loss. The most a technician can show for the time he spent in his business is the income he earned, the feeling he had of being 'independent,' and whatever few assets he may have acquired with the income he earned over the time he was in business.

The entrepreneur on the other hand, builds an enterprise that liberates her, creates endless amounts of energy, and increases her financial, emotional, and mental capital exponentially. In the end, there is significant equity to show for her investment. The enterprise runs itself in the hands of professional management. It has real value in the world. The entrepreneur is now free to invest what she's learned in another enterprise, depending on what she wishes to do with the rest of her life. In any event, she has learned how to grow an organization, how to utilize her creativity in the real world, how to expand her reach, and how to add value to many people, all while creating income that she no longer has to 'work' for, not to mention an estate for herself and the people she loves.

Same amount of time invested, significantly different return on investment.

The technician goes to work *in* his business.

The entrepreneur goes to work *on* his business." —*E-Myth Mastery*, pp. 6-7.

This is such an important concept to understand and why this book is so important and so powerful. When you understand the systems that make up your business and focus on implementing them, you will be so much more successful than you will by just working in your business.

It is so easy to lose focus when you are working in your business. Why?

Simply put, because we all have too much to do and too little time to do it in. It is difficult if not impossible to catch up. There is always more to do. It doesn't stop. Instead, we have to choose what we will focus on. What we need to focus on is doing more *on* our business and less *in* our business.

In the foreword of *The E Myth*, Michael Gerber makes this observation:

"...The people who succeed in business don't do so because of what they know, but because of their insatiable need to know more. Conversely, the problem with most failing businesses is not that the owners don't know enough about finance, about marketing, about management, about operations....the problem is that they think they know enough. And so they spend their time defending what they know, rather than discovering what they don't." —*The E-Myth*, p. xiii.

With that in mind, let's talk about the three stages of business (Infancy, Adolescence, Maturity):

1. Infancy - The Entrepreneurial Phase

Gerber says:

"It's easy to spot a business in Infancy—the owner and the business are one and the same thing. If you removed the owner from an Infancy business, there would be no business left. It would disappear! In Infancy, you are the business....you love it!...but then it changes. Subtly, at first, but gradually it becomes obvious. You're falling behind. There's more work to do than can possibly get done. The customers are relentless. They want you, they need you. You've spoiled them for anyone else. You're working at breakneck speed. And then the inevitable happens. You, the Master Juggler, begin to drop some of the balls!

...What do you do? You stretch. You work harder. You put in more time, more energy. If you put in twelve hours before you now put in fourteen. If you put in fourteen hours before, you now put in sixteen. If you put in sixteen hours before, you now put in twenty. But the balls keep dropping....There's simply no way in the world you can do all of that work yourself!

...Infancy ends when the owner realizes that the business cannot continue to run the way it has been; that in order for it to survive, it will have to change. When that happens—when the reality sinks in—most business failures occur. When that happens, most of The Technicians lock their doors behind them and walk away." —*The E-Myth*, pp. 22-24.

Here is a comment I heard recently from a bridal store owner who is currently in this stage:

"I always feel overwhelmed lately as well. I have a new sales person so that means I am here 24/7 with very little relief. Yes, the economy is hurting my business so much that I truly don't think it's worth it for me. My husband keeps topping it up with money that should be going into our retirement. But more importantly, I just don't think I like this business enough to keep it up. I think I'm almost done. I long for my previous job where I worked 4 days a week at home doing medical case management and legal nurse consulting. I found it very challenging and I didn't go to bed worrying about payroll, marketing, EEs, etc. I'm trying to figure it all out this week. But, I think I want my old life back. One of my biggest problems is I can't find consistent, competent sales people who can fill in the gap. They're very much spoiled down here and don't have to work. The older women as well just want to work here because it may be fun. You mention Saturdays to them and they're out the door. I thought at this point I would have someone I could count on to be a real manager so I could get relief. I'm just more and more exhausted so I think this is not working for me. Sorry, but I just don't love the no paycheck, b——y brides and unstable staff enough to keep me in this business."

Have you ever felt these emotions?

If so, you are not alone. The key is to avoid the temptation to quit and move into the next phase or stage of business.

2. Adolescence (Second Phase)

As Gerber points out:

"Adolescence begins at the point in the life of your business when you decide to get some help. There's no telling how soon this will happen. But it always happens, precipitated by a crisis in the Infancy stage. Every business that lasts must grow into the Adolescent phase." —*The E-Myth*, p. 25.

This stage is initially a great stage for the overwhelmed and overworked store owner. When you hire help and delegate some things and it goes well, it is a moment of great happiness since you now feel freer to do other things. The technician part of you starts to go to sleep (since someone else is doing the work) and you put on the manager hat. But, as Gerber says, here is where a new challenge begins since we aren't used to being the manager:

"...Unaccustomed as you are to being The Manager—your newfound freedom takes on an all too common form. Management by *abdication* rather than by *delegation*. In short, you give [someone the assignment] and run."

For a while this is great, until you walk by and see someone doing something or you get a call from a customer and you hear that someone wasn't treated exactly like they should be treated. In short, what happens is we immediately shift from being the manager to being the technician because "if you want something done right, you have to do it yourself."

Here is where many of us make a big mistake. We get back into doing the technical work (like selling, steaming, etc.) instead of training and making sure that it is understood and then done correctly. When we get back into the technician role (we will quickly find ourselves stressed out, overworked, and frustrated again).

Instead, what usually happens is what Gerber illustrates:

"This is the beginning of a process which occurs in *every* Adolescent business, once the owner's Management by Abdication begins to take its toll. It's the beginning of the process of deterioration, in which the number of balls in the air not only exceeds *your* ability to juggle them effectively, but your *people's* ability as well.

The balls begin to fall, faster and with greater confusion than they ever did when you were doing everything yourself. And as the thud of their landings becomes deafening, you begin to realize that you never should have trusted [the person you hired to help you]. You never should have trusted anyone. You should have known better.

You begin to realize that no one cares about your business the way you do. No one is willing to work as hard as you work. No one has your judgment, or your ability, or your desire, or your interest. If it's going to get done, you're the one who's going to have to do it.

So, you run back into your business to become the Master Juggler again. It's the same old story. One finds the owner of every Adolescent business doing, doing, doing—doing the work of the business—*despite the fact that he [or she] now has people who are supposed to be doing it for him [or her].* And the more *he [or she]* does, the less *they* do."
—*The E-Myth*, pp. 29-30.

Pretty soon, you are right back where you started. Is this where we are all doomed to end up in our businesses? Thankfully, the answer is no. Instead, we have to learn a new set of skills. That of being a manager and an entrepreneur.

The problem is that many times, technicians won't stop doing the work of the business long enough to learn the skill sets of managers and entrepreneurs.

To truly grow your bridal business and have it be what you want, you have to get out of your comfort zone and learn a new set of skills. You have got to learn how to lead and how to delegate.

Learning these new skills will require some stretching and some growing—but it is critical to the future success of your store.

Michael Gerber makes this important point:
"Every Adolescent business reaches a point where it pushes beyond its owner's Comfort Zone—the boundary within which he feels secure in his ability to control his environment, and outside of which he begins to lose that control."

Technician	Manager	Entrepreneur
How much I can do myself	How many other technicians (bridal consultants) or assistant managers I can supervise effectively and organize into productive effort	How many managers and leaders on your team can you engage in the pursuit of your store's vision

Instead of learning the new skill sets required, most store owners will do one of three things:

1. **Get small again (return to infancy) to stay in control.** When this happens, you own a job, not a business.

2. **Quit**.

3. **Hang on for dear life.** The business survives, but eventually you become completely consumed with the business and you do everything you can to save it. Unfortunately, the business doesn't explode, but you do. As Gerber says: "You're like a twelve cylinder engine working on one cylinder, pumping away, trying with everything you have to produce twelve cylinder's worth of resutls. Finally, there's nothing left. There's simply nothing more you can do, except face the fact that one cylinder can't produce twelve cylinders of results, no matter how hard it tries. Something has to give, and that something is you."
—*The E-Myth*, p. 36.

Of course, the best thing to do is learn the truth about what works and do it.

What works is what the rest of *The E-Myth* is about and what I would like to focus on during the rest of this chapter. In a nutshell it is this:

1) Create systems for every aspect of the business.

2) Set up the business to be run by systems.

3) Then have your staff (manager, assistant managers, and bridal consultants) run the system.

This requires discipline, standardization, and order, and requires a new set of skills that you may or may not have developed yet. This is the key to having a successful and profitable bridal store.

A great example of how a company has grown through systems is Weight Watchers.

"In 1961, founder and New York housewife Jean Nidetch was thirty-eight, weighed 195 pounds, and described herself, her bus-driver husband, her two sons, her poodle, and most of her friends as overweight. A 'When are you due?' question tipped Nidetch over the edge and she decided to do something about her ballooning weight. She began her battle to overcome an addiction to chocolate cookies, which she would eat by the packet, and took herself to the New York City Department of Health obesity clinic for a diet plan.

Months later, Niedetch invited a group of six 'fat friends' around for coffee and announced that she had lost 40 pounds, challenging them to get with her program. The group began meeting regularly: Nidetch would hand out diet sheets and everyone would assess their weekly progress. Two months later, they all chipped in and bought some scales. 'We weren't going to blame our genes, our hormones, or our mothers anymore,' says Nidetch. Demand was huge. Soon there wasn't enough chairs or space in her apartment.

Al Lippert, an overweight buyer for a coat company, and his wife, Felice, heard about Nidetch's meetings and invited her to their home for a meeting. As well as quickly starting to lose weight (one of the Lipperts' sons had described his parents as being 'like two beach balls'), the Lipperts immediately saw the business potential in these meetings.

Nidetch and the Lipperts hatched a plan at the Lipperts' kitchen table for an enterprise they called Weight Watchers. They would run weekly motivational, empathetic meetings and charge a fee.

The first commercial Weight Watchers meeting was held in 1963. The company charged $2 per person, per session, the same price as a movie ticket at the time. After the first meeting, Nidetch recalls stuffing more money than she had ever seen in her life into her bags. Within a year they were selling Weight Watchers franchises. The business expanded through a system where franchisees paid a few thousand dollars for a license and agreed to pay 10 percent of their revenues back to Nidetch and the Lipperts. Within three years, they were generating $160,000 and by 1970, $8 million.

With the combination of Al Lippert's business administration and marketing prowess, Felice's writing and support skills, and Nidetch's natural leadership, motivation, and speaking skills, Weight Watchers was the perfect way to make money at a time when the post-war generations were packing on the pounds. Nidetch was the 'Energizer bunny', Al was the marketing genius, and Felice the creative force.

In 1978, the Lipperts and Nidetch sold the company to H.J. Heinz for $72 million. Heinz sold the business to European investment firm Artal Luxembourg in 1999, and today the company is worth $4.8 billion.

There are more than 46,000 weekly Weight Watchers meetings in 30 countries around the world, with sixty million people attending meetings in 2004."—*100 Great Businesses and the Minds Behind Them*, pp. 54-56.

The kind of growth Weight Watchers experienced and has sustained is the result of well thought out and executed systems.

Even if you never plan on growing past the store you have, you should still think through and start implementing systems in your business.

Before we get into more detail about the systems for your store, let's talk about the third phase of business.

3. Maturity (Third Phase)

The third phase of the business is Maturity. This is the stage of growth that is exemplified by the best businesses in the world. The important thing to remember is that these businesses didn't end up as mature companies. They started out that way. The original owners planned the business before it was begun. The owners saw their job as working on the business instead of working in it.

Look at great companies like Microsoft, Google, Starbucks, and IBM. These owners had a model in their minds of a business that was already working. They had vision. They saw and see the business fulfilling the needs of a specific group of customers in an innovative way.

These are the companies that Jim Collins talks about in his books *Good to Great* and *Built to Last*. The people who started these successful businesses started out with the vision of what it would be like.

Tom Watson, the founder of IBM once said: "IBM is what it is for three special reasons. The first reason is that, at the very beginning, I had a very clear picture of what the company would look like when it was finally done. You might say I had a model in my mind of *what it would look like when the dream—my vision—was in place.*

The second reason was that once I had that picture, I then asked myself how a company which looked like that would have to act. I then *created a picture of how IBM would act when it was finally done.*

The third reason IBM has been so successful was that once I had a picture of how IBM would look when the dream was in place and how such a company would have to act, I then realized that, ***unless we began***

to act that way from the very beginning, we would never get there. " — *The E-Myth*, p. 39.

Here are a couple of differences in how the different personalities think from one another.

Entrepreneur	Technician
How must the business work?	What work has to be done?
Vision – You see business in its entirety (Where do I want the business to go? What do I want my store to become?)	***Business in parts*** (buying at markets, receiving gowns, steaming, selling, doing alterations, prepping gown to be picked up, following up for referrals)
Customer is opportunity Couldn't (shouldn't) I also be selling ____ to this bride? I know something about this...	***Customer is a problem*** Why do I keep getting all of these bridezillas? Why do these customers keep interrupting my work (sewing, doing alterations, etc.)?
How will my business stand out from the rest?	How will my business look to the consumer?

I think the best explanation of the type of mindset it takes to succeed in business can be found in Robert Kiyosaki's excellent book: *The Cashflow Quadrant*. If you haven't read that book, I would strongly encourage you to do so. It will change the way you think about your business and more importantly will teach you the skills you need to move from one quadrant to the other.

I love this statement he makes on page 18:

"When it comes to money and the emotions attached to money, we all respond differently. And it's how we respond to these emotions that often determines which quadrant we choose to generate our income from [and what type of business owner we will be]." —*The Cashflow Quadrant*, p. 18.

He also makes this observation:

"Changing quadrants is often a change at the core of who you are, how you think, and how you look at the world. The change is easier for some people than for others simply because some people welcome change and others fight it. And changing quadrants is most often a life-changing experience." —*The Cashflow Quadrant*, p. 18.

He also asks this question (which really tells you what phase your business is in or as Kiyosaki puts it the difference between being self-employed and owning a big business):

"Can you leave your business for a year or more and return to find it more profitable and running better than when you left it?" —Robert Kiyosaki, *The Cashflow Quadrant*, p. 46.

Now, that is not likely going to be completely achievable in your business, yet it is a good question to think about as you build it.

A good way to build systems that Michael Gerber points out in the book is to think of your store as a prototype. In other words, how would you pattern your store if they were going to replicate 5,000 of them across the country?

Now, obviously, you nor I are going to become the next David's. Most people who get in the bridal business have no intention of opening other stores (and that is totally fine). It's plenty enough work to have one or two. But, the key here is to standardize and create a system that can be operated by individuals with a low level of skill. Discipline, standardization and order are the keys.

The franchise model works. Where 80% of all businesses fail in the first five years, 96% of all Business Format Franchises succeed. Why?

Because the prototype suits the technician because all the entrepreneurial and management factors are established by someone else. You can then be a technician and have the other two aspects of the business figured out for you.

Here are six rules for creating systems that are found in *The E-Myth*:

- The system will provide consistent value to and exceed expectations of brides.
- The system will be operated by people with the lowest possible level of skill.
- The system will stand out as a place of impeccable order.
- The work done in the system will be documented in operations manuals.
- The system will provide a uniformly predictable product and/or service to the customer.
- The system will use a uniform color, logo, dress and facilities code.

Building a system and defining the prototype of what your store should look like is a continuous process. Here are nine areas of your business in which you should develop systems for your store.

1. Strategic Objective Systems

   How is the business going to help you realize your life purpose? This is the strategic plan. Your business is a means to an end. Your strategic objective is a list of standards that well enable you to achieve your objectives.

2. Advertising and Marketing Systems
3. Sales Systems
4. Organizational and Internal Business Process Systems
5. Management and Leadership Systems
6. People (Employee) Systems
7. Inventory and Buying Systems

8. Customer Service Systems

9. Productivity Systems

You should work on developing the systems for each of these areas in your business. Create checklists and systems within your store that will help you become a world class organization. When you have better systems, your store will be more successful and you will be happier. You'll be able to take more time off. You'll make more money and you will be more profitable. You will be able to work *on* your business and not just *in* your business. And that will make all of the difference.

There is an old Chinese proverb which says:

When you hear something, you will forget it.
When you see something, you will remember it.
But not until you do something, will you understand it.

My hope is that you will move from skills thinking to systems implementation and do something about it to transform your business to new heights.

CHAPTER 9

OVERCOME RESISTANCE

We all experience resistance. Resistance is the powerful force that stops us from doing what we know we need to do every day. In order to get anything done and to stay focused on your personal and business goals, you have to beat resistance every day of your life.

Stephen Pressman in his excellent book, *The War of Art* makes this observation: "Most of us have two lives. The life we live and the unlived life within us. Between the two stands Resistance."

If you've ever started an exercise routine and haven't followed through for more than a few days, you've experienced resistance. If you've ever set a goal to follow a new routine or start a new habit (or eliminate a bad one), you've experienced resistance. And, if you've ever tried to change anything or do anything outside of your comfort zone, you've experienced major resistance.

The interesting thing is that breaking through resistance is the only way we can really get ahead and move up to the next level in anything. As

Steven Pressfield points out in *The War of Art*, "Resistance obstructs movement only from a lower sphere to a higher." That means that staying stagnant or plummeting to a lower level won't cause much resistance on the way down. You do feel resistance when you *recognize* how far you've fallen and how much harder you'll have to work to get to where you used to be, or where you really want to be.

This is especially true in our new economy, where many retailers are opting to give up or give in instead of effectively dealing with the major resistance they are experiencing from all sides.

I sincerely believe that our inability to break free of resistance is at the heart of why we don't achieve more in our bridal businesses. It is easier to *stay* where you are than it is to battle the resistance necessary to climb to the next level. It is easier to *accept* where you are now than it is to battle the resistance you will continually encounter on your way up.

The truth is that all of us let resistance beat us much more than we would care to admit. In this chapter, I will show you four specific areas of your business and personal life where you are likely being beat by resistance and what you can do about it to get back on track and be more productive, focused, and successful.

1. Resistance from brides to buy now.

Brides today are waiting longer to buy their wedding gown. They are much more resistant to buy. If you have been frustrated because you have experienced this resistance, take heart. You are not alone. But in order to stay on top of your daily and weekly sales goals, you have to learn how to overcome this resistance. Using old, outdated approaches will cause you to feel even more overwhelmed because the new resistance you are experiencing now *is* almost insurmountable. We have all felt the pressure and strain in recent weeks and months because of this strengthened resistance to our marketing and sales efforts. Unfortunately, being overwhelmed and scared about a lack of sales causes sellers to push harder and brides to resist even more. Instead, you have to break through resistance in a different way.

Author Kurt Mortensen makes this point in his book *Persuasion IQ*:

"Ever-smarter consumers have built up a lot of resistance to the old style of persuading; many people have a brick wall of resistance up before you've even started....They assume you're going to be the sleazy, manipulative sales guy before you've even had a chance to speak. They are all ready to resist you before you start. What must you do to overcome this tendency? Your persuasion attempts must be nonthreatening and very natural. Forget loud and flashy. That strategy only encourages resistance. And most definitely forget about high pressure. Not only does that solidify the wall of resistance in that particular moment, but the wall will increase in size. When people feel they have been pressured, bullied, or coerced into buying or doing something they don't need or want, they are resentful....The moment people sense that you are attempting to persuade them, the brick wall increase in size and strength, and they will resist you. To counter this tendency, persuasion and sales must take place below the conscious radar."—Kurt Mortensen, *Persuasion IQ*, pp. 22-23.

The timeless parable of the wind and the sun is applicable here. As you read through this parable, think about how its powerful lesson applies to you right now at your store:

"The sun and the wind were always arguing about which of them was the strongest. The wind believed he was stronger because of his destructive powers in tornadoes and hurricanes. He wanted the sun to admit he was stronger, but the sun held fast to his own opinion and could not be convinced."

"One day, the sun decided he wanted the matter settled once and for all, so he invited the wind to compete with him in a contest. The sun chose the contest carefully. He pointed out an old man taking a walk, and challenged the wind to use his power to blow the man's jacket off.

The wind felt this would be an easy contest to win and began to blow. To his surprise, each gust of wind only made the man cling more tightly to his jacket. The wind blew harder; and the man held on tighter. The harder the wind blew, the more the man resisted. The powerful blows of wind even knocked the man down, but he would not let go of his jacket. Finally, the wind gave up and challenged the sun to succeed in getting the man to take off his jacket. The sun smiled and shone radiantly upon the man. The man felt the warmth of the sun, and sweat began to appear on his forehead. The sun continued pouring out warmth and sunshine upon the man, and at last, the man took off his jacket. The sun had won the contest." —Kurt Mortensen, *Persuasion IQ*, pp. 36-37.

The obvious lesson from this simple parable is that if you push harder to get brides to buy they will resist even more. In order to be successful at selling today, you have to become a better persuader and help *pull* brides in to buy from you now instead of pushing them to do so.

A big part of the approach that works today to reduce resistance and get brides back on track to buying their dress now is to ask better questions that break the trance brides are in. I go into great detail about three specific questions we are using now to help us do this at our store in a recent conference call I did entitled "How to Shift Brides to Buyers Faster and Watch Your Sales Soar During the Recession". To learn the secrets of these three questions and more specific strategies about how to overcome the bride's resistance to buy now, simply go to www.bridaltrainingsystems.com and register to receive my monthly conference calls and I'll send you a copy of this CD and detailed notes you can use to train your staff for free.

2. Distractions that lead to decreased productivity.

The biggest resistance we encounter to productivity is distraction. If you've ever come into your store with a list of things you need to get accomplished and then find at the end of the day that you haven't accomplished any or all of them, you have come face to face with the resistance of distraction. What has happened is that one distraction after another has held us back from getting to our most important listed priorities. We let the crisis of the moment overcome the discipline of staying on task to accomplish what we know we need to get done.

Author Chet Holmes asks this question in his excellent book *The Ultimate Sales Machine* on page 9:

"Do you function most in a reactive or proactive mode? In my experience most business people don't take the time to plan and take action because all of their time is consumed by reacting to the business they've already built. To build your business...you need to be in a primarily proactive mode. Time management is crucial."

Most of us have taken a course on time management over the years or know how important it is to manage our time better. But, when you objectively look at how you use your time day in and day out (and if you are honest with yourself), you know that you could be much more productive than you are. You are experiencing resistance to managing your time. Why do we do this to ourselves? Why do we resist what we know we need to do? Here are five reasons:

1) **We do lesser priority things either because we haven't established our true priorities or because it is *easier* to give into lesser priority things. More often than not, it is the second reason.**

   All of us would agree that the essence of time management is to set priorities and then to organize and execute our daily activities around them. Stephen Covey refers to this as beginning with the end in mind. The great philosopher Winnie the Pooh said, "It is wise to ask someone—perhaps yourself—what you are looking for, before you begin looking for it." When you know what it is that you really want, it is easier to say no to things that you don't want.

   If your priorities aren't set, it is easy to allow yourself to be distracted by lesser things first. Why? Because *it is easier to give in* to the resistance of doing something else than it is to *focus on* working on the task that will give you what you really want.

Fortunately, organizing around priorities is a skill and can be learned. Everyone can learn to become extremely well organized, efficient, and effective. The payoff for good planning is huge. You save ten minutes on execution for every minute that you spend planning. Another way of looking at this is realizing that you get a 1000% return on your investment every time you plan.

2) **We resist planning out our time on paper because *it is easier not to* or because we recognize that we have failed with this method in the past. Instead, limit the list to six things each day.**

All of us know that we are much more effective when we think through our day on paper first. Why don't we do this more often? The reason goes back to resistance. The answer is simply because *it is easier to begin and get distracted* on other activities than it is to take five minutes to plan out your day first and focus on these things systematically throughout the day.

The biggest reason why we don't work off of lists very well is because we have too many things on the list in the first place and it is easier to get distracted by easier things than it is to focus on all of the many activities on the list itself.

Chet Holmes says it very well:

"The key to being productive is to stick to the six most important things you need to get done that day. You'll find that when you have a long list, it becomes the management tool for your time. When you want to feel productive, you go to your list and just pick something and do it. It feels good. When you have a long list, you generally do the easier, less productive tasks just to trim down the list. At the end of the day, you find that the most important things on the list didn't get completed because they are either the hardest, the most time-consuming or both. Long lists also mean that you will never finish your list. There is a negative psychological impact to not finishing your list. But there is an enormous psychological boost to crossing off that sixth item on your list, especially when all six of them were the most important things you needed to do that day. So here's the rule: list the six most important things you need to do and, by hook or by crook, get those six things completed each day. That doesn't mean you don't keep a side list of running items that need to be done. When you plan each day, you can go to your long list and use that as a menu of items from which to build your list of the six most important things for that day." –*The Ultimate Sales Machine*, p. 14.

Take more time to think before you begin each day. You can do this in the mornings or at night before you leave the store, but the critical element is that you should make time for at least 15 minutes each day of uninterrupted thought. That means that you should remove yourself from an environment with interruptions. Turn off your cell phone. Don't answer the phone if you are in the store. Don't turn on your computer and look at your emails or favorite web sites.

Instead, think on paper about the upcoming bridal shows you have, the challenges you're facing with your staff, how to bring more brides into the store, how to help your staff sell more, etc. The key is to take time every day to think and to plan. Make the decision that you won't start your day without finishing it on paper first. Write down the six most important priorities you need and will get accomplished that day before you go home. Do your best to get back on task as quickly as you can. Avoid distractions and resistance.

3) **We don't begin with a timeframe in mind. Instead, have a start and end time for what you have determined you will do.**

All of us procrastinate. We all allow ourselves to get distracted. Sometimes it is easy to welcome the distraction if we don't want to face the challenges we have in front of us. One of the big secrets to being successful at time management is to manage your time in small chunks of time. Because we all know our tendency to procrastinate and get distracted, I have found it best to have a start *and* end time for what I am working on each day. This will help you focus on the task at hand when there are many other things that also need to get done. We all have numerous activities we have to work on at our stores. When you break these activities into small chunks, they are much manageable. Also, by having an end time, you know there is a deadline that you have to work under. Even if you don't finish what you set out to do, you can reschedule more time to get it done later (but make sure there is a start and end time). If you don't manage your time in this way, it will get away from you. Remember the Old Scottish proverb: "What may be done at any time will be done at no time."

4) **We don't control the environment we work in.**

The reality is that we can't be productive in environments that aren't conducive to productivity. In today's information age, where we are all so wired and connected, it is nearly impossible to not be constantly distracted by incoming emails, faxes, text messages, phone calls, and numerous interruptions from others around us in the form of questions or idle chatting and gossip. The only way we can eliminate these distractions is to purposefully take ourselves out of this environment. Remember, distractions will always be constant *if* you allow them to be.

Even if we value our time and are trying to focus on getting things done in bite size chunks, we may have bridal consultants on our staff who constantly interrupt us. You may need to set some very specific parameters in place to ensure that you are not interrupted when you are trying to think through the specific things that you are working on.

For example, sometimes advertising or sales people who call your store each day can be sneaky. They may say, "She is expecting my call." Or, "It is a private matter." Your bridal consultants should always answer these calls the same way. They should say to those who call to sell something:

"She can't take your phone call right now as she is working with a bride. The best thing for you to do is to send a proposal of what you do via email and then she can get back to you if it is something she is interested in."

Or, (if it is someone you need to talk to and you can let your staff know who these individuals are) you can have a set time when you call back those who call. The script should be:

"She takes time at 1:00 pm to call back all those who call. I'll be sure to have her give you a call then."

Remember, you are in control of your time. Don't let others rob it from you by dictating your schedule. It can usually wait.

Another example of this revolves around a weekly meeting I have with myself every Monday morning on the marketing for my store. In this meeting, I plan and work on all of the marketing promotions that I have coming up at our store. In addition to this meeting, I have numerous time periods each week that I have blocked off to focus on specific areas of our store that I want to work on. My staff knows not to interrupt me during that time. Things can wait 90 minutes while I finish what I am working on.

5) **We don't recognize how much "multi-tasking" really disrupts our focus.**

Over the past several years, we have all been taught that multi-tasking is an essential and important part of getting things done. Unfortunately, multi-tasking is what causes us to be less productive than we could be if we would just focus on one thing for an extended period of time.

Research has shown that those who stay focused on one thing for a specific period of time are able to get much more accomplished than someone who is trying to get multiple things done at the same time.

One of the biggest lies we can tell ourselves is that we are great multi-taskers. If you doubt this, consider this study:

"Beginning in 2004, [Gloria Mark] persuaded two West Coast high-tech firms to let her study their cubicle dwellers as they surfed the chaos of modern office life. One of her grad students, Victor Gonzalez, sat looking over the shoulder of various employees all day long, for a total of more than 1,000 hours. He noted how many times the employees were interrupted and how long each employee was able to work on any individual task.

When Mark crunched the data, a picture of 21st-century office work emerged that was, she says, "far worse than I could ever have imagined". Each employee spent only 11 minutes on any given project before being interrupted and whisked off to do something else. What's more, each 11-minute project was itself fragmented into even shorter three-minute tasks, like answering e-mail messages, reading a Web page or working on a spreadsheet. And each time a worker was distracted from a task, it would take, on average, 25 minutes to return to that task." —Clive Thompson, The New York Times, October 16, 2005 http://www.nytimes.com/2005/10/16/magazine/16guru.html?ei=5088&en=2864cc65d74cefb8&ex=1287115200

That's amazing. When people get off task, it takes an average of 25 minutes to return to that task because they are constantly interrupted. Think about the consequences of this in your life and at your store. One of the things I continually work on with the top bridal retailers I coach in my Quantum Leap program is this area of carefully measuring how productive they *really* are. Most store owners I've interviewed on this topic have privately admitted to me that they are not as productive at their store as they could or should be. They all attribute it to being constantly interrupted or distracted.

Tony Schwartz in his book *The Power of Full Engagement* says that "the greatest power of the human mind is the ability to focus on one thing at a time." The problem with distraction and interruption is that it causes us to lose our natural ability to focus. This is a very difficult habit to overcome. It is so much easier to log on and check our email and let others control what we do. This causes us to be reactive in our businesses instead of proactively determining and doing what needs to be done.

I think Steven Pressman says it best in his book, *The War of Art*. He says: "Resistance cannot be seen, touched, heard, or smelled. But it can be felt. We experience it as an energy field....It's a repelling force. It's negative. Its aim is to shove us away, distract us, prevent us from doing our work." –p. 7.

Get control of yourself. Don't fall for the lie that multi-tasking makes you more productive. In reality, it spreads you thinner so that nothing really gets done as well as it could if you would just focus on one thing single-mindedly for a period of time.

3. Resistance from bridal consultants to stick to established standards and resistance on the part of store owners to enforce them.

I often hear from other bridal store owners that they are not happy with the results they are getting at their store. When I ask them what standards they have in place for hitting daily and weekly sales goals and how they enforce them, I often get a blank look. When I ask what they do to enforce those standards, I hear all kinds of excuses about why the standard can't be met.

As Mark Victor Hansen, co-writer of the *Chicken Soup for the Soul* books says: "You can't get right answers when you're asking the wrong questions."

When you set standards of any kind, you will experience resistance to them from your staff. There are two parts of setting a standard. One is actually setting a standard and two is making sure that you stick with the standards. If you don't stick with your standard, pretty soon it becomes meaningless and can be de-motivating to the people who actually do reach it, especially if there is no consequence for those who don't.

One of the benefits of having standards and sticking to them is that everyone rises to the standard or they don't. This makes it easier for you to make adjustments in your personnel if someone is not hitting the standard.

I like what Jim Collins says:

"The only way to deliver to the people who are achieving is to not burden them with the people who are not achieving." —*Good to Great*, p. 53.

The reality is that if you don't have standards and if you don't enforce them, you will always be frustrated with your results because people will live up to the expectations you have for them. Jim Collins in his book *Good to Great* makes this great point about the importance of standards and sticking to them. He says:

"The good-to-great companies probably sound like tough places to work—and they are. If you don't have what it takes, you probably won't last long. But they're not ruthless cultures, they're rigorous cultures. And the distinction is critical. To be ruthless, means hacking and cutting, especially in difficult times, or wantonly firing people without any thoughtful consideration. To be rigorous means consistently applying exacting standards at all times and at all levels, especially in upper management. To be rigorous, not ruthless, means that the best people need not worry about their positions and can concentrate fully on their work." —Jim Collins, *Good to Great*, p. 52.

What standards should you set for your staff? This is really up to you, but as a bare minimum you ought to have at least five:

1) A specific $ amount of sales per hour

2) A goal of a specific number of dresses sold per week

3) A specific goal of outbound phone calls made each day (we require at least 2)

4) Sending out a thank you card for every purchase made

5) Getting a testimonial from every bride you sell a dress to

Look at the critical success factors that you know lead to a sale and then measure and reward those activities.

Another important area where you need to have standards is in the area of what your employees do when it isn't busy at the store. This means having a very firm policy on no texting or cell phone use during their shift, not accessing the Internet or cell phone to access their MySpace, Facebook, or Twitter account and most importantly doing productive things when there aren't brides in the store. If you find that your bridal consultants aren't doing productive things when it is slower, this is your fault. Put together a list of things they can do in slower times. Quiz them on overcoming objection flashcards, make phone calls, or put together their own marketing campaigns to bring brides into the store.

If you have a list of things for them to do in slower times and they still will not do them, it is your fault if you allow this behavior to go unpunished in any way. I'm not trying to be rude here, but the point is that your bridal store is a workplace that should be a place of work and productivity, not spending time on the Internet and texting their friends. If you don't have standards and expect your bridal consultants to live up to them, you have no one else to blame but yourself for a lack of results.

If you have employees who would rather spend time working on their projects rather than working on the business of selling and helping brides and prom customers in the store, it is time to replace those individuals with caring bridal consultants who will help you and the other members of your staff get the work of each day completed.

No one wants to pick up the slack of ineffective or unproductive bridal consultants. Do yourself and your bridal consultants a favor and let go of those who will not comply with the standards you've set at your store. David Cottrell in his book *Monday Morning Mentoring* makes this point:

"The single greatest 'demotivator' of a team is to have members who are not carrying their load. It takes courage to address issues honestly and then let people go when that's necessary. Your emotions are involved, the employee's short-term livelihood is involved, and it is a tough conversation to have. But, if you have provided someone every opportunity for success and yet his [or her] performance fails to meet expectations, summon your courage and allow him [or her] to go where he [or she] can be successful. It is not a personal mistake of yours, nor is it the employee's mistake—the job is just not right for him [or her]." —p. 47.

When everyone understands ***and*** follows the rules, it is amazing how much more productive we really are. Don't let the initial resistance that your bridal consultants give you to following these standards dissuade you from actually implementing them at your store. It will make all of the difference in being more productive at your store.

A final aspect of this is the resistance you may receive from bridal consultants regarding implementing a training program to improve their skills. Most of us believe that our skills are better than they really are. Quizzing your consultants on their skills and having evaluations after they work with brides can help them see the areas where they need improvement. Stick with this regimented training approach and you will see your bridal consultants approach true mastery much faster.

Any time you invite someone to start a new training regimen, you will experience resistance. Think about yourself. If you've ever started an exercise routine, you may be excited about starting it the first few days. Then, when your muscles are sore, you find it harder and harder to actually overcome the resistance to get out of bed and go do the work. The same is true with training your bridal consultants. They may be excited the first day or two after you've done any kind of training event. But the rigorous discipline it takes to master anything is what really will help you internalize and use what has been trained. Make the commitment to always be training and to strive for mastery.

4. Resistance to changing anything that affects the status quo or stepping outside of your personal comfort zone.

If you've ever felt resistance to changing how things have always been done at your store, you have experienced this type of resistance. Everyone knows that change is the only way we really make progress but we all resist it. A closed-minded approach to new ideas is one of the most common manifestations of this type of resistance. You have likely experienced or thought these things before. For example, have you ever heard yourself say:

- " We don't do it that way."
- "We don't care what anyone else is doing. We have all of the answers right here."
- "We're doing okay. That may get results for them, but it would never work for us because...."

The problem with this kind of thinking is that the things that have worked in the past won't always work in the future. It is a good idea to be constantly seeking out new ideas to old and challenging problems.

A great example of this comes from the life of Henry Ford, who invented the automobile. He was once asked about customer demand for the automobile. He said: "If we had asked the public what they wanted, they would have said faster horses." Because he was willing to reach out of his comfort zone and think differently, he achieved legendary success during his lifetime. Later in his life, he became closed to new ideas. He thought he had all of the right answers. This attitude started him on the path of decline. He once famously said that the public could have their Model-T car in any color as long as it was "black." His closed minded approach allowed competitors to gain the upper hand and shatter the momentum that Ford had created in the marketplace.

Think about the resistance of the big three automakers in the past to making different types of cars and continuing to make gas-guzzling SUVs when other competitors were offering alternatives. These companies are in trouble largely for their inability to get outside of the comfort zone that they got used to. As a result, they have been declining for years.

The question to ask yourself is: Are you open to new ideas **or** do you close yourself off to suggestions by others who are successful saying, "That will never work here."?

For example, I know many retailers who invest in private lines that give them a higher profit margin. Many retailers have resisted this over the years saying that only branded merchandise would sell in their stores. Now, they are looking at it again much more closely because being a generalist has caused them to be shopped solely on the basis of price.

The best way to avoid becoming closed minded is to ask questions: find out what others are doing and how you can do the same.

I have five children. I've always been amazed how children ask better questions than adults. They aren't afraid of looking dumb or silly. And they don't try to impress with the quality or caliber of their questions. They sincerely want to know the answers. Most questions that kids ask are "How Come..." questions like "How come the sky is blue?" or "How come dogs have cold noses?" or "How come we don't have dessert after breakfast?"

Avoid the resistance to change by being open to new ideas. Ask questions of others who are where you want to be. As Charles Steinmetz once observed: "No person really becomes a fool until that person stops asking questions."

Many times we resist change because that is the only way we know to do things. There is a story told of a family who moved into a new neighborhood. One morning they got a late start, and the six year old missed her bus to school. Though it would make him late for work, the father agreed to take her to school if she could give him directions.

They left the neighborhood, and the young girl began directing her father to take one turn after another. Following twenty minutes of circuitous driving, they arrived at the school, which turned out to be only eight blocks away. Steaming, the father asked the kindergartener why she had him drive all over the place when the school was so close to home.

"We went the way the bus goes," she said. "That's the only way I know."

How many of us are like this young girl?—we go where we go in our bridal business—because that is the only way we know how to do it. We can't be like Alice in Lewis Carroll's *Through the Looking Glass*, who asks for directions in this way during her encounter with the Cheshire Cat: "Would you tell me please, which way I ought to go from here?" she asks.

"That depends a good deal on where you want to get", the cat replies with a grin.

"I don't care much where", she answers.

"Then it doesn't matter which way you go", the cat responds.

If we are undecided about the direction of our businesses, we will merely *drift* along (and will likely not achieve the success we could if we would just focus in on what we need to do).

What do you *really* want your business to do?

Are you focusing on the right things that will lead you to that goal moment by moment and day to day or do you get easily distracted and lose your focus?

You can overcome this resistance by recognizing what you don't know and asking lots of questions of those who do.

Drifting with the status quo or just going with the tide can give the false appearance of ***motion without direction***. Drifting is dangerous because we feel as though we are making progress (and sometimes we are), but we will never get to our desired goals with the speed and momentum we could if we focused in on the actions required to get us where we want to go.

I like what Mark Sanborn says in his book *You Don't Need a Title to Be a Leader:*

"Without focus, it is impossible to move forward to achieve your goals. Effective leaders...are able to keep themselves and those around them on task. Those who lack focus in their personal lives and in their careers tend to drift.

Years ago, on one of the first cruises my wife and I ever took, I visited the bridge of the behemoth ocean liner we were sailing on and spoke with the captain. I asked him about the biggest seas he had ever sailed in with that ship. He told me he had been in seas with ninety foot waves.

Impressed, I inquired about how he had managed to keep the ship intact. He told me that while ninety-foot waves were daunting, the ship could negotiate them quite handily as long as it didn't lose power.

'If you lose power in big seas in any boat, you're in serious trouble. Under power,' he explained, 'the boat can stay perpendicular to the waves. Without power, the boat would drift parallel to the waves and be capsized or swamped.' That is the danger of drifting.

In acting as a leader, you can handle just about anything that comes your way as long as you don't lose power and drift. Power, in this sense, is the ability to stay engaged in what is going on. It doesn't mean that you have control over every situation, any more than a boat has control over the waves. Rather, it is the ability to engage the situation with intent, with *focus*.

Drifting and waiting are very different things. Waiting is an intentional choice. It requires patience and deliberation. Drifting takes away your power of choice.

When you wait, you believe that something will happen, although you may not know when. Instead of acting rashly or impetuously, you pause to gather information and seek insight.

Drifting results from rudderlessness and lack of direction. When you drift, it doesn't even take particularly large waves to capsize the boat.

It's all too easy to become distracted or lulled into complacency. Before you know it, you are drifting. A simple lack of attention can cause you to lose the power of purpose and engagement. Instead of initiating action, you become paralyzed. Rather than acting, you find yourself acted upon." —pp. 42-43.

Resistance has both positive and negative aspects to it. It has been said without resistance a person or vehicle could not move about, or if already in motion, could not be stopped except by collision. Simple things like nails, screws, and bolts would not stay in place; a cork would not stay in a bottle, a light globe would drop from its socket; a lid would not stay on a jar.

Yet, if you let resistance prevent you from doing what you know in your heart you should do, you will be stopped in your progression. Learn to break through resistance and let it be what propels you to achieve your goals.

A great analogy of how you can use resistance to propel you forward is that of a boat. When you pull the oars against the resistance of the water, it creates the force that causes the boat to move forward. Well designed boats also have a prow that helps the boat cut through and divide the water in order to help overcome the resistance that slows down the speed of the boat.

Don't give in to resistance. Learn to overcome these four areas of resistance in your life and at your store. When you overcome its daily assault on your life, you *will* rise above it.

CHAPTER 10

TAKE ACTION AND DO IT NOW

There is power in taking action. While many businesses today are waiting out the recession and cutting back on their advertising, the smart ones are expanding their marketing and increasing their market share. Consider this example and the lesson of two very different responses of Kellogg and Post during the Great Depression.

"In the late nineteen-twenties, two companies—Kellogg and Post—dominated the market for packaged cereal. It was still a relatively new market: ready-to-eat cereal had been around for decades, but Americans didn't see it as a real alternative to oatmeal or cream of wheat until the twenties. So, when the Depression hit, no one knew what would happen to consumer demand. Post did the predictable thing: it reined in expenses and cut back on advertising. But Kellogg doubled its ad budget, moved aggressively into radio advertising, and heavily pushed its new cereal, Rice Krispies. (Snap, Crackle, and Pop first appeared in the thirties.) By 1933, even as the economy cratered, Kellogg's profits had risen almost thirty percent and it had become what it remains today: the industry's dominant player.

You'd think that everyone would want to emulate Kellogg's success, but when hard times hit, most companies end up behaving more like Post. They hunker down, cut spending, and wait for good times to return. They make fewer acquisitions, even though prices are cheaper. They cut advertising budgets. And often they invest less in research and development. They do all this to preserve what they have. But there's a trade-off: numerous studies have shown that companies that keep spending on acquisition, advertising, and R. & D. during recessions do significantly better than those which make big cuts." –James Surowiecki, "Hanging Tough", *The New Yorker*, April 20, 2009

The difference between financial success and mediocrity in any business is action and implementation. All of us know more than we do. As General H. Norman Schwarzkopf once observed, "The truth of the matter is that you always know the right thing to do. The hard part is doing it." The key to thriving and not just surviving the troubled times we find ourselves in is to do more of the right things. Here are five suggestions of things that must be done now at your bridal store.

1. Stay focused on your top priority every day. Eliminate productivity killers.

There is so much that needs to be done at our stores every day. If we don't have a plan and priorities for action, we are likely to get sucked into the day's activities and merely drift through each day instead of focusing on the most important priorities of each day.

Why don't more of us get things done more productively at our stores? The problem in large measure is us. We don't clearly define what it is that we want and make sure that every activity we do moves us closer to that goal. Jim Rohn was once asked why more people don't become millionaires. His answer is very interesting. He said, "The reason more people don't become millionaires is because they don't have enough reasons to."

Do you have enough reasons to keep you productive? Or do you allow yourself to get easily distracted from the things that you do that create profit for your store?

What this really means is that you have to control yourself and many people really have a challenge with this.

Most people have never been around someone who is extremely productive. They haven't observed the success habits of those who get more done than others do. But, if you study this, you'll find that the most productive people are those who have learned to control themselves and what they do.

They put themselves in an environment where they can focus and where distractions are eliminated. In many cases, they use their environment to control their behavior. Great writers like David McCullough and Dan Brown have revealed that they work in a secluded environment where there can be no distraction from what they are doing, which in their case is writing. Some writers even have special computers they use to write that do not have a plug in connection for the Internet or wireless connectivity so they can focus on the task at hand.

To help you be more productive, you must learn to eliminate distractions that will prevent you from accomplishing the tasks you need to get done. This may mean working on marketing campaigns or other projects you need to get done out of the store or in the store earlier before anyone else arrives. You have to discipline yourself to unplug the phone, turn off your cell phone, not connect to the Internet, and avoid anything that will distract you from the priority in front of you. Distractions today are incredible. Many are completely consumed by technology and have an automatic tendency to constantly be checking email, text messages, voice mail, Facebook and Twitter updates, phone calls, updates on their favorite web sites, etc.

Even if you are the most productive person on the planet, you will still have productivity issues with those around you who interrupt you or who aren't as focused on the task at hand as they could or should be. You must first learn to control yourself and your environment and then help your bridal consultants to do the same.

Everyone has some form of productivity kryptonite—something that interrupts you and prevents you from performing at peak productivity. Just like Superman, you have to shield yourself from these productivity killers so you can get done what must be done. So, here is a question you need to carefully think about. What is your productivity kryptonite?

What can you do to shield yourself from this deadly productivity killer? What changes will you have to make to your behavior or your environment to ensure maximum productivity?

For example, if you know you should have a Monday Morning Marketing meeting with yourself every Monday morning and you are being interrupted, what changes will you have to make in order to make this meeting more productive so you can focus and get things done?

The other thing you need to think about is this: What is the productivity kryptonite of your staff?

For example, if looking at and constantly updating Facebook or another online forum is your productivity killer, what constraints do you have to put in place to prevent you from constantly getting online? For example, you might want to:

- Limit yourself to ½ hour every day when you will get online
- Install software on your computer that blocks Facebook unless you enter a password. This will help you get out of the electronic OCD loop (where you do something without even thinking about it).
- Unplug your Internet connection when you are working on your priority.

A big part of increasing your productivity is to put constraints on others. If you are your own biggest enemy, everyone else at your store and outside your store that wants to talk to you are your next biggest enemy. You have to let people know how you work so that you can get things done. For example, if you are the primary salesperson at your store, you can't be constantly interrupted by sales reps or others constantly calling you on the phone.

You need to have some controls in place. For example, you may decide that you will return phone calls from 1:00 to 2:00pm every day. Then, you have to train your staff when they answer the phone to tell the other party that you aren't available then, but will return their call sometime that day between 1 and 2pm.

This will disappoint, frustrate, annoy and inconvenience some, but you will disappoint, frustrate, annoy and inconvenience yourself if you don't have these types of parameters in place since you will have fewer sales and less productive time in your office and at your store.

I would strongly encourage you to work on this. To be more productive, you must understand and control yourself and those around you.

The last thing I'll say about this is that you have to be clear about your priorities. When you are clear, you can stay focused on the task at hand. You may need to write down what your rules will be and post them on your wall.

For example, during my Monday Morning Marketing meeting, I will not:

- Answer the phone or take phone calls (I turn off my phone or take the phone off the hook before I start working to ensure the environment is conducive to this type of focus).

- Check my email (my email browser will be closed)

- Be distracted by web sites that don't pertain to my specific objective or focus

- Get up from this meeting with myself until I have a comprehensive plan in place with lists and steps for what needs to be done next, who will do it, and when it will be completed by so I can stay on track for launching and creating a successful event. The 2nd CD on the Advertising Your Bridal Store CD set offers tips on how to schedule and think through this type of planning for events.

In addition to my weekly Monday Morning Marketing meeting, I have numerous time periods each week that I have blocked off to focus on specific areas of our store that I want to work on. My staff knows not to interrupt me during that time. Things can wait 90 minutes while I finish what I am working on.

The key to being more productive is to focus on one thing at a time and compartmentalize your thinking so that you allow yourself to focus on one thing at a time. The other part of this is being really clear about why you are staying focused. In other words, what is the reason behind the need for increased focus? Are you really motivated to stay on task because of the goal you have set for yourself? We'll talk more about this in chapter 13 when I discuss understanding the true value of your time.

The questions you should ask are:

- What is driving me?
- Does it really motivate me to stay on track?

Until you gain clarity on this issue, you will never have the personal discipline to control yourself, your environment and others around you because the priority won't be strong enough to overcome the resistance you'll feel.

2. Delegate more.

Face it – you can't do it all. Trying to do it all will burn you out and prevent you from reaching your true potential. Instead, get good at assigning the right job to the right person in the right way. This means that you think through the job *before* you delegate it. Determine who the best person to delegate a task to will be. Ask them to write down what you've asked them to do and have them summarize for you what needs to be done. Then, set up a time to review progress or completion. One of the biggest mistakes made when delegating is to think you can forget about something once it has been delegated and believe that it will still be done. Instead, help others remain accountable to the task you've delegated by carefully explaining and overseeing what needs to be done. To help you find out what activities you can delegate, carefully think through these five questions.

1) List all of the business activities at your store that take up your time. Include everything (including five minute tasks). Be specific, clear, and brief.

2) Describe three things that you are brilliant at doing in your store.

3) Name the three most important activities that produce income for your bridal store.

4) Briefly outline your daily schedule. What do you spend most of your time doing? Can you delegate out some things you are weak at so you can focus more on what you are brilliant at?

5) Name the three most important activities that you don't like to do at your store or that you feel you are weak at doing. Then ask yourself, "Who could do these for me?"

Now that you've determined what time consuming activities you can delegate, what is the *first* thing you are going to say 'No' to or delegate right away? **Don't put it off any longer. Delegate this activity now.** There will be an immediate benefit to your store because of your choice to delegate and focus on what you are best at.

3. Spend more time every week working on marketing your store. Stop guessing and start tracking results.

How much time do you really spend on marketing at your store?

If you're like many store owners, it is not nearly enough as it should or could be. We can all do better at this and if you have the right framework with a marketing calendar planned out for the year and you put in the time, this will have a dramatic impact on the number of brides coming into your store.

The best marketing strategies in the world won't work if you don't utilize them. As I already mentioned, you should be having a meeting weekly where you plan your marketing promotions. You should also set aside at least 5-10 hours a week where you can work exclusively on the marketing of your business. If you find that you are too busy, find someone who can help you with this critical function of your business. This can be one of the most profitable things you'll ever do for your business.

In every successful business, someone takes time to carefully evaluate the numbers. You should take time to carefully evaluate how successful each campaign you have done has been. I have a worksheet I've developed that will help you evaluate the cost for each marketing campaign you have. If you would like a copy, email me at info@bridaltrainingsystems.com.

Here are two reasons why you should track your results more closely:

1) If you know what works and what doesn't, you will be able to know what to do to increase your business.

2) Once you see an increase in sales due to good marketing decisions, you will see a drop in client visit cost. In other words, let's say you spend $1,000 on an advertising campaign that brings in 10 brides. The cost of attracting each of these brides is $100 ($1000 divided by 10). On the other hand, if you use proven strategies that will help you bring in 30 brides and you spend the same $1,000, these brides now only cost you $33.33 each ($1000 divided by 30). When you track your results, you can make better decisions about how to spend your advertising budget.

As an assignment, here are four questions for you to consider about your marketing and advertising decisions:

1) What has been the most successful marketing promotion you've done this past year?

2) Why was it so successful?

3) When can you run this promotion again? Is there any way you can change it to make it even more effective?

4) What promotions do your competitors use that are successful? Which ones can you adapt and use now?

Find out what works and keep repeating it. If you would like some ideas of marketing promotions I've done at our store that have helped bring in brides, get the CD I've created entitled "12 of the Best Promotional Ideas and Strategies I've Used to Flood Our Store with Customers This Past Year." This CD and the accompanying notes are packed with examples of the promotions we've used to help us generate tens of thousands of dollars in sales. The bottom line is that if you want to be successful in marketing your store, stop guessing, start implementing, and track your results to determine how you can be even more effective.

4. **Build and take control of your personal brand. Do everything it takes to become an authority figure in your market niche in your area.**

In Chapter 2, I explained the price/power matrix which shows you how to position your store as unique and necessary so that you can differentiate yourself from your competitors to stand out and avoid being lumped into the commodity classification. Unfortunately, the majority of bridal stores today rely on manufacturers to brand the dresses they sell in their stores instead of branding their own stores. They are finding out that having what everyone else has gives them no unique or meaningful edge and so as a result, they have seen their business decline and suffer.

Consider this statement by Robyn Spizman and Rick Frishman on page 33 of *Where's Your Wow?*:

"If your product or service has no unique or meaningful edge, no amount of marketing is going to make it a success."

When you brand your store, you can create brides that are loyal to *your store* **and** *the experience* they will have at your store as compared to anyone else.

There is a great book called *Personality Not Included* by Rohit Bhargava that details the seven elements that make up the personality of a brand on page 257. He identifies these as:

1) **Uniqueness** – you are different from anything or anyone else.

   How are you different from every other store in your area? If you are perceived to be the same because you carry the same lines, are you really different?

2) **Authentic** – you are real, believable, and not fake.

   Brides today want authenticity. They want to believe in someone that can help them have their wedding dreams fulfilled but they are nervous that they may have their dreams dashed because they have made poor choices in the past. Blogs, newsletters, and social networking sites give brides a chance to get to *know* **and** *trust* you. Stephen Covey's recent book *The Speed of Trust* details this important component of gaining trust.

3) **Talkable** – you are interesting, simple, and viral (you have created a way for people to start talking about you) – a lot of this is done today through YouTube and social networking sites such as Facebook and Twitter.

   Are you doing things at your store that brides want to talk about? Our referral program is one that has gotten brides in our area talking. You should carefully think about how you are getting brides in your area to talk about you.

4) **Soul** – you are significant, honest, and not superficial.

   This ties into authenticity. What drives you at your store? The essence of this is "What is your mission?" At our store, I want every bride who walks out of our store to feel more beautiful than she did when she walked in. People can sense that you have depth of character and a sincere desire to help them find their dream dress.

5) **Brand** – you have a brand on your product, service, company, or your own personal brand.

   No one cares as much about your business as you do. Relying on manufacturers to brand you may save money on initial marketing costs, but the long-term cost is much higher than branding your store on your own.

6) **People** – the people who make up your store are amongst the most important part of your brand (your partners, employees, yourself and of course the brides and prom girls you serve)

   A lot could be said about this. Brides buy from the bridal consultants at your store and they make up your brand – especially what they remember about you. Is each member of your staff communicating the brand image that you really want?

7) **Passion** – you are loyal, vocal, and have deep belief about your business

   Brides can sense your passion for this business and more particularly your passion for helping them plan the wedding of their dreams. You either exude passion or you don't. Leave your challenges and problems at your desk. When you are in front of a bride, let her feel your passion for this business. When you do, you'll be amazed at how quickly you will develop trust and make the sale.

The most important part of branding is to stand for something. You can only stand for something when you specialize. Many bridal stores today try to be all things to all people. As a result, the lines they carry become commoditized because there isn't anything unique about them.

To help you understand this, look at this illustration of the bridal business hierarchy. I first learned how power and authority are related and tiered from marketing expert Dan Kennedy.

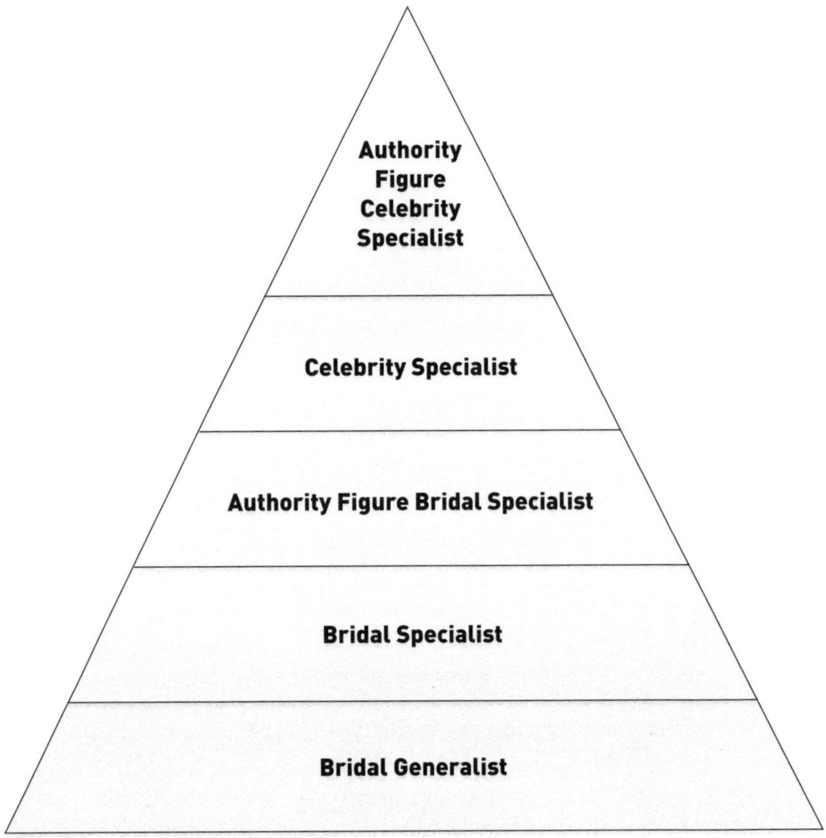

Dan Kennedy says: "At the bottom of the hierarchy of any business is a generalist. A generalist has very little authority and they have very little power. Why? Because they are fundamentally interchangeable and generalists are viewed as interchangeable by everybody who does business with them.

A great example of how this works is in medicine. If you go to a general doctor or a general practice (you may not even see your doctor), you can get the care you want from pretty much any doctor there. If your doctor isn't in, you can get help from someone else. The doctor is interchangeable with any other doctor because they are not a specialist. If the doctor is out on vacation when you come, you can still find someone else to give you service.

This means that you as the patient have the power. You can decide if you like that group of doctors or not. If you don't, you can go down the street and find a new group of doctors (provided that your health insurance covers their care).

However, if you need cardiac surgery or brain surgery, you go to a specialist. You go to the best one in the business.

How are you treated when you call a specialist? You have to have an appointment. They can't just see you anytime (in other words, they are in control).

The people who have the most power in any market are those who have specialized their businesses into a specific niche."

I want to encourage you to become a specialist in the bridal business. Why? Because when you are a specialist instead of a generalist, you will be more valued, remembered, and brides will value doing business with you to a much higher degree.

Here is what the hierarchy looks like in the bridal industry followed by the attitude of power and control that each type of bridal store has. As you read through these, you'll probably notice where you and your competitors currently fall. Your goal should be to move up the hierarchy where you will have more power and control and where you'll also be the most profitable.

Classification of Bridal Store	Attitude of Power and Control
Bridal Generalist	**This is the bridal store that says:** "We carry every line and can price match any dress, anytime, anywhere. I want to help you anyway I can. I'll keep my store open or you can come in anytime and I'll meet with you. Come in and try on anything you want and then see if you can find it cheaper on the Internet because we make it easy to find out where we get our dresses from." This is not necessarily a bad thing – but the reality is that you are not in control.
Bridal Specialist	**This is the bridal store that says:** "We only carry these exclusive lines and no one else in our region carries them. We specialize in serving a specific demographic (whatever that might be)."
Authority Figure Bridal Specialist	**This is the bridal store that says:** "We are recognized by the community and brides as an **expert** (often ***through the passage of time*** – for example, if the mother bought her dress from you) ***or as a result of being perceived as an expert*** (writing newspaper columns, interviewed on the news as a fashion consultant, etc.)."
Celebrity Specialist	**This is the bridal store that says:** "We design and fit dresses to celebrity brides." Pictures are very valuable here especially pictures with a recognized celebrity designer or bride.
Authority Figure –Celebrity Specialist	**This is the bridal store that says:** "I am the designer. We design dresses for celebrity or wealthy clientele." Your picture and celebrity status should be played up in every ad that you do.

So, in order to build a powerful store brand and be more successful in selling, you need to have more power as a store and as a person.

There are so many personal tools that you can use to build your brand in today's crowded marketplace. In order to expand your outreach and build your authority and celebrity, your bridal store should have a blog, a business Facebook and Twitter account, and a good website.

You need a coordinated place to showcase your store, why you're different and your specialized bridal knowledge. You need to take control of your personal brand. Don't expect anyone else to do this for you. The best thing you can do for your store is to decide what you want to be known for, what you want brides to say about you, and what you are willing to do every day to be sure it happens. Once you decide and commit to the actions required to do that, you can build your bridal brand quickly.

5. Pay the price. Be willing to change and make sacrifices to reach your goals.

Even if your store is doing very well, you always have to be willing to make changes. John Maxwell has four ideas in his book *The 17 Indisputable Laws of Teamwork* that explain the price you have to be willing to pay if you want to keep improving and get better. He says:

1) *The price must be paid by everyone.*

   "It is so critical that every member on your team is willing to pay a price and that they pay the price to win. Because if they don't, then you will pay the price of losing." We are in the bridal business to win. I know you are too or you wouldn't be reading this right now.

   I like what former Notre Dame coach Lou Holtz once said, "The freedom to do your own thing ends when you have obligations and responsibilities. If you want to fail yourself you can but you cannot do your own thing if you have responsibilities to team members."

2) *The price must be paid all the time.*

John Maxwell observes: "Destination disease is as dangerous for a team as it is for any individual. It makes us believe that we can stop working, stop striving, stop paying the price—yet still reach our potential."

Dwight D. Eisenhower once said: "There are no victories at bargain prices."

3) *The price increases if the team wants to improve, change, or keep winning.*

John Maxwell writes on p. 139 of his book *The 17 Indisputable Laws of Teamwork* that "there are few back to back champions in sports. And few companies stay at the top of *Forbe's* magazine's lists for a decade. Becoming a champion has a high price. But remaining on top costs even more. And improving upon your best is even more costly. The higher you are, the more you have to pay to make even small improvements. World champion sprinters improve their times not by seconds, but by hundreths of a second."

Are you constantly striving to improve or do you sometimes stop to admire the view?

If you want to improve, change, and keep winning in the bridal business, you always have to be making improvements and pushing the envelope. Otherwise, you will start to decline.

4) *The price never decreases.*

Maxwell observes: "Most people who quit don't give up at the bottom of the mountain; they stop halfway up it. Nobody sets out with the purpose of losing. The problem is often a mistaken belief that a time will come when success will suddenly get cheaper. But life rarely works that way.

He concludes with this thought:

"When it comes to the Law of the Price Tag, I believe there are really only two kinds of teams who violate it: those who don't realize the price of success, and those who know the price but are not willing to pay it. No one can force a team member to have the will to succeed. Each person must decide in his own heart whether the goal is worth the price that must be paid."

What about you? Are you willing to pay the price to succeed in your bridal business?

Here are some questions for you to consider about the price to be paid to succeed:

- Do you have a track record of looking for the "easiest and fastest" route to get things done?
- Do you have a track record that indicates you are willing to do whatever it takes, which includes making sacrifices, in order to move your store to the next level?
- What are you not willing to sacrifice to move to the next level?
- What is the greatest sacrifice you have ever made? Why did you do it? Would you do it again?
- What sacrifice have you avoided, that if you "bit the bullet" you could launch your store to the next level? What prevents you from doing it? Is there someone you can team up with or partner with?
- Are the key personnel and bridal consultants around you willing to sacrifice whatever is needed for the store to reach its full potential? If not, why?

In business, you can have anything you want, but you cannot have everything you want. All of life is a trade. For example, you may choose to open a second or third location, but you also choose to sacrifice personal time with your family and friends. You must choose what you will sacrifice. Sacrifice comes in a variety of price tags, but author Steve Chandler says there are two questions that let you know if you are really committed to paying the price to get good at something:

1. **Have you asked for help with it?** Are you going around to get help? This is important, because in order to ask for help you have to drop your pride (or in other words you have to stop saying "I should be able to do this on my own"). When you ask for help, you are *really* trying to learn how to do something.

2. **Are you measuring it?** You can't improve what you aren't measuring. If you don't know what you are measuring or how you are doing something, there is really no commitment to getting better at it. Start taking action and measuring the specific areas of your business where you want to improve. When you do, you'll see change and results.

Today is the best day to take action to get what you want. In his book *Action! Nothing Happens Until Something Moves*, author Robert Ringer says:

"There are two kinds of actions. One is proaction, which puts you on the offensive and, all other things being equal, gives you a great deal of control over events. The other is reaction, which puts you on the defensive and relegates you to an inherent position of weakness. An interesting way of looking at inaction is that it's really just a negative form of action—a sort of black hole of action that sucks energy away from you much the same as the black holes of the universe pull matter into the deep recesses of their cosmic bowels. This is why inaction often yields consequences by default. Nothing happens until something moves, so if you wait for something, or someone, to act on you, you likely will be unable to control the consequences."

Don't wait on what you know you should do. Take action. Nothing will happen at your store until you move. Carefully consider the five actions I've recommended here and keep moving forward. Being proactive every day on the critical success factors of your business will help you create what you want.

Chapter 11

Build and Surround Yourself with an Excellent Team

Brad Smart, an expert on hiring and the author of *Topgrading* has observed that "the cost of the average mis-hire costs business 23x their yearly salary." If this is true, then hiring a full time employee at $40,000 a year who is not the right person for your business will cost you $920,000.

If you have a part-time bridal consultant who is paid $8 an hour and she is not the right person, this will cost you $184,000. [(8x20 hours/week x 50 weeks per year) = $8,000 x 23 = $184,000]

Why is this number so high? There are two reasons:

- This includes the opportunity cost of what they could have sold if they would have been the right person
- The employee who you've just trained for a year or two isn't doing the right job and it is costing you big money.

The reality is that one person can kill your business. Brad Smart says that three out of four people that are hired are mis-hires. That statement should scare you to death. Why does this happen?

The reason is because when you ask people ten standard questions in your interview, they know great answers to these questions since they've been out in their car before they came in reading, "How to Answer Interview Questions Like a Pro" and you think: "Wow, what great answers!"

To counter this, you need to understand what top performers look like. Brad Smart, author of *Topgrading* says that there are three types of employees: C Players, B Players, and A Players. He says that most people that are hired are C players. C players are great at creating job security for themselves at your company (since they create processes at your company that only they know how to run and you feel like you could never get along without them). The biggest problem with C players is that they are also great at scaring off A players.

Most of us don't know what an A player (superstar) really looks like. It is rare to find these individuals because they are usually very happily employed at another business. Here are three mistakes that you are making when hiring bridal consultants at your store that are preventing you from hiring superstars that will help you reach your sales goals:

1. You are hiring people *you* like.
2. You are hiring people *like* you. Why is it bad to hire another person like you? You're the entrepreneurial one. So, they come to work for you and then go out and start their own bridal store too.
3. You are hiring someone because you want to help them.

You are a professional business. If you were a major league baseball team, would you hire amateurs to play for you or would you hire professionals? The reality is that if you hired amateurs you wouldn't play very well as a team in competition with other professional teams. You need to see your store the same way. You have to hire professionals and not amateurs. You don't have time to help someone by hiring an amateur. You are hiring professionals who can help you reach your business goals. Don't ever forget this important lesson.

Another important thing to remember about this is that A players hang out with other A players. They don't like hanging out with C players. Ask these top professionals that you meet in your interactions with other people to come work for you or ask them to introduce you to their friends – because they are likely superstars as well. Remember, it is mostly C players that answer ads. A and B players are usually already employed somewhere else. There is a direct correlation between a C player and why they don't currently have a job. They're looking because they probably weren't a top performer for their previous employer either. Now, there are some exceptions to this but keep this in mind when interviewing and hiring bridal consultants to work at your store.

Here are several realities about hiring today:

- Some candidates believe they can change themselves and their circumstance and some don't
- Some candidates are driven to develop, learn, and improve themselves and some aren't
- Some candidates have emotional and social intelligence and some don't – this is one of the most important things I'm looking for in our third interview when we're watching them sell
- Some candidates want to create and contribute to others and some don't
- Some candidates are comfortable with who they are, and are authentic, and some aren't
- Some candidates are optimistic and some aren't
- Some candidates live in a friendly, abundant, and opportunity-filled universe, and some don't

What this should teach you is that you should hire people who already have the values you want and who are already motivated from within.

When you give these individuals incentives and goals, you'll be amazed at the results. You can't change people. Start with what you want and they will help you build your store.

On the other hand, if you only hire A players and sellers at your store, what happens?

- These stars amplify each other and will collectively enhance your store's sales goals like never before
- Your store will shatter your previous sales records
- You will attract more like-minded A players/sellers because people like being around other leaders and achievers.

In order to accomplish this you have to create a culture of leadership.

I learned from business consultant Eben Pagan how to know if you have an A player on your team. He said to ask them to give you a daily update. He says this update should be composed of three things.

These things are written from the point of view of the person giving the daily update. They should tell you:

1. What I did today and what results I got today.
2. Problems and challenges I experienced today.
3. Questions I have for you.

After reading this chapter, meet with your key personnel one on one. Share with them some of the things you've learned. Then ask them to email or write you with a quick daily update every day. At the end of each day for 30 days, you will know via a pulse reading what kind of an individual you have *really* hired.

I am grateful for all of the wonderful leaders we have at our bridal store, especially our excellent manager Deidra Breckon. Each member of our team is an "A" player and a true professional.

Be committed to hire only A players. You are a professional business. Hire professionals. Always be on the lookout for professionals you can work with to help you reach your goals.

Another critical function of hiring and creating a great staff is to understand what everyone on your bridal team does. I have created a chart for you to write in your bridal store support team so that you can grade each of the employees you have in your store now on an A-F grade. Decide to make changes and keep only the A and B players. Then, strive to help your B players become A players.

My Bridal Store Support Team

Business Area	Who Works in This Area	Grade	Changes Required	Action Steps – What Needs to Be Done?
Administrative (Receptionist)				
Marketing & Promotion				
Sales				
Management				
Suppliers (Dress lines, accessories, etc.)				
Financial (bankers, investors, partners)				
Accountant				
Bookkeeper				
Tax Specialist				

My Bridal Store Support Team (cont.)				
Business Area	**Who Works in This Area**	**Grade**	**Changes Required**	**Action Steps – What Needs to Be Done?**
Legal Consultant				
Staffing (hiring, training, coordinating)				
Fashion Team Coordinator				
Bridal Special Projects				
Prom Special Projects				
Other: Advisors, Mentors, Coaches				

The second part of hiring is to create a culture of leadership and constantly be developing great leaders around you. To help you understand this principle, see what lessons you can learn from the life of Edmund Hillary as detailed in John Maxwell's *The 17 Indisputable Laws of Teamwork* on pages 42-46. Hillary is known by most people as the first man on top of Mount Everest. His story and the story behind that story is instructive for the following reasons:

1. Failure precedes accomplishment. Seven major expeditions tried and failed (over a period of 32 years – 1920 and 1952) before Tenzing Norgay and Edmund Hillary made it to the top. Norgay was on six of those expeditions and was also the lead guide on major expedition #8 (which was successful) as well as making many other high climbs to other notable mountains.

2. No one gets to the top of any mountain or achieves any significant goal alone. Teamwork is required to accomplish anything of significance.

Two to three hundred people were hired just to get the supplies (nearly two and a half tons of equipment and food) in the vicinity of the mountain. Another forty Sherpa porters helped carry supplies from the base camp higher up the mountain. The team that climbed thc mountain included Norgay and Hillary and also ten high-altitude climbers. One set of men would exhaust themselves just to get the equipment up the mountain for the next group. Two-man teams would work their way up the mountain, find a path, cut steps, and secure ropes for the next team to continue to move ahead or press ahead.

Norgay made this statement about the necessity of teamwork in climbing:

"You do not climb a mountain like Everest by trying to race ahead on your own, or by competing with your comrades. You do it slowly and carefully, by unselfish teamwork. Certainly I wanted to reach the top myself; it was the one thing I had dreamed of all my life. But if the lot fell to someone else I would take it like a man, and not a crybaby. For that is the mountain way."—James Ramsey Ullman, *Man of Everest: The Autobiography of Tenzing*, p. 250.

Ultimately two sets of the men climbing the mountain made an attempt for the summit. The first set (Tom Bourdillon and Charles Evans) tried and failed leaving the opportunity to Tenzing Norgay and Edmund Hillary.

Norgay made this statement about the first team and the effort it took from both teams to succeed:

"They were worn out, sick with exhaustion, and, of course, terribly disappointed that they had not reached the summit themselves. But still...they did everything they could to advise and help us. And I thought, Yes, that is how it is on the mountain. That is how a mountain makes men great. For where would Hillary and I have been without the others? Without the climbers who had made the route and the Sherpas who had carried the loads? Without Bourdillon and Evans, Hunt and Da Namgyal, who had cleared the way ahead? Without Lowe and Gregory, Ang Hyima, Ang Tempra, and Penba, who were there only to help us? It was only because of the work and sacrifice of all of them that we were now to have our chance at the top." — James Ramsey Ullman, *Man of Everest: The Autobiography of Tenzing*, p. 255.

Why do I share this story to start off a discussion about developing great employees around you? Because it is easy to spend more time focusing on your ***dream*** than it is on your ***team***.

John Maxwell is right when he says: "When the team you have doesn't match up to the team of your dreams, then you have only two choices: give up your dream or grow up your team." –*The 17 Indisputable Laws of Teamwork*, p. 50.

The topic we are going to be covering in the remainder of this chapter (that of growing and developing your team) is a big concern for all small business owners, especially those in the bridal business.

I recently visited with a store owner who has been in the bridal business for a relatively short period of time. She is doing everything in the store by herself. She told me, "I can't find anyone I can trust. I just have to do everything on my own."

When my wife and I first started our store, we faced the same dilemna. We had three young children (ages 5, 3, and 18 months) at the time. We split our schedules and drove our kids to the store and switched places. We hired a babysitter on Saturdays and worked together at the store. We hired our first employee several months after we started our business. Those were challenging times. Our first employee was a bride that we sold a dress to. Shortly, thereafter, we hired two more people to help us on Saturdays.

We have had as many as twenty-seven people working at our bridal and prom stores. As we have grown, it has been critical to find and train up great leaders who can help us to grow our store to new levels of success. It is my hope to share some of the things I have learned and am still learning about how to lead and help those around me to lead as well.

Helping people become leaders and develop their true potential is one of my passions. I believe very strongly in the potential of people and I want to help everyone that I hire to become extraordinary. I don't take this for granted because I am always working on improving myself and expect the same from those that work with us at our store.

As I've thought about the dilemna of growth and making a conscious decision to develop those around us into great leaders, I've identified 5 reasons why many store owners don't make the leap to build a powerful group of leaders with them at their store. These reasons are:

1. They fear that those they train will leave and become their competition. Insecure leaders don't empower others to become leaders.

2. They aren't sure how.

3. They personally feel inadequate to develop others because they recognize their own weaknesses.

4. It isn't a priority. They know it is important, but are so overwhelmed with the day-to-day responsibilities of the business that they don't take the time to develop those around them.

5. They are not good leaders themselves so few really want to follow them (they have high turnover).

John Maxwell identifies six reasons why we need to develop leaders around us at our stores in his book *Developing the Leaders Around You.* I'll be quoting from this book extensively in this chapter and I highly recommend that you get, read and study it on your own. These six reasons are:

1. **Those closest to the leader will determine the success of that leader.**

    - Who are the five or six people closest to you at your store?

    - Are you developing them?

- Are they growing?
- Have they been able to lift your load?

Andrew Carnegie once explained the importance those close to you this way:

"I wish to have as my epitaph: 'Here lies a man who was wise enough to bring into his service men who knew more than he.'"

2. **Your store's growth is directly proportional to the growth of your bridal consultants.**

   Maxwell states:

   "Grow a leader—grow the organization. A company cannot grow without until its leaders grow within."

   If we want to grow in any area at our bridal stores, we first have to train the members of our staff to make the changes necessary to create and cause the growth.

   As we grow from one level to the next, the numbers will change (number of wedding gowns or prom dresses sold), but the principles involved to make these changes won't.

   As Maxwell points out: "The strength of any organization is a direct result of the strength of it's leaders. Weak leaders equal weak organizations. Strong leaders equal strong organizations. Everything rises and falls on leadership."—p. 6.

3. **Potential leaders help carry the load.**

   Peter Drucker once said:

   "No executive has ever suffered because his people were strong and effective."

   Here are two ways that developing leaders around me have helped our store and will help yours as well:

1) *They are a sounding board for my marketing ideas.* Members of my staff help me clarify the ideas I have and help me make them happen.

2) *They possess a leadership mindset.* They don't just work with me, they think like leaders. Since I am not always in the store, they take charge and jump in and do what needs to be done. I am so grateful for the great leaders that we currently have and that we have had at our store who have all made great contributions to our store's success. This is such an important principle. If you only have followers at your store and without help from other leaders to help carry the load, you will become fatigued and get burned out very quickly.

4. **Leaders attract potential leaders.**

When you are a strong leader, you are not threatened by people with great potential. Instead, you will attract people who have great strengths that can help you grow in new ways that you couldn't have by yourself.

I really like this statement by Calvin Lloyd: "Nobody rises to low expectations."

This is another reason why it is so important to develop ourselves as the leaders of our stores. As we grow to new levels, we want to attract leaders (or inspire latent ones in our stores) who are drawn to the excitement of what we are doing.

5. **Leaders who mentor potential leaders multiply their effectiveness.**

Together, we can accomplish so much more than any one person can accomplish on their own.

As Bob Moawad says:

"Help others get ahead. You will always stand taller with someone else on your shoulders."

John Wooden once observed that if you oversee people and wish to develop leaders, you have four responsibilities. These are:

1) "Appreciate them for who they are
2) Believe that they will do their very best
3) Praise their accomplishments
4) Accept your personal responsibility to them as your leader." —John Wooden, as quoted in *Developing the Leaders Around You*, pp. 1-2.

John Maxwell says this: "Great leaders—the truly successful ones who are in the top 1 percent—all have one thing in common. They know that acquiring and keeping good people is a leader's most important task." *—Developing the Leaders Around You*, p. 2.

I think we can all agree that acquiring and keeping good people is our most important task as a leader. What I hope you will realize as you study this chapter and topic is how to create the environment to grow leaders and how to specifically make this happen in your store.

Consistent accomplishment is what generates momentum. Creating the environment of momentum is critical to your success as a leader.

When you have an environment of momentum in your store, leaders will be attracted to your store and will want to be a part of what you are creating and doing.

Fascinating research has been done on the importance of the environment with regard to growth. Sharks have been found to adapt to their environment based on how big it is. If a shark is caught when it is small and confined, it will only grow to a size proportionate to the aquarium in which it lives. Sharks can be six feet long when they fully mature, but can be kept at a much smaller size in an aquarium environment. When these same sharks are released into the ocean, they grow to their normal size.

This is an interesting observation about nature – but it is true about the leaders in your store as well.

Is the environment in your store **confining** growth or is it **encouraging** growth?

As I mentioned before, there is a big distinction in the results that come from being a thermostat leader vs. a thermometer one. Decide to be a thermostat leader.

Remember, **good leaders can *sustain* momentum. Great leaders can *increase* it.**

By creating the right environment and developing the leaders at your store, you can increase your momentum as well.

Colin Powell said it best:

"How many immerse themselves in the goal of creating an environment where the best, the brightest, the most creative are attracted, retained, and most importantly—unleashed?" — Oren Harari, *The Leadership Secrets of Colin Powell*, p. 258.

Here are four ways you can establish the right environment at your store to develop and unleash leaders:

1. Surround yourself with those who can help you accomplish your goals.

In his book *8 Ways to Great*, author Dr. Doug Hirschhorn shares this insight from how Roger Bannister broke the four-minute mile. The lesson is one we can all better apply at our stores. He says:

"One of the most compelling illustrations of how setting short-term goals and committing to the process leads to extraordinary achievement is the story of how Roger Bannister became the first person to ever run a mile in under four minutes. At the time, many people believed that running a sub-four-minute mile was humanly impossible, but Bannister had a plan. He ran with two pacemakers. The first pacemaker, Chris

Brasher, ran under the four minute pace with Bannister slotted to run behind him for the first half mile. Then, when Brasher began to tire, Bannister signaled to his second pacemaker, Chris Chataway, to take over. Chataway moved up and ran under the pace with Bannister right behind him until they were two hundred yards from the finish, at which point Bannister sprinted ahead and crossed the finish line in 3 minutes, 59.4 seconds. The point is, Bannister didn't start out saying he had to run the mile in under four minutes. Instead, he had short-term goals—keeping up first with Brasher and then with Chataway—and when those two things were added together, Roger found himself being the first person to break the 'impossible' four minute mile."

I love that story because it illustrates what leaders do They think through the process and challenge in front of them. Bannister broke down his goal and then had others around him set the pace for his achievement. Each of us has this task and challenge as well. In our stores each day, we have to figure out what will work and what we need to do to reach our goals. When obstacles arise as they always do, you have to remain optimistic and lead by taking action. Great leaders have a plan and a process. They make adjustments and improve. They lead by getting out and making the first sale. They lead by being more enthusiastic than anyone else. When you lead with enthusiasm and stick to a process and plan, you will be unstoppable.

2. Invest in those with the most potential.

It is valuable and wise to make leadership development available to everyone at your store, but important to invest more in the ones with the greatest potential. They will give the greatest return.

I train everyone at our store to be great salespeople and I strive to train our leadership team to be great salespeople *and* great leaders. They in turn are to train everyone else to be great salespeople and great leaders too.

Here are five key characteristics you want to watch for to know the potential of an individual to be developed as a leader as outlined by

John Maxwell:

- "The person has influence with others. (It does not matter how much or little.)
- The person is hungry to grow as a leader. They are teachable.
- The person is receptive to input and guidance from a "mentor" leader.
- The person's character and general competence stand out as excellent.
- The person is willing to pay the price of commitment."
  --Developing the Leaders Around You, pp. 37-43.

3. ***Devote yourself to the process and provide the necessary resources for growth.***

Leadership development is not a quick fix, or add-water-and-stir proposition. It is not a one-time event, like a seminar or a conference. Leadership develops daily, not in a day. Do not compromise the process by expecting amazing results in 30 days when what is needed is an entire year or more.

A big part of this is to provide growth opportunities to members of your staff that you would like to develop into leaders. Always be looking for ways to develop each member of your staff. Don't assume that this will just happen on its own.

Give your best people opportunities to shine by giving them more responsibility over a specific project or area of your store. If you give proper training and assistance and provide guidance along the way, you will rarely be disappointed by how well your bridal consultants can accomplish what needs to be done.

But, here is the key: you have to provide the right tools in order to succeed. Or, as illustrated in this humorous story, you will have disastrous results:

"A woman went to a pet store and purchased a parrot to keep her company. She took her new pet home but returned the next day to report, "That parrot hasn't said a word yet." The storekeeper asked "Does it have a mirror? Parrots like to be able to look at their reflection in a mirror." So she bought the mirror and returned home.

The next day she was back, announcing that the bird still wasn't speaking. The storekeeper said "What about a ladder? Parrots enjoy walking up and down a ladder." So she bought the ladder and returned home.

Sure enough, the next day she was back with the same story - still no talk. "Does the parrot have a swing? Birds enjoy relaxing on a swing." She bought the swing and went home.

The next day she returned to the store to announce the bird had died. The storekeeper said "I'm terribly sorry to hear that. Did the bird ever say anything before it died?" The lady replied "Yes, it said, 'Don't they sell any BIRD FOOD in that store?'" —*Developing the Leaders Around You*, pp. 25-26.

Devote yourself to the process and provide the *right* resources for growth.

4. Keep growing yourself as a leader.

This is vital. When you stop growing as a leader, the leaders around you stop growing. Soon after that, your store will stop growing as well.

John Maxwell points this out on page 20 of *Developing the Leaders Around You*:

"When people follow us, they can only go as far as we go. If our growth stops, our ability to lead will stop along with it."

Here are three questions to consider about your own personal growth:

1) Do I have a game plan for personal growth?

2) Is my life an example for others to follow?

3) Am I willing to pay the price to become a great leader?

Thomas J. Watson, the former chairman of IBM, once said: "Nothing so conclusively proves a man's ability to lead others, as what he does from day to day to lead himself."

John Maxwell adds: "The smallest crowd you will ever lead is you—but it's the most important one."

When you can lead yourself, you can lead those at your store to new and greater heights.

Here is an assignment for you:

What is your personal plan for growth? Do you have one?

Here are four suggestions:

1. **Come up with a plan.**

   If not, you need to develop one – my assignment is for you to put this together in the next couple of days. Determine what your daily disciplines will be.

2. **Apply quickly what you learn.**
3. **Grow with someone.**
4. **Plan your growth and follow it for a year.**

The reality is that if you want to lead your bridal consultants and reach the next level in your business, you have to have a plan for growth. Growth has to be intentional. It doesn't happen automatically.

Rick Warren, author of *The Purpose Driven Life*, says, "The moment you stop learning is the moment you stop leading."

If you want to lead, you have to learn. Help your bridal consultants become leaders by becoming readers. I periodically will buy copies of a great book I have just read for my management team to read and study and discuss with me. These discussions have been great ways for us to grow and learn together.

Philips Brooks, the minister who spoke at Abraham Lincoln's funeral was right when he said:

"Sad is the day for any man when he becomes absolutely satisfied with the life he is living, the thoughts he is thinking and the deeds he is doing; when there ceases to be forever beating at the doors of his soul a desire to do something larger which he seeks and knows he was meant and intended to do."

Some people reach this point in their life where they don't want to keep growing.

I have met many people in this business and I'm sure you have as well who don't have any desire to keep learning (they already think they know everything they need to succeed).

"They are a little like the little girl who thought she had exhausted mathematics when she had learned the twelve times tables. When her grandfather said with a twinkle in his eye, "What's thirteen times thirteen?" she scoffed, "Don't be silly, Grandpa, there's no such thing." —John Maxwell, *Leadership Gold*, p. 129.

How do you identify who you should develop as a leader at your store?

Andrew Carnegie was once asked how he had managed to hire 43 millionaires. Carnegie told the reporter that these individuals had not been millionaires when he hired them, but that they had become millionaires when they started working for him. The reporter then asked how Carnegie had developed these individuals into such remarkable and successful leaders. His answer is quite insightful. He said:

"Men are developed the same way gold is mined. Several tons of dirt must be moved to get an ounce of gold. But you don't go into the mine looking for dirt. You go in looking for the gold."

This is how you should decide at your store who you should develop into a leader. You have to look for the good, not the bad.

Here are some suggestions for deciding who you are going to promote to be an assistant manager or to start developing into a leader at your store:

1. **Who is available?** It is difficult to really develop someone into a leader who isn't at the store very often. Taking inventory of your current staff can help you determine if you have the right group to select from. You may find that you don't have the right person. If so, you should consider the following characteristics of individuals who you want to become your leaders:

    - ***Strength of character*** - as we've seen recently with the numerous scandals involving politicians, sports stars, or other celebrities, character flaws cannot be ignored. They will eventually make a leader ineffective.

    - ***Influence*** – potential leaders are *going somewhere* **and** *can persuade others to go with them* (that is why noticing a bridal consultants selling ability is a key indicator of their ability to become a great leader – sales is really all about influence)

    - ***Positive attitude*** – people with a positive attitude are determined to walk to the very edge of their potential before they accept defeat; they have fewer self-imposed limitations and can do things that others can't.

    - ***Excellent people skills*** – many of the challenges we face in this business stem from an inability to communicate effectively and deal with brides the way they want to be treated. Since your leaders will be dealing on the front line with customer service issues, you want someone who already has genuine concern for others, understand where people are coming from and can solve challenges as they come up.

    - ***Proven track record*** – they have a knack for getting things done.

- ***Self-discipline*** – potential leaders realize that they have to give up in order to go up. They are willing to sacrifice and discipline themselves to get things done.
- ***Discontent with the status quo*** – leaders who love the status quo quickly become followers (people who are never satisfied with current performance, but are always stretching to become better are obviously ideal candidates to sell and lead at our stores.)
- ***Effective communication skills***

2. **Who has some leadership ability?** Who has shown promise already at the store by rising to the top? I have noticed that many of our best leadership candidates also seem to be the ones who are our top sellers. This is important because it shows the other consultants at the store that leadership roles are given based on 1) achieving results and 2) modeling results for others. In other words, I want someone leading our staff who has shown that our minimum standard can be reached and achieved.

   Coach John Wooden made this statement about finding potential leaders:

   "Some people are automatic leaders. Some can never be leaders. But many who don't think of themselves as leaders have the potential to become such if they understand the fundamentals of getting individuals to work together. Those fundamentals can be learned. I learned them." —*Wooden: A Lifetime of Observations and Reflections On and Off the Court*, p. 112.

3. **Who is willing? Who has the most positive attitude?**

   A great salesperson with a bad attitude who selfishly takes from others to get what she wants can bring down the morale of your team very quickly. Be sure you look for someone who is not only willing and has a positive attitude, but also understands how to increase excitement and momentum. Remember, you are looking for potential leaders who are willing to make changes *within* instead of looking to change everyone around them.

As John Maxwell says: "You can look at others to place the blame, or you can look at yourself to discover your opportunities." —*The Difference Maker*, p. 68.

4. **Who gets things done and who gets results?** Who does more than is expected of them?

   I think a great example of what I'm talking about here can be found in the life of Pleasant T. Rowland, a schoolteacher, who in 1986 founded Pleasant Company because she was frustrated with the uncreative textbooks she was provided with where she taught. She developed her own materials and later began working in educational research and publishing and then began offering dolls with the books she developed. Today, the American Girl company has nine historical dolls (each with a back story and book and literally hundreds of products to accompany them). The company has sold more than 61 million books and 5 million dolls and over 700,000 individuals subscribe to their magazine. In 1998, American Girl was acquired by Mattel and Pleasant Rowland became Mattel's vice chairman. Mattel was impressed by Pleasant's business skills, sense of mission, and her ability to turn her vision into reality (or, in other words, achieve results).

   Many people may have never expected a school teacher from Madison, Wisconsin to have and achieve such a remarkable vision. But, that is what is so great about finding and developing leaders: people who have a tendency to get things done and achieve results are prime candidates for developing into greater leaders.

If you don't feel like you have any candidates to draw from that meet the criteria we've just discussed, you may want to listen to the training CD I created discussing the book *9 Lies That Are Holding Your Business Back*.

It is part of the training set I created entitled "Attitude and Business Success." On this CD, I explain that you need to make hiring these kinds of leaders a want based activity instead of a needs based activity. This type of focus and clarity will help you find the leaders who can help you take your business to the next level.

How do you nurture potential leaders?

Here are five recommendations about how you can nurture potential leaders into great leaders from *Developing the Leaders Around You*:

1. **Explain expectations and set the standard.**

John Wooden makes this statement about the importance of getting off to a good start with your first introduction to a new team member or new leader (someone you have just promoted):

"Getting off to a good start is important. It sets the tone for your team in many ways—expectations, values, attitude, behavior, rules, and much more. This is especially true with individuals who are new to your organization, but it also applies to the others under your leadership who may need a reminder from time to time of how you expect things to be done." —*Wooden on Leadership*, p. 237.

When I promote someone to be an assistant manager at our store, we have a meeting where we discuss expectations and set a standard for their performance. This meeting is critical to setting up the parameters for how you will help them become a better leader.

I think one of the most important aspects of this meeting and all training with your leaders has to be **mutual respect**. Even though you recognize that she is likely going to make some mistakes as she learns to lead in different ways, you have to avoid projecting yourself as superior in any way.

Developing people is hard work.

I really like the story John Maxwell tells on page 107 in his book *Developing the Leaders Around You* about a preacher who quit the ministry after twenty years and became a funeral director.

When asked why he made the change, he replied, "Well, I spent three years trying to straighten Fred out, and Fred is still an alcoholic. And I spent six months trying to straighten out Susan's marriage, and she filed for divorce. Then I spent over two-and-a-half years trying to straighten out Bob's drug problem, and he's still an addict. Now at the funeral home, when I straighten them out—they stay straight." —*Developing the Leaders Around You*, pp. 107-108.

2. Employ BEST.

Believe in them. It is great to believe in your bridal consultants, but it is even more powerful when *they know* that you believe in them. When your bridal consultants work in your store and know that you personally care about them, they will contribute a lot more than their paycheck dictates.

Encourage them.

J.M. Barrie, the playwright who wrote Peter Pan said: "Those who bring sunshine into the lives of others cannot keep it from themselves."

When I was 14, I was given a copy of this poem by a great friend and leader and to this day it is my favorite poem:

"If with pleasure you are viewing any work a man is doing,
If you like him or you love him, tell him now.
Don't withhold your approbation till the parson makes oration,
And he lies with snowy lilies o'er his brow.
For no matter how you shout it, he won't really care about it,
He won't know how many teardrops you have shed.
If you think some praise is due him,
Now's the time to slip it to him,
For he cannot read his tombstone when he's dead."

Share with them. Share with your bridal consultants what you are learning in this book and what you learn from other books and resources you study and learn from.

Trust them. One of the best ways to help your leaders grow is to trust them with responsibility.

3. **Offer hope.**

Bob Eaton, former chairman and CEO of Daimler-Chrysler Corporation said:

"A leader is someone who can take a group of people to a place they don't think they can go."

Napoleon observed:

"Leaders are dealers in hope."

When you set a goal and you are training your staff and your leaders to achieve it, there are only two ways to offer hope that they can achieve it. Offering hope is so important since if you don't have hope, your bridal consultants won't take action to achieve the goal.

I have seen bridal consultants demotivated and demoralized by setting our goal too high or conversely when they just didn't believe in themselves. When you see this, you have to immediately do two things to turn the situation around:

1) **Help your bridal consultants change their way of thinking.**

The best way to do this is to motivate them by talking about their past successes and training them to improve.

2) **Help your bridal consultants win some small victories.**

As the saying goes, "Positive thinking must be followed by positive doing."

Too often, we give our bridal consultants pep rallies at our training meetings, but don't help them achieve the small victories. Once the small victories have been achieved, it is easier to believe and hope that the bigger goals and victories are possible.

4. Reward production and results.

Former Kansas City Chiefs Coach Dick Vermeil once observed: "Few people, on their own initiative, set their standards high enough."

Since this is often true, we must reward production ***and*** results. You have to be careful to not contaminate your rewards system by rewarding those who don't deserve it. In other words, you must not reward mediocrity. If you do, you will lose credibility as a leader.

Recently, one of our prom consultants begged me to lower the sales amount she would have to sell in order to qualify to win a gift card to Nordstrom's that I was going to give to the highest seller that day. I told her I couldn't lower the standard. She needed to rise up to the standard. This is what leaders have to do. If you lower the standards, you cheapen the reward. As a leader, the best way to reward production and results is to only give rewards to those who deserve them.

Here are three motivation questions that John Maxwell points out on pages 109-110 of *Developing the Leaders Around You*:

1) What do they want?

The more you know the reasons behind what motivates and drives each of your bridal consultants, the better you will be able to motivate them and help them reach their potential.

2) Do they have a way to get what they want?

If your bridal consultants want something, but do not think they can get it from what they are doing at your store, they will not be motivated. One of the most important roles as a leader you can fill for your team members is to show them a way to have what they really want.

3) ***Will they be rewarded if successful?***

   Good leaders are great listeners. When you understand the concerns or needs that your bridal consultants have and you help them see how they will be rewarded for their performance, you will see tremendous growth. Help those around you see that the rewards outweigh the cost of what needs to be done (whether that is to reach a financial goal, learn to master overcoming objections, handle a difficult customer service problem, etc.)

5. **Offer time and be available.**

   It is so important to be available so you can communicate issues that come up in their development and challenges that are facing the store.

   Here are a couple of things to remember when you are communicating with those you are training to be leaders:

   - Poor communication or no communication guarantees that there will be problems
   - Allow people to freely express their ideas. Let your bridal consultants know that you will always respect their thoughts and ideas. No one of us is smarter than all of us.
   - Lack of respect stops communication.

What is the difference between nurturing (caring) for your bridal consultants, equipping (training them) and developing (helping them become someone better)?

There is a great chart on page 108 of *Developing the Leaders Around You* that really illustrates the difference between these key functions as you train up bridal consultants and leaders at your store.

Everyone you hire needs to be nurtured and equipped (or trained) for the job. And with time, everyone should be developed into a leader.

Consider the following comparisons of these three vital roles:

Nurturing	*Equipping*	*Developing*
Care	Training for Work	Training for Personal Growth
Focus is on Need	Focus is on Task	Focus is on Person
Relational	Transactional	Transformational
Service	Management	Leadership
Maintains leadership	Adds leadership	Multiplies leadership
Establishing	Releasing	Empowering
Helping	Teaching	Mentoring
Need Oriented	Skill Oriented	Character Oriented
What They Want	What the Organization Needs	What They Need
A Desire	A Science	An Art
Little to No Growth	Short-Term Growth	Long-term growth
All	Many	Few

—John Maxwell, *Developing the Leaders Around You*, p. 108.

I love this list of principles that Coach John Wooden employed with his team of basketball players at UCLA:

1. "Basketball is a game of habits." Isn't selling and succeeding in the bridal business a matter of habits as well?

2. "Never become satisfied.

3. Don't give them too much, but teach well.
4. Don't tie them down so rigidly that they lose their initiative.
5. Have an offense that gives equal opportunity to all.
6. Don't overlook little details. You must prepare to win to be a winner.
7. Convince your players of the importance of condition-mental, moral, and physical.
8. Nothing is as important as the proper execution of the fundamentals.
9. Confidence comes from being prepared and properly conditioned.
10. Development of team spirit is a must and selfishness, envy, and egotism must be eliminated.
11. Both coach and players must be industrious and enthusiastic if success is to be achieved.
12. Teach respect for all and fear for none.
13. Use the positive approach and develop pride in your own game.
14. Have one team, not regulars and substitutes.
15. Give public credit to your playmakers and defensive men at every opportunity."
    —*Wooden on Leadership*, p. 253.

He also had this list of coaching methods that he employed that have great application to us as well.

1. "Be a teacher. Follow the laws of learning—explanation and demonstration, imitation, criticism of the imitation, repetition until habit is formed.

2. Use lectures, photographs, movies, diagrams, mimeographed material, etc. to supplement your daily practices.

3. Insist on punctuality and proper dress for practice.

4. Insist on strict attention.

5. Permit no 'horse play.' Practice is preparation.

6. Show patience.

7. Give new things early in the practice period and then repeat daily until learned.

8. Avoid harsh, public criticism. Use praise as well as censure.

9. Encourage teamwork and unselfishness.

10. Do considerable individual coaching of individuals.

11. Use small, carefully organized groups.

12. Have a definite practice plan—and follow it."
—*Wooden on Leadership*, p. 252.

When you develop leaders at your store, you will achieve astonishing results. John Maxwell details the power of this principle by detailing the growth of Papa John's Pizza in his book *The 21 Irrefutable Laws of Leadership*.

"In 1984 at age 22, John Schnatter started his own business. He began selling pizzas out of a converted broom closet at Mick's Tavern. He worked hard and built his tiny pizza business into a success. He named his pizza place Papa John's. He started franchising the stores and by the beginning of 1991, he had 46 stores. That in itself is a great success story. But what happened during the next couple of years is even better.

End of 1991: 110 stores

End of 1992: 220

1998: 1,600

He said of this growth that it happened because he focused on developing leaders. "Between 26 and 32 [years old], the hardest thing was I had a lot of John Schnatters around me [people with great potential who needed to be mentored]. They needed a lot of coaching, and I was so busy developing myself, trying to get myself to the next level, that I didn't develop those people. As a result, I lost them. It's my job to build the people who are going to build the company. That's going to be much harder for me than the first 1,200 stores."

Developing leaders at our stores is a challenge for us as well. Many times you may think it is easier to do things on your own. The reality is that you'll get there a lot faster with the help of others.

Here are 3 suggestions to help you develop the leaders at your store:

1. **Narrow your focus. Think huge, act narrow.**

John Maxwell makes this statement:

"A fascinating irony of leadership is that if you want to something really big that involves a lot of people, you need to narrow your focus to a few people. That may not seem to make sense. It goes against the grain of our natural inclinations. But it's true nonetheless. Great things aren't achieved by the crowd. They're accomplished by the core. If you think huge, you need to learn to act narrow."

2. **Stay committed to the process.**

I love this story that illustrates the importance of commitment:

"Several years ago, the Great Gadzoni had just completed a challenging and dangerous tightrope walk over Niagara Falls. The wind was howling around the aerialist's ears, and stinging rain pelted him as he inched across the rope.

Met with enthusiastic applause from those waiting on the other side, the Great Gadzoni was wringing the water from his cape when an excited fan approached, urging him to make a return trip, this time pushing a wheelbarrow, which the fan just happened to have with him.

The Great Gadzoni was hesitant, having barely made the first trip across in the high winds and pouring rain. But the spectator insisted. "You can do it — I know you can," he urged.

The Great Gadzoni thought a moment. "You really believe I can do it?"

The spectator nodded excitedly, "Yes, yes. Definitely - you can do it."

"Okay," said the aerialist, taking the wheelbarrow from the man. "Get in."

—David Cattrell, *Monday Morning Choices*, p. 23.

3. **Foster an environment where rotten attitudes and selfishness are quickly quenched. Remember, the goal is more important than the role.**

This is so important in creating an environment where leadership can grow. I have personally seen how destructive selfish and rotten attitudes can be to the growth of an organization and I'm sure you have too. I have had to fire individuals who created huge conflicts at our store because of their own selfishness.

John Maxwell wrote about this problem in his book, *The 17 Essential Qualities of a Team Player*: "Anyone who loves her opinions more than her teammates will advance her opinions but set back her team." —John C. Maxwell, *The 17 Essential Qualities of a Team Player*, p. 107.

Here are six common rotten attitudes that ruin a team and notice that they are all the result of selishness (from pages 110 and 111 of *The 17 Indisputable Laws of Teamwork* by John Maxwell):

1. ***"An inability to admit wrongdoing.*** Have you ever spent time with people who never admit they're wrong? It's painful and not much fun. Nobody's perfect, but someone who thinks she is does not make an ideal teammate. This wrong attitude will always create conflict.

2. ***Failing to forgive.*** Holding a grudge is never positive or appropriate. When there is unforgiveness between our

managers or bridal consultants, it definitely hurts our team.

3. ***Petty jealousy.*** The desire for equality feeds petty jealousy. People who are consumed with petty jealousy believe that every person deserves equal treatment, regardless of talent, performance or impact. This is simply not true—we are all unique and perform differently and as a result should be treated as such.

4. ***The disease of me.*** Pat Riley in his book, *The Winner Within* describes the 'disease of me.' He says of team members who have it, 'They develop an overpowering belief in their own importance. Their actions virtually shout the claim, 'I'm the one.'' Riley asserts that the disease always has the same inevitable result: 'The Defeat of Us.'

5. ***A critical spirit.*** When someone on the team has a critical spirit, everybody knows it because everyone on the team can do no right.

6. ***A desire to hog all of the credit.*** This attitude is similar to the 'disease of me.' But where the person with that disease may simmer in the background and create dissension, the credit hog continually steps in the spotlight to take a bow—whether she has earned it or not.

   The attitude we should have should be like NBA Hall of Fame center Bill Russell, who said of his time on the court, 'The most important measure of how good a game I played was how much better I made my teammates play.'"

Ask yourself: "How can I create the attitude at our store that 'My best day is when I help the bridal consultants I work with to sell better.'?"

Do any of your team members or you believe or think that:

- The team wouldn't be able to get along without us?

- Secretly (or not so secretly) believe that recent team successes are really attributable to your personal efforts, not the work of the whole team?
- Keep score when it comes to the praise and perks handed out to other team members?
- Have a hard time admitting when you make a mistake?
- Bring up past wrongs from your teammates?
- Believe that you are being grossly underpaid or underappreciated?

If someone is putting others down, sabotaging teamwork, or making himself or herself out to be more important than the team, you can be sure that you have someone on your team who has a bad, rotten and destructive attitude.

Establish team objectives and goals that everyone clearly understands. Lou Holtz created a group of covenants for the football players at the University of South Carolina to help them understand how they should work together as a team. I have modified these below for you to consider at your bridal store.

Our Bridal Store (______________________________)

1. We will accomplish what we do together. We share our success, and we never let any one of us fail alone.
2. We are all fully grown adults. We will act as such, and expect the same from the people around us.
3. We will not keep secrets. Information that affects us all will be shared by all of us, and we will quickly and openly work to separate fact from fiction.
4. We will not lie to ourselves or to each other. None of us will tolerate any of us doing so. We will depend on each other for the truth.

5. We will keep our word. We will say what we mean, and do what we say. We trust the word of others to be good as well.

6. We will keep our head. We will not panic in the face of tough times. We will always choose to roll up our sleeves rather than wring our hands. We will work together to set things right.

7. We will develop our abilities and take pride in them. We will set our own standards higher than our most challenging competitor and we will please our customers by pleasing ourselves.

8. We will treat our break room like home and our fellow bridal consultants like friends. We spend too much time together to allow these things to go bad.

9. We will be unselfish and expect that everyone else will exhibit this same quality. We will care about each other without expectations.

10. We will look out for each other. We truly believe that we are our brother's keeper.

11. We all have individual goals to achieve and work to do our part. We take pride in the achievement of our individual and team goals and expect our teammates to do the same.

12. Failure cannot and will not be tolerated in anything we do. Failure to achieve our goals is unacceptable and is not an option. There is no excuse for losing not achieving our goals at our bridal store.

    —*The 17 Indisputable Laws of Teamwork*, pp. 123-124.

There is tremendous power in unity. But, on the converse side, the greatest enemy of unity is personal ego.

I love this statement by former Kansas City Chiefs Coach Dick Vermeil:

"Don't be concerned with who gets the credit. Now that we've gotten back into the playoffs, there will be enough credit to fill the need for personal recognition for everyone on the staff. My belief is if you need credit, go to the bank! I repeat—leave the letter "I" in your office." —Dick Vermeil

He also made this observation which I think is dead on:

"Unity is not a result of agreement. It is a result of commitment."

Ask yourself:

How committed are you to supporting other members of the team?

Are you supportive of everyone?

Are you open and vulnerable?

Do you have any grudges against anyone on the team?

Do you gossip about others or choose not to help others who are newer to this business than you are?

Supporting others is a choice and I hope it is the one we all choose to make each day.

I want you to ask yourself:

What one thing could you do to help someone else on your team? Resolve to start tomorrow to help that individual become a leader.

We can all grow and we need each other's help. It reminds me of the story of Edmund Hillary, who I started talking about at the beginning of this chapter. In 1952, Edmund Hillary attempted to climb Mount Everest, more than 29,000 feet straight up. A few weeks after his failed attempt, he spoke to a group in England. Hillary walked to the stage, made a fist, and pointed at a picture of the mountain saying, "Mount Everest, you beat me the first time, but I'll beat you the next time because you've grown all you're going to grow...but I'm still growing!" On May 29, one year later, Edmund Hillary became the first man to reach the summit of Mount Everest.

Andrew Carnegie once observed: “It marks a big step in your development when you come to realize that other people can help you do a better job than you can do alone.”

Helen Keller said: “Alone we can do so little, together we can do so much.”

Commit to developing the leaders around you and you will do more than you ever dreamed possible at your bridal store.

Chapter 12

Stay On Track and Eliminate Distractions

As the end of each year approaches you should take time out of your schedule to get away from the store and write down business goals for your store for the following year. Determine what it is that you want. Then, build a marketing calendar for the entire year to help you put together your plan. Once the goals are set, the big challenge is to get everyone around you who will help make the goal happen buy into the goal and do the work necessary to accomplish the goals. This is always a challenge because you typically have to go against the grain to get things done. Change is always required and when change is required, there *will* be resistance. The greater the change with your goals over the previous year's accomplishments, the greater the resistance you will experience. In order to help you with this struggle, here are eleven suggestions to help you stay on track, eliminate distractions and jump start your business.

1. Accept the responsibility to motivate yourself. Accepting responsibility means being creative and initiating change where it is needed.

If you are thinking that next year is going to be more of the same of last year, you are likely going to move slower towards accomplishing it.

Why? Because if you don't feel like you have something to jump to, you won't have much of a desire to jump-start your business. In reality, we don't jump up because we feel beaten down and have lost hope for the future.

The other reason that we don't take the initiative to jump-start our lives and our businesses is because of procrastination, which is the biggest killer of progress in the world today. Now is the time to align or re-align your bridal business with the energy you had when you started. We all chose to be owners in this wonderful, yet crazy business. Choosing to be an owner of anything requires responsibility. Besides being responsible to our employees and our brides, we have a responsibility to ourselves. When anyone accepts responsibility in their life, they simultaneously embrace initiative. When you get into a rut or a routine and don't continue to be creative and initiate change, you have dumped your responsibility and are looking to someone else to bail you out.

2. Stop doing the stuff that isn't helping your business achieve your goals and start doing what will.

You likely got into the bridal business because you were passionate about it and it was something that you really wanted to do. Along the way, you may have started focusing on things that may not help you reach your goals because you think your brides or customers (Mothers, Flower Girls, etc.) really have to have other products. The most powerful word for accomplishing more of what you want is to specialize. Specialization requires you to simplify down what you do to the core elements that will bring you the greatest profitability, the highest return on your time and energy, and to focus on what really matters.

If it isn't making a difference in your store, stop doing it and start doing something that does.

John Maxwell says: "Winners stop doing things that are not good for them and losers stop doing things that are good for them."

3. **Plan ahead and focus on goals that motivate you. If you have an outdated goal that no longer excites you, drop it and focus on what will motivate you this year. Then put together a to-do list for each goal you have.**

In order to do this, use John Maxwell's acronym for **PLAN AHEAD.**

Predetermine your objectives.

Lay out your goals.

Adjust your priorities.

Notify key personnel.

Allow time for acceptance.

Head into action.

Expect problems.

Always point to the successes.

Daily review your progress.

Lawrence J. Peter once observed: "If you don't know where you are going, you will probably end up somewhere else."

Once you have established your goals, you create an action plan for each goal on your list and include starting dates and target dates for their completion.

4. **Eliminate distractions. Think about the implications of each action item under your goal. If it sidetracks you from the actual goal, refocus on what will get you what you really want.**

Your energy can be tied up in things that drain and distract you if you let them. Find ways to free up your time to do what's important to you. Don't try to be all things to everybody. Focus on what you can be the best in the world at. Read Jim Collin's book *Good to Great*. In this book, he talks about The Hedgehog Concept which basically has three components:

1) What you are deeply passionate about

2) What you can be the best in the world at

3) What drives your economic engine

Jim Collins makes this statement on page 118 of the book:

"The key is to understand what your organization can be the best in the world at, and equally what it cannot be the best at—not what it wants to be the best at. The Hedgehog concept is not a goal, strategy, or intention; it is an understanding."

What can your bridal or prom store be the best in the world at? You choose. You focus. The key is to specialize and simplify. The very best bridal stores focus and become very good at what they do in a couple of key areas. They don't try to be all things to all people.

5. See your business and what you want to have happen in it as a choice, not an obligation. Set the direction for your business. You are the navigator.

Here are ten practical steps that can help you accomplish your bridal store goals.

1. ***See the end before you begin***. Break down your goals into daily, weekly, and monthly components. Know and do what needs to be done each day to reach your monthly and yearly goals.

2. ***Chart the course in as much detail as possible.*** Think through every facet of how your business is impacted by your bridal

consultants, the brides coming into your store, the marketing promotions you use to get them in the store, etc. Put together a marketing calendar for the entire year.

3. ***Determine what resources are needed.*** Five key resources to consider are:

    - Financial
    - Inventory
    - Staff (bridal consultants, receptionists, steamers, seamstresses, etc.)
    - Time
    - Your experience and expertise – how well can you set the pace?

4. ***Anticipate the obstacles that will slow or sabotage the achievement of your store goal.*** Take time to make a list of every imaginable obstacle that could prevent you from achieving your desired result. This exercise will help you really think through the obstacles that may hold you back from doing what needs to be done. For example:

    - Consider the effects of having a major competitor move into your area.
    - How will your store be affected by the economy this year, next year, and three years from now?

5. ***Seek wise counsel from successful bridal store owners who have "traveled" before you.*** Ask questions, listen, and study successful stores. Implement the best ideas of those who have gone before and have more experience than you.

6. ***Do not cut corners.*** Cutting corners is a poor choice that may get you ahead in the immediate scenario, but you will undoubtedly reduce if not destroy your overall and long-term results.

7. ***Gather the right people*** – if you don't have the right staff, you are killing yourself in the long run.

8. ***Monitor your progress along the way***. Evaluate, evaluate, evaluate. Always be looking for ways to improve.

9. ***Embrace change when needed.*** It is so easy to get caught in a rut. Be sure to get better by embracing change, even when it is painful.

10. ***Put your confidence on paper***. Write your business goals and marketing plans on paper and work around and execute on these priorities.

6. Be a leader that creates a climate where your staff can outdo their goals each week and month in order to help you hit your monthly and yearly goals.

Be a leader who cultivates the 3 R's in your store:

The 3 R's:

1. **Result** – What is the final outcome desired?

2. **Reward** – What are the desired financial goals desired? How will excellent bridal consultants be rewarded?

3. **Reason** – I love what Brian Tray says: "Reasons are the fuel in the furnace of achievement." What are the reasons you want to hit your daily, weekly and monthly goals? Your reasons will drive you to accomplish your goals.

7. Do the little things each day and the weeks and months will take care of themselves.

Don't settle for any less than your very best each day. One of the biggest keys to achieving our business goals is to be willing to do whatever it takes.

Ask yourself: If you make a list of all of the things you need to do to be successful, are you willing to do everything on the list?

Do you sometimes say, "I'm willing to do whatever it takes to sell ___ number of bridal gowns and sell _____ dollars this year at my store, ***but*** I can't do this or I'm unwilling to do that."

When a bride comes in at the last minute and you are ready to go home and haven't hit your goal, do you say, "We're getting ready to close," or do you say, "I'm going to help her find her dress today and make this sale so that we can reach our goal."

The willingness to do anything it takes is key. When you frame each day as the most critical one in accomplishing your goal, your actions will be different. When you focus on achieving your critical success factors each day, the weeks and months will take care of themselves.

8. Find a coach or an accountability partner who can help you where you need help. Don't try to do it all alone.

The best thing is to find someone who is where you want to be who can help you.

At the very least, you should find someone who:

- wishes for your success
- is mature
- asks questions to help you discover your true potential
- can help you when you need help

9. Find out how to nourish or feed yourself. Be sure to sharpen the saw.

Take time to sharpen the saw as Stephen R. Covey says in his book *The Seven Habits of Highly Effective People.*

John Maxwell recently said that there are ten areas you can look to when you feel down or discouraged.

1) Music – is there a song or songs that lift you when you are feeling down?

2) Thoughts – is there a book whose thoughts speak to you?

3) Experiences – are there experiences at your store that you can reflect on that can remind you of why you got into this business?

4) Friends – are there other store owners in the bridal industry who you can talk to? Friends can make such a big difference in offering encouragement.

5) Recreation – is there an activity or sport you can engage in that will rejuvenate you? How often do you plan to participate in it? Could you do it more often?

6) Soul – are there spiritual exercises or routines that can strengthen you like prayer?

7) Hopes – what dreams inspire you? What helps you have hope for the future?

8) Home – what family members care for you and encourage you?

9) Gifts – what gifts or talents do you have that you can share with others?

10) Memories – what memories make you smile? How can you create memories for those around you?

10. Start talking about what you want, instead of what you don't want.

Successful bridal store owners think about **what they want and how to get it.** They look to the future and refuse to consider the possibility of failure. They say things like:

- We're going to increase our sales 15% this month over what we did last year.

- I have the best staff in the nation and our sales are improving every day.

- We are the most profitable bridal business in our area.

- I sell a veil and tiara with every bridal gown.

On the other hand, pessimists think about **what they don't want and why they've got it.** They think about people they don't like, problems they're having and who is to blame for their situation. They are heard saying things such as:

- I've got too much inventory.

- Our staff isn't selling.

- I can't seem to get the bridal gown sale, but luckily I get the accessory sale.

- Our competitors seem to be getting all of the sales.

- We're doing worse than we were last year.

- Everyone seems to be making more money than me.

- I seem to be working harder than ever before with little results.

What do you think about most of the time? Do you think about the future?

or

Do you think about what has already happened in the past?

Instead of beating yourself up about the past, write your own future. Think about a clear, exciting future vision of what is possible and make it happen.

11. Celebrate your successes with your team.

Be sure to have celebrations with your staff after you accomplish a great target or goal. Let them know how proud you are of them. Reward them. Everyone wants to be a part of something and you can create this for them by how you treat them and act around them.

What kind of leader are you? Are you creating a climate where your staff can outdo their goals each week and help your store grow to new heights?

Are you the type of leader who is willing to pay the price to create a climate in which your people can follow you and emerge as the leaders of tomorrow?

There are so many great things to hope and believe in. Your future is so bright. It's all up to you and the decisions you make each day. I wish you a very prosperous, successful and exciting adventure as you implement these ideas to grow your business.

Chapter 13

Reinvigorate Your Bridal Business and Marketing Message

It can be easy to lose perspective. Many store owners have realized this as they experience whiplash form the up and down roller coaster ride with their sales. When this happens, some are tempted to emotionally throw in the towel. In this book, I have outlined ways to think differently and given you many strategies you can implement to help your bridal store experience a quantum leap in growth. At the end of this book, I'd like to give you some suggestions to help you reinvigorate your business and marketing message in these challenging times. This shift in perspective can help you act decisively towards putting together marketing promotions and better training your sales staff to help you get better results. Here are eight suggestions for how you can go about reinvigorating your business and marketing message:

1. **Don't get bogged down in the past day's successes or failures. If you make a mistake, learn from it and move on.**

While you may not be able to prevent being affected by the recession, you can definitely choose your attitude on how you deal with it. Instead of being overcome with fear and anxiety, your daily focus should be: My bridal store is leading the way towards an economic recovery.

Selling has its ups and downs. You may feel positive that a bride is going to buy a dress from you and then find out there is a last minute objection that blindsides you that you aren't prepared to overcome. In this economy, I've found that we've experienced some of our highest highs and have also had days where we under-performed and didn't hit our daily goal. Through the ups and downs, you have to be careful to not let your emotions get the best of you. When you have a great day, be grateful, positive, and ask yourself: "What can I learn from this that will help me stay higher longer?" When you have a lousy day, ask, "What can I learn from this?"

Tennis great Chris Evert once said: "If I win several tournaments in a row, I get so confident I'm in a cloud. A loss gets me eager again." That is great perspective for how you should react to both the day's successes and failures. Strive to bounce, rather than break by the small defeats of each day.

Our bridal consultants look to us as leaders for how they should respond to what is happening around them. Your attitude, outlook, and encouraging words are critical. If you run around scared, bewildered, and out of control of your emotions because of the fluctuations in the economy, your bridal consultants will do the same. As playwright Lister Sinclair once observed: "A frightened captain makes a frightened crew."

We all make mistakes from time to time. I like the story John Maxwell tells in his book *Failing Forward* about *Three Musketeers* author Alexander Dumas that teaches us that we shouldn't beat ourselves up if we stumble and fail. The story goes as follows:

"The novelist and a friend had a heated argument, and one challenged the other to a duel. Both Dumas and his friend were expert marksmen, and they feared that if they proceeded with the duel, both would die.

So they decided to draw straws to determine which of them would shoot himself. Dumas picked the short straw.

With a sigh, he picked up his pistol, walked into his library, and closed the door, leaving behind him a group of worried friends. After a few moments, the loud report of a pistol echoed from the library. His friends immediately charged into the room, and there stood Dumas with the pistol still smoking in his hand.

'An amazing thing just happened,' said Dumas. 'I missed.'" —John C. Maxwell, *Failing Forward*, p. 142.

Don't let mistakes or poor sales performance from the day before kill you. Recognize it for what it was ('a miss') and move on.

2. Focus on the *present* and increasing the sales you have with brides who are coming in.

You may not be able to control what happened yesterday, but you can focus on the bride in front of you and give her the most amazing experience she has ever experienced in a retail setting.

Don't get caught up in the past. In today's uncertain economy, brides are already hesitant and unsure of what to do. If they encounter a bridal consultant who is even more fearful than they are, their confidence will erode even more and they will not buy. This will happen because if the bride can sense your fear (because you are worried about paying your store bills or being stressed out about because of lost sales the day before), you will panic and do something that will kill the sale. Confidence is critical in selling. If you panic, the brides who come into your store can sense it and it won't help you create the sales you need. Instead, focus on the present and the bride you have in front of you.

This is not easy. It is much easier to be caught up in a cycle of missing out on future sales because of how badly we feel about not making the last sale or the last several sales. The best thing to do is to focus on the fundamentals and the process of selling. If you do this well, the result will take care of itself.

We get into trouble when we only think about the result and ignore the fundamentals that make the result a reality. As I mentioned, this happens when we panic, press too hard for the sale, get down on ourselves because we didn't overcome a certain objection that seems to keep plaguing us, or we get mad because we think the bride is lying to us. When these emotions are present over a period of time, eventually you will shut down mentally and quit.

However, if you can focus on giving the brides in front of you an amazing experience, you'll overcome any last minute smokescreen objections that brides might throw your way because of their fears and insecurities and you will close the sale. Don't get caught up in the past. Be confident and express confidence to the brides coming into your store and the result will take care of itself. The key is to separate yourself from the bad times you may be experiencing and have a positive approach to what you can do next (instead of what you should have done in the past).

3. Intensify *and* implement better advertising and promotional strategies to bring in more brides and make more sales.

One of the biggest mistakes bridal store owners make during periods of economic slowdown is to cut back on their marketing. I've found that intensifying and focusing on better marketing has helped us keep our store busy when many other stores I've talked to are slower.

One of the reasons why I have my marketing calendar marked out a year in advance is that I always know I have a specific strategy or promotion coming up in the next week or two to help to get more brides into the store. If you don't, it is easy to stop promoting the store and get into a mindset and behavior (of little to no action) that is not healthy.

I think that always looking for new ways to improve is so critical and important. Ask questions of others to find out what is working. Don't be content with how things are. Constantly seek to be learning and improving your marketing.

If you aren't familiar with the changes in social networking sites and how to tie these into your store, you need to learn how. Brides and prom prospects are online and using social media in a big way. Learn how to create an online community that you can use to help promote your store and bring in more referrals and sales.

4. Let go of your limitations. Instead, re-evaluate your strengths and focus on new, creative, and better ways that you can reach your goals.

Dr. Daniel Drubin in his book, *Letting Go of Your Bananas* makes this interesting observation:

"Ricky Henderson, the greatest base stealer in the history of baseball, had a decision to make each time he contemplated stealing a base. He could choose not to steal the base and remain exactly where he was, or he could run the risk of leaving safety and comfort for the possibility of something greater. Ricky understood that if he wanted to get to second base, the first thing he had to do was take his foot off first base....The same could be said of a trapeze artist. To get from one side of the net to the other, he or she must be prepared to let go." —*Letting Go of Your Bananas*, pp. 3-4.

In order to get where you want to go, you are required to let go of something else. Like a trapeze artist, if you do not let go of the bar, you will never perform to your potential. Many store owners will go to market year after year and continue to pick up a line because they are afraid that someone else will get it or have it, regardless of whether the line really makes them money or not. Sacrifice is a simple concept to understand, but very difficult to put into practice because it requires change.

After reading this chapter, ask yourself: "What limiting factors am I holding onto that are preventing me and my store from going to the next level?" Take some time to write these down. Then, take time to mentally see yourself letting go of each one of them. *Remember, you can't get to the next level without letting go of where you are now.*

5. Re-organize and re-prioritize the time you spend in your store so that you are only doing things that help you get what you want.

When was the last time, you seriously looked at the way you spend your time at your store each day? Are you really spending each hour of each day at your store on the most critical things that can help you get your store to where you want it to be?

Carefully analyze the time you spend at your store each day. Take the time to write down your typical daily schedule and the activities you do each day. Now, look at the chart below. What is your time really worth? Circle your answer.

Your Income	Income / Hour	Your Income	Income / Hour
$30,000	$15	$120,000	$60
$40,000	$20	$130,000	$65
$50,000	$25	$140,000	$70
$60,000	$30	$150,000	$75
$70,000	$35	$160,000	$80
$80,000	$40	$170,000	$85
$90,000	$45	$180,000	$90
$100,000	$50	$190,000	$95
$110,000	$55	$200,000	$100

Based on working 250 days/year, eight hours per day.

Continually ask yourself, "Is what I am doing right now, contributing to me making $___/hour?"

If it is not, immediately stop doing it, delegate it to someone else and start doing activities that will make you $___/hour.

There are certain things at your store that only you can do that will have the greatest return on your energy and help you generate the most income.

When you carefully take time to write down your daily schedule and evaluate how effectively you are using your time, you will likely discover that you need to restructure your daily schedule so that you are spending more of your time on the 20% of activities that bring the most value to what you do and less time on the things that don't bring value to you or to your bridal store.

This question (Is what I'm doing right now, contributing to me making $____/hour?) is one of the most important questions you should be asking throughout each day. Doing so will help you re-invigorate your business since you will be able to spend more time focusing on marketing activities that will bring more brides into your store. It will also allow you to seriously evaluate the administrative things that currently occupy much of your day that you may be able to delegate to others so you can put your priority and focus on activities that will help you bring in and sell the brides at your store.

6. Re-engineer your systems.

I talked about this topic in depth in chapter eight. Here are four questions to consider as you reflect on your current business systems.

- When was the last time, you seriously looked at the systems you are using to run your business?
- Could you simplify them?
- Could you make things faster or easier?
- Is there a way to reduce the number of steps involved?

Unfortunately, most businesses don't have systems. The reality is that the very best businesses in the world are run entirely around them. The biggest difference between McDonald's and the corner hamburger stand is that McDonald's is run entirely on systems.

What I have found is that most bridal stores don't have systems or if they do, they don't interact well with other aspects of their store. I would encourage you to take the time to think through each aspect of your store's systems and how they interact with one another. There is a completely different mindset between a systems- based business owner and a skills-based business owner.

The bottom line is that when you have better systems, your store will be more successful and you will be happier. You'll be able to take more time off. You'll make more money and you will be more profitable. You will be able to work *on* your business and not just *in* your business. And that will make all of the difference.

7. Re-invent your marketing message.

If you could completely start your bridal store over again, what would you do differently?

What unprofitable areas of your business would you eliminate?

What profitible new niches would you get into?

If you would do those things when starting over, why not do them now?

Here are some questions for you to consider when moving into a new market niche:

The goal is to get 3 YESes. The essence of what you are doing is finding brides and prom customers who are *looking for you.*

1) **Are brides in my area experiencing pain + urgency or irrational passion?**

2) **Is my bride (or prom customer) proactively searching for solutions?** Where is she searching and how can I get in front of her?

3) **Does my bride (or prom customer) have few or no perceived options?**

When the answer to these three questions is yes, you have a really good idea for a niche that you can develop and get into. Don't pick up a new bridal or prom line without considering these three questions for a niche you plan to pursue.

Choose your area of focus. You can choose to specialize in several areas, but your marketing has to be different for each area. In other words, you don't market strapless gowns to brides who are looking for sleeved gowns. Focus your marketing and your message on your specific target bride. You will become known for that specialty and will become more successful as a result.

8. Regain control of your life.

Most of the problems that result from feeling that our lives or our businesses are out of control result from trying to do too many things at once (multi-tasking) and not staying focused on key result areas in uninterrupted blocks of time.

Since our bridal stores consume so much of our daily lives and the work is never done it can be easy to lose control of our own lives. Even when our stores become successful we often find that we now don't have enough time to enjoy the fruits of our success because we are so busy. I remember hearing my four year old son (who is now eleven) tell someone once when they came to our bridal store, "This is where my daddy lives." That comment caused me serious reflection and brought on the challenge to re-prioritize my life so I could spend more time with my wife and children. We are all short on time in almost every area of our lives. The key is to view time differently and start having it work for you.

The reality is that all of us have 168 hours in every week. If you sleep 8 hours a day you have already used up 56 of your 168 hours. If it takes an hour each morning from the time your alarm goes off through showering, brushing your teeth, eating breakfast and heading out to the store, here is another 7 hours a week. We'll add another 3 ½ hours at 30 minutes every day for the amount of time it takes to wind down, get ready for bed and go to sleep. Now there are 101.5 hours left in the week. If you commute each day to your store, you probably could spend another 3-7 hours every week just driving in your car commuting.

Then if your store is physically open 8-9 hours a day, you have used another 48-56 hours depending on how many hours your store is open and if you are open on Sundays. And that doesn't even count the amount of time it takes to open and close your store. When you factor in your time that you run errands and eat dinner, you are left with less than forty hours a week (or an average of 5-6 hours a day, to get done everything else that really matters to you). With essentially 75% of our life consumed each week by the work at our stores and other necessary activities, we are essentially left with a small percentage of time left to do things for:

- Our spouse
- Our children
- Hobbies or interests
- Sports and or exercise
- Friends
- Personal errands
- TV Shows or entertainment - I recently heard author Jim Cathcart talk about the "EVE Ratio". This is the Education vs. Entertainment ratio in our lives. He mentioned that the most successful individuals he has ever met have always put a high emphasis on education. I know we are all busy and I enjoy a great movie as much as anyone else, but I wholeheartedly agree with his assessment. We have to put a priority on educating ourselves and learning each day. What we choose to do over time defines us and what we have in our lives.

- And I'm sure that you could add a dozen or more other items that take up your remaining time as well.

Brian Tracy once observed:

"Time is inelastic; it cannot be stretched. Time is indispensable; all work and accomplishment requires it. Time is irreplaceable; there is no substitute for it. And time is perishable, it cannot be saved, preserved, or stored. Once it is gone, it is gone forever."

In the hustle and bustle of our businesses, it is so easy to let our bridal stores consume our lives. When we have so much to do and too little time, it is easy to get overwhelmed and feel that we are losing control of our time. Time management helps us control the **sequence** of events in our day so that we can better **control** our lives.

Consider these questions as you strive to regain control of your life:

1. What really matters to me?
2. Where do I want my store to be in five years?
3. Why? Am I sure?
4. How do I want my life, at work and outside it, to be different?
5. What key changes must I make to get there from here?

Remember, we are always free to choose what we do **first**, what we do **second**, and what we choose **not to do** at all. Our lives are the sum of the choices we make each day. By making better choices and better decisions we can redirect the course of our lives so that we can be happier.

Epilogue

Remain Optimistic in Challenging Times

All of us struggle with disappointment and discouragement. That is a part of business. Yet, as leaders, we have to be optimistic about the future while still confronting the brutal facts of reality. This means that we keep moving forward and take steps and actions that will help us get through the challenging times. Here are several suggestions to help you get through these challenging times with your store and sanity still intact.

1. Fight your fear with action.

There is a tremendous amount of fear and anxiety today. Much could be written about the role fear has had in recent weeks as the stock market has bounced up and down. Everyone feels fear. It is easy to get sucked into these emotions when prognosticators on the news proclaim doom and gloom every day no matter what happens. The uncertainty can cause and has caused fear and panic.

Since all of us experience the emotion of fear, what separates those who are paralyzed with fear from those who overcome their fears to accomplish great things even in the face of tremendous challenges? The difference is that those who are successful have *learned to fight their fear with action*. They have learned to channel the emotion of fear into action that will help create a more hopeful future. Joe Tye, author of *Never Fear, Never Quit* says:

"The only way to escape from the prison of fear is action. You cannot wish your way out, you cannot wait your way out. You can only work your way out. Every time you escape the prison of fear, you grow stronger."

A tremendous amount of energy can be expended through worry about your fears. You might be worrying about:

- Did I buy too much inventory at market?
- How am I going to make it through this slow period?
- How can I compete and remain profitable with Internet vendors and other competitors who are slashing prices?
- Why aren't we seeing more brides in our store?
- Why aren't I closing more sales?

We all feel the emotion of fear from time to time and probably all of us have felt it strongly in the past few weeks and months. The key is to work your way through the emotions until you achieve results.

I really like this statement by John C. Maxwell in his book *The Difference Maker*. He says:

"Fear can be very destructive in a person's life. The root of the word fear comes from the Old English word *fǽr*, literally meaning sudden attack, and is akin to the Old High German word *fāra* meaning ambush or snare. That's what fear does to us: It attacks us and makes us captive. As psychiatrist and Nazi concentration camp survivor Viktor Frankl observed, 'Fear makes come true that which one is afraid of.'"

Maxwell continues:

"Fear makes us afraid of doing something that might be beneficial for us. Taking action will require us to move into the unknown. That can be scary. But if we give into our fear, we don't move forward. We don't receive the benefit of what we've avoided, nor do we gain the valuable experience that would make us better informed. As a result, we remain ignorant about that area of life, and ignorance almost always breeds more fear, making it that much harder to push ahead and get things done." —*The Difference Maker*, pp. 125, 128.

Another way to conquer your fears is to look to others who may be able to look at your situation more objectively and ask for help. They can help you beat your fears by encouraging you to take action.

Ralph Waldo Emerson said: "Do the thing you fear and the death of fear is certain."

A book I read once had a very interesting observation by a Dr. Hinz. He said:

"You can't just wish and plan. At some point, you have to jump in and take action or else your fear, your perfectionism, whatever is blocking you from taking that step, will keep you in your present mess...."

That is some great advice.

Now is a great time to take action and do what others are not doing because they are paralyzed by fear. Bill Brooks in his excellent book *Niche Selling* makes this observation:

"Never let an economic turndown take your focus off the only thing that will bring you success in today's crowded marketplaces: fulfilling your customers' needs. Your customers are probably retrenching, too, and that is the best time to ask yourself, "How can I serve my [bride's] deepest needs?" More than ever, your customers need someone who will focus on their needs, which may be getting desperate. A downturn in the economy, therefore, can be used to leave your competitors in the dust."

Opportunities are seldom labeled as such. Take some time to think about how you can take action when others may be hesitating because of their own fears. When you can control your own fear by taking action, you will accomplish great things. I know I am continuing our marketing promotions now more than ever since many of our competitors are not.

2. Lead with optimism.

Our bridal consultants look to us when they are scared or nervous to see how we respond. We all instinctively do this. I think one of my favorite stories about the importance of leading with optimism can be found in the way Thomas Edison approached a tragedy that occurred when he was in his late sixties.

"He had a lab that he built in West Orange, New Jersey and it was world famous. He called the fourteen building complex his invention factory. Its main building was massive—greater than three football fields in size. From that base of operations, he and his staff conceived of inventions, developed prototypes, manufactured products, and shipped them to customers. It became a model for modern research and manufacturing.

Edison loved the place. He spent every minute he could there. He even slept there, often on one of the lab tables. But on a December day in 1914, his beloved lab caught fire. As he stood outside and watched it burn, he is reported to have said, 'Kids, go get your mother. She'll never see another fire like this one."

Most people would have been crushed. Not Edison. 'I am sixty-seven,' he stated after the tragedy, 'but not too old to make a fresh start. I've been through a lot of things like this.' He rebuilt the lab, and kept working for another seventeen years."—John Maxwell, *The 21 Indispensible Quilities of a Leader*, pp. 89-90.

Many of the inventions that we take for granted were invented after this tragedy. His staff and his workers pushed through the difficult times to become even more successful.

When you suffer a devastating blow or a crushing defeat in your bridal business, how do you respond?

The reality is that the way you respond makes the difference.

In his book, *Good to Great*, author Jim Collins talks about an interesting duality he has observed in great companies. He calls this duality the Stockdale Paradox. The Stockdale Paradox is "accepting the brutal facts of reality and at the same time maintaining an unwavering faith in the endgame, and a commitment to prevail as a company regardless of the brutal facts." Collins says:

"The name refers to Admiral Jim Stockdale, who was the highest ranking United States military officer in the 'Hanoi Hilton' prisoner-of-war camp during the height of the Vietnam War. Tortured over twenty times during his eight-year imprisonment from 1965 to 1973, Stockdale lived out the war without any prisoner's rights, no set release date, and no certainty as to whether he would even survive to see his family again."—*Good to Great*, pp. 83-84.

When author Jim Collins read Stockdale's book, he found himself getting depressed when he knew how the story ended up. Later, when Collins interviewed Stockdale he asked, 'how on earth did [you] deal with it when [you] were actually there and *did not know the end of the story*?'

Stockdale replied, "I never lost faith in the end of the story. I never doubted not only that I would get out, but also that I would prevail in the end and turn the experience into the defining event of my life, which, in retrospect, I would not trade.'

There is a key lesson to be learned from this lesson as we struggle through the uncertainties we face in today's economy. We have to live by the Stockdale Paradox which means accepting the brutal facts of reality that our economy is struggling and that buying patterns of brides are changing, yet on the other hand, maintain an unwavering faith in the endgame, and a commitment to prevail as a store despite the brutal facts.

How we can successfully operate our stores on both sides of the Stockdale Paradox is the subject of this month's Bridal Edge newsletter. We're not talking about just being blindly optimistic in the future. Successful store owners who make it through these challenging times will do so because they have the discipline *and* do what it takes to succeed (sell and market better) while never losing faith in what got them into business for themselves in the first place.

An important thing to remember about optimism is that it is *not* a simplistic view that everything is going to be all right. A very interesting thing about the interview Jim Collins had with Admiral Stockdale is found in his exchange about those who didn't make it out of the prison. Collins asked, "'Who didn't make it out?'

'Oh, that's easy,' [Stockdale] said. 'The optimists.'

'The optimists? I don't understand,' I said, now completely confused, given what he'd said [before].

'The optimists. Oh, they were the ones who said, 'we're going to be out by Christmas.' And Christmas would come, and Christmas would go. Then they'd say, 'We're going to be out by Easter.' And Easter would come, and Easter would go. And then Thanksgiving, and then it would be Christmas again. And they died of a broken heart.'"

Stockdale concluded, "'This is a very important lesson. You must never confuse faith that you will prevail in the end—which you can never afford to lose—with the discipline to confront the most brutal facts of your current reality, whatever they might be.'"—*Good to Great*, p. 85.

I love this statement that Collins makes in his book as a summary of what he learned from this conversation. He said:

"That conversation with Admiral Stockdale stayed with me, and in fact had a profound influence on my own development. Life is unfair—

sometimes to our advantage, sometimes to our disadvantage. We will all experience disappointments and crushing events somewhere along the way, setbacks to which there is no 'reason,' no one to blame....What separates people, Stockdale taught me, is not the presence or absence of difficulty, but how they deal with the inevitable difficulties of life. In wrestling with life's challenges, the Stockdale paradox (you must retain faith that you will prevail in the end *and* you must also confront the most brutal facts of your current reality) has proved powerful for coming back from difficulties not weakened, but stronger—not just for me, but for all those who've learned the lesson and tried to apply it." —*Good to Great*, pp. 85-86

He concludes with this observation:

"The good-to-great leaders were able to strip away so much noise and clutter and just focus on the few things that would have the greatest impact. There were able to do so in large part because they operated from both sides of the Stockdale Paradox, never letting one side overshadow the other. If you are able to adopt this dual pattern, you will dramatically increase the odds of making a series of good decisions and ultimately discovering a simple, yet deeply insightful, concept for making the really big choices." —*Good to Great*, p. 87.

The challenge we face as bridal store owners is that we live in a very pessimistic and cynical society. It is very hard to focus on the few things that will have the greatest impact and not get caught up in all of the hoopla and emotion when we are constantly being bombarded by doom and gloom from the so-called experts about the global economy, downturns in housing and retail shopping, and new unemployment numbers.

In recent weeks and months, we have all seen a shift as the usual happy and excited brides have become cautious, apprehensive, and nervous about spending money. My purpose in writing this is to address how you can and should stay optimistic about the end-game when the stark reality of your current situation has left you feeling frustrated and discouraged with what is happening in your business.

Ask yourself this: Have you become paralyzed by fear because of the uncertainty of the future?

Have you lost faith in the endgame – what you got into the bridal business to achieve?

We all experience cycles and trends in this business. Sometimes you'll have a great day; sometimes you'll have a lousy day. When you think about it, virtually nothing turns out exactly as we had hoped. I remember reading a statement when we first started our bridal business by Brian Tracy. He said, "When you are trying to figure out how long it is going to take to do something, give it your best guess and then multiply it by three." I have always thought that was an interesting statement.

The thing to remember is that you and I aren't remembered by how many times we fail, but by how often we succeed. Most people never see our failures, our discouragements and our dark moments. We all have these.

For example: Did you know that Michelangelo failed more than 200 times trying to produce the perfect sketch for the ceiling of the Sistine Chapel?

Or that the only reason Oprah Winfrey went to work on a talk show was because she failed as a news reporter?

Or that Henry Ford went through two failed companies and eight car models before he developed the Model T?

Or that Bill Cosby dropped out of high school and worked as a shoe repairman and in a muffler shop?

Most of us look at successful individuals and think they just fell on the top of a mountain. The truth is that very few see all of the falls, scrapes, bruises, bumps, and painful steps it took to get to there. I have always loved the poem "Along the Road" by Robert Brown Hamilton because it teaches a great truth about what we learn from the frustrations of life and business:

"I walked a mile with Pleasure;
She chattered all the way,
But left me none the wiser
For all she had to say.

I walked a mile with Sorrow,
And ne'er a word said she;
But oh, the things I learned from her
When Sorrow walked with me."

One of the most important reasons we have to lead with optimism is because people are not persuaded very often by pessimistic individuals. The truth is that **optimistic individuals sell more than those who are pessimistic.** Kurt Mortensen makes this point in his book *Persuasion IQ*. He says:

"Optimistic persuaders out persuade pessimistic persuaders every time. Not only is optimism essential to influencing others, but it is also critical for success in life. Optimism is more than a positive mental attitude. It is not constantly saying positive things to yourself and then hoping they will come true. Rather, true optimism is a state of mind that dictates how you look at the world. An optimistic view of life and the world around you can inspire hope and courage in others. We all want to feel inspired and encouraged. When a persuader can deliver this type of message, we want to follow that person. This tendency is how optimism helps you in influencing others.

Pessimism on the other hand is always taking the negative view. Others will consider a pessimist as irritable and always looking for the negative in every situation. Pessimists are the ones who will be the first to complain and tell everyone else that nothing goes right. As a result, they never get the success or recognition they deserve.

Countless studies have shown that optimists do better in school, persuade better, have more friends, perform better in their careers, and live longer than pessimists. Pessimists, on the other hand, frequently battle depression, have fewer friends, find it difficult to persuade, and give up faster and more easily. To illustrate this point, in one study, those who sold insurance were monitored on their optimistic or pessimistic outlook in relation to setbacks. The optimistic persuaders sold more policies and were half as likely to quit.

Great persuaders have what we call 'influential optimism'. This means that they see the positive in all situations. Rather than focusing on disappointment, cynicism, or negative feelings, they look for ways to move forward. People want to be persuaded by individuals who have a positive view on life. As an optimist, you see the world as a series of exciting challenges. You inspire positive feelings about everything you stand for. People want to be around you because they live in a very pessimistic world. The optimistic mindset is contagious and helps to empower other people to believe in you and in themselves. As an optimist, you help others see failure or setback as temporary. You have no doubt that success will happen.

To achieve true optimism, you have to learn to control your pessimistic voice. We all have both an optimistic and a pessimistic voice inside of us. Which one do you listen to?

Can you be overly optimistic? It depends on the situation. You can have too much false cheer—taking optimism to nausea-ism—but I think it is rare to have too much realistic optimism. The only time optimism will backfire is when you are persuading a die-hard pessimist. If you start off with too much optimism, you will clash with your audience. If, on the other hand, you gradually offer small doses of pessimism, you can turn even the pessimist around. Great persuaders find that it is essential to mirror their audience's reality and to gradually raise their optimism level.

Work on refining your educated optimism—that is, the ability to see around corners, to anticipate challenges, and to still maintain a positive outlook, while preparing for bumps in the road." –Kurt Mortensen, *Persuasion IQ*, pp. 166-168.

I think Winston Churchill put it best:

"Success is going from failure to failure without loss of enthuasism."

The best way to go from failure to failure and still have enthusiasm is to ***continually seek the valuable lesson in every problem or difficulty you encounter.*** Optimists believe that each temporary failure or obstacle has been sent to teach them something. They continually ask, 'What am I meant to learn from this situation?' And they always find something.

We can learn a lot from jet pilots. For one thing, they don't use rearview mirrors. They have others help them back up and get on the runway. They look forward and side to side as they fly. They know their destination before they take off. They make course corrections in midair as they journey to their destination. They arrive at their destination just like they planned even though they may have gone through serious turbulence and storms on the way there. No one would want to fly with a jet pilot who was unconfident in his ability to fly or make it to where he or she was flying.

Lead with optimism. If you aren't feeling optimistic, get around those who are. Associate with successful business owners through reading their biographies and learn what they have done to get past the tough times. I think you'll discover as I often have that we have it relatively easy when compared to the challenges others have been through.

3. Don't let despair, doubt, and discouragement keep you down.

Winston Churchill once said, "If you're going through hell, keep going." There is no reason to stop and admire the view. The only way out of challenges and problems is through them. The biggest obstacles to persevering through challenging times are despair, doubt, and discouragement. These emotions will keep you down if you let them because they will paralyze you from taking the actions necessary to ensure your ultimate success.

Reading business biographies helps me to realize that I'm not the only one who has ever experienced heartache, frustration, disappointment, doubt, fear, discouragement and despair. I am currently reading *The Snowball* about Warren Buffet's successes and defeats in business and life. Like all successful business leaders, he persevered through tough times and came out on top.

One of my favorite quotes about this is by Thomas Edison. He said: "Many of life's failures are people who did not realize how close they were to success when they gave up."

Williams James said:

"The greatest discovery of my generation is that human beings can alter their lives by altering their attitude of mind."

All of us suffer disappointments, discouragements and failures. As I mentioned before, the difference is how we deal with them.

Many of us watched or have heard about how Lance Armstrong won a record breaking seven Tour de France titles and placed third in the 2009 Tour de France. It is a two thousand mile race that takes place over a grueling three week period.

His story as detailed in his book *It's Not About the Bike* and as summarized in John Maxwell's *Today Matters* (pages 54-58) is one of tremendous heartache and the possibilities that lie within each of us when we overcome pessimism and have optimism for the future.

Lance grew up in a single parent home. His mother was only seventeen when he was born. They struggled financially and Lance often felt like an outsider. In Texas, where he is from, the big sport is football. Lance says that he was always uncoordinated for any sport with a ball so he gravitated to activities that required endurance.

In fifth grade, he ran a distance race and won. He became a swimmer. Within a year he became the fourth best swimmer in Texas in the 1,500 meter freestyle.

At thirteen, he entered a junior triathlon competition called Iron Kids. He won easily.

When he was fifteen, he started competing against men in running competitions.

In his first race, he came in thirty-second place. He told a reporter, "I think in a few years I'll be right near the top, and within ten years I'll be thc best." He was mocked by his friends and was seen by many as extremely cocky.

When he was sixteen, they stopped laughing when he won 5th place in the same race and earned over $20,000 a year entering and winning triathlon competitions.

As he competed in these triathlons he found that he really liked cycling. Over time he began to focus all of his energy entirely upon cycling. After competing a while in the US, he decided he wanted to compete in Europe, where the best athletes competed.

His first professional race was memorable. It was a bitterly cold day with pouring rain. He came in dead last, a full twenty-seven minutes behind the winner – a terrible finish. The Spanish crowd lining the course laughed at and made fun of him. This is what he said about this humiliating experience:

"A few hours later, I sat in the Madrid airport, slumped in a chair. I wanted to quit the entire sport. It was the most sobering race of my life; on my way to San Sebastian, I had actually thought I had a chance of winning, and now I wondered if I could compete at all. They had laughed at me....I pulled a sheaf of unused plane tickets out of my pocket. Among them, I had a return portion to the States. I considered using it. Maybe I should just go home, I thought, and find something else to do, something I was good at."

Have you ever felt that way? Have you ever felt like quitting because people laughed at you? Have you ever felt so discouraged that you just wanted to find something else to do?

Sitting in that airport, alone and discouraged, Lance remembered what his mother had told him growing up:

"Make an obstacle an opportunity. Make a negative a positive. It you can't give 100%, you won't make it. Never quit!"

Those words drove him back to racing and by 1996 at the age of 25, Lance Armstrong was the top-rated cyclist in the world. "It looked as if he had finally made it. He was making a good living. He was at the top of his form. And he was winning races against the best in Europe.

But then, he started experiencing intense pain in his groin and began coughing up blood. When he saw a doctor, he found out he had testicular cancer. But the news kept getting worse. The cancer had spread, it was pervasive in his lungs, and his prognosis was grim. Through all of that he kept his positive attitude, his fighting spirit.

But then they found cancer in his brain.

'I met a wall,' Armstrong said, 'Much as I wanted to be positive and unafraid, all I knew was, when people get tumors they don't live.'—John Maxwell, *Today Matters*, pp. 56-57.

Have you had a similar prognosis for your store?

- David's is opening a store down the street or 15 minutes from my business. How will we survive?
- One of my best employees just decided to quit. What am I going to do?
- Sales have been so bad this month – How am I going to pay rent and survive?
- Have you recently experienced a personal loss that you thought you would never make it through?
- Or perhaps, you've felt: "I'm so deeply in debt and sales are so down that I'm not sure how I will even make payroll next week."

"Armstrong underwent brain surgery and a procedure to remove his cancerous testicle. Then he started the excruciating process of chemotherapy. After he finished his treatment and his recovery seemed certain, one doctor admitted that his case was the worse he had ever seen, and he had only given Armstrong a 3% chance of living.

Through it all, Armstrong managed his attitude so that he would remain positive. He believes that hope is the only antidote to fear.

Surviving cancer with a positive attitude is quite an accomplishment. But Armstrong wanted more. He wanted to start racing again. He had some difficult moments during his comeback. At one point, he actually quit in the middle of a race—something he had never done before." —John Maxwell, *Today Matters*, p. 57.

But he came back from that setback and has now won seven consecutive Tour de France victories. He even came out of retirement in 2009 to compete in the Tour de France where he placed third.

Listen to this statement by Lance Armstrong:

"Without belief, we would be left with nothing but an overwhelming doom, every single day. And it will beat you. I didn't fully see, until the cancer, how we fight every day against the creeping negatives of the world, how we struggle daily against the slow lapping of cynicism. Dispiritedness and disappointment, these were the real perils of life, not some sudden illness or cataclysmic millennium doomsday."—Lance Armstrong, *It's Not About the Bike*, p. 114.

After Lance won his first Tour de France in 1999, he told reporters this (and I hope you remember it as you are building your businesses through these challenging times):

"I would just like to say one thing. If you ever get a second chance in life for something, you've got to go all the way."—Lance Armstrong, *It's Not About the Bike*, p. 257.

If you have been feeling discouraged, I hope you now have the optimism and courage to do what needs to be done.

There was a great *Peanuts* cartoon several years ago where Charlie Brown pours out his heart to Lucy telling her that "[he] would never be a big-league player." He told her "I just don't have it! All my life I've dreamed of playing in the big leagues, but I know I'll never make it!

Lucy replies, "You're thinking too far ahead, Charlie Brown. What you need to do is set yourself more immediate goals. Start with the next inning, for example. When you go out to pitch, see if you can walk out to the mound...without falling down."

There will be many who will tell you what you can and can't do. One reason why our store grew so quickly is because we set a direction for what we wanted to accomplish and learned from others who were where we wanted to be. My encouragement to you is to remember that when writing your own future, don't listen to the "experts."

A good example of why this principle is so important can be found in the life of Olympic athlete Parry O'Brien. He won a gold medal at the 1952 Olympics by throwing a 16-pound shot 57 feet. In 1953 he set a new world record by throwing the shot 59 feet, ¾ inch. Experts at the time said O'Brien, the best in the world, might beat his record by a few inches if he practiced, but they were certain that no one would ever be able to break the 60-foot barrier.

Luckily, O'Brien didn't think like an expert. He chose to be a leader and go out and do what hadn't been done before. As an athlete he was determined to continue improving himself. He began experimenting with different styles and invented a new technique for his event, which would become the universal style of putting the shot until the mid-1970s.

In 1956, O'Brien won at the Olympics again—not by a few inches, but by a few feet. He also broke the unbreakable record by tossing the shot 60 feet, 11 inches (what others said could never be done). O'Brien set his final record in 1959 when he threw the shot 63 feet, 4 inches. From that time on, every competitive shot-putter has tossed the shot beyond that length. Today, the record is over 75 feet.

The same is true of the four-minute mile. No one, the experts said, would ever be able to run the mile in less than four minutes. Then, in 1954, a young medical student named Roger Bannister did the impossible by breaking that barrier. Today, every world-class runner can run the mile in less than four minutes. Why? Because one man decided to keep improving. One man decided to pay the price of personal growth. One man was willing to lead. As a result, he created a climate for those achievers who followed him.

My question for you is this: What kind of leader are you? Are you creating a climate where your staff can outdo their goals each week and you can help your store grow to new heights?

Are you the type of leader who is willing to pay the price and create a climate in which your people can follow you and emerge as the leaders of tomorrow?

George Foreman tells this story in his book, *Knockout Entrepreneur*, about the importance of listening to those who can help you get where you want to go and not listening to the voices of dissent around you. He says:

"My son George III ('Monk') was at home watching one of my boxing matches on television when he heard a person in the audience call out an extremely derogatory remark to me. 'I just knew that Dad had to have heard that guy,' Monk said, 'because he was so loud and obnoxious. The remark hurt me as Dad's son, and I was sure it must have hurt Dad.' Later when Monk asked me about the nasty remark, I didn't even know what he was talking about. I hadn't heard the loudmouthed fellow. 'I never listen to the crowd,' I told Monk. Many arenas in which I fought held twenty or thirty thousand people, but I could not allow myself to hear their voices, whether positive or negative. I concentrated on listening only to the men in my corner."

He then gives this advice: “In the same way, when it comes to your career or business, you cannot allow the crowd to influence you. In every crowd you will find some who cheer you on and others who jeer you and try to destroy your confidence. Don’t pay attention to either group. Stay focused on the job at hand.”—*Knockout Entrepreneur*, pp. 47-48.

That is what true leaders do. They focus on the job at hand. When things look bad, they remain optimistic and lead by taking action. They lead by making the first sale. They lead by being more enthusiastic than anyone else. Don’t be discouraged by what the “supposed experts” tell you that you can and can’t do. You create the future by choosing to be a leader every day.

Another great example of being a leader and pushing through disappointments and setbacks can be found in George Foreman’s comeback. He says:

“In 1987, I had made up my mind to get back into boxing, but in the ten years since I had been in training, I had allowed my weight to balloon up to 315 pounds. I planned my physical workout routine to firm up my muscles as I lost the weight, and part of my regiment involved chopping down trees...The axe exercises proved extremely effective in helping me drop the excess weight and firm up my torso.

About two months before my first fight, I was outside chopping on an oak tree, when suddenly the axe head richocheted off the tree and slammed into my leg, slicing through the flesh all the way down to the bone...I was in a mental zone, a focused training mode, so although the pain seared through my leg, I was not about to let it keep me from training. I sat down on the ground, took off my boot and sock, and used the sock as sort of a tourniquet above the spot where the blade had gashed me. Then I picked up the axe and began whaling away at the tree again.

After finishing his workout, he went to the doctor who used a ‘large number of sutures to sew me back together. After he finished, I said to him, 'Doc, I gotta get back to runnin' and choppin' again. I have an important boxing match coming up in about two months. 'Well, I don't think you're going to be doing much running for a while,' he said...The next day I headed out of the house to run, but I could barely walk. I had to hop on one leg just to move around the house. My mental state bounced back and forth between being mad and disappointed. I had scheduled a boxing match and had been training for several months, and now with only weeks before the fight, I couldn't run. What was I to do?

I decided that I would continue my training as best as I could. I got a stool and placed it in front of the punching bag, and then I had my brother Robert hold the bag firmly while I sat on the stool and punched the bag from a sitting position. I couldn't do anything else. The pain was intense, but I didn't dare take anything for it because the drug might remain in my system...I just gritted my teeth and kept punching. Day after day I sat on the stool and punched that bag. In the process I developed a different punching style, using my upper body movement more than my lower body and legs. Eventually, when I finally was able to get back on my feet, I was ready for the boxing match. That injury could have wiped out my comeback career before it even started. But I was determined to work my way back to the top of the boxing world. The kids at my youth center were depending on me, and I wasn't about to let them down."—*Knockout Entrepreneur*, pp. 63-65.

Be a leader. Don't allow yourself to become discouraged. Refuse to take failures and defeats personally. Don't let them get you down. Remember what Winston Churchill said, "Success is the ability to go from failure to failure without losing your enthusiasm." You can do it. I know you can. It's your time to make it happen. I wish you all the best in your endeavors and look forward to hearing of your successes.

What Bridal Store Owners are Saying About Jim Butler's Training Materials

"We have really made a huge effort to use Jim Butler's new training video. It is working so well as I walk through the bridal salon today I am hearing my consultants use so many of his ideas they have learned and we are having a fantastic day. THANK YOU to Jim! It is the best training DVD worth every penny!"—*Barbara Antonacci, Marry and Tux Bridal Shoppe, Nashua, New Hampshire*

Thank you...we have been enjoying the CD's. We had a staff meeting Saturday morning, and I had one consultant apply and use some of the techniques from the "Closing Sales, Opening Relationships" module: she sold 6 dresses ($4800)! We are excited to listen, absorb and apply the remaining techniques. Thanks again."
—*Stacy Van Dusen, Fantasy Bridal, Salt Lake City, Utah*

"Jim has prepared a ton of valuable information in an easy to use format by way of CDs and a workbook. Now if I have an employee who is not performing well in a certain area, I not only speak to them myself, I also have Jim backing up what I am saying by way of his materials. I think this is some of the best money that I ever spent. Thank you Jim! I also just want to say how much I am enjoying Jim Butler as a mentor. I signed up with Jim in Tampa last December and I have to say that he has surely given me far more than my money's worth already. His advertising and promotional ideas are limitless and he is so willing to personalize them for me to meet my store's needs.

At the beginning, I was somewhat embarrassed to have to confess to him that I was a real 'marketing dummy' and did not know how to advertise effectively. I was stuck in the 90's when it came to my marketing ideas. However, I should never have felt intimidated by this marketing genius who has taught me so much since December. He has helped me to implement at least 10 of his ideas over the past 2 months that are working for us, and I am looking forward to further success during these difficult economic times under his tutelage.

Jim is a true gentleman and a joy to work with. I would highly recommend him to any of you who need to learn the tricks of the trade regarding bridal marketing and promotion. He's the best!"
—Mary Marr, Marilee's Bridal & Social Occasion Dressing, Fonthill, Ontario, Canada

"Jim's presentation was awesome and taught us so much... He is a walking wealth of information."
—Cynthia Leonard, Brass & Bows Bridal, Roxboro, North Carolina

"The seminar was amazing. Three minutes into 25 Objections and How to Overcome them my store manager looked at me and said "This is definitely worth it - I'm so glad we came. We are having another training session on Monday with Jim's materials. He is a godsend. The ideas and sales techniques he has gathered are indispensible."*—Michelle McFarland, The Wedding Shoppe, Berkley, Michigan*

"Just wanted to let everyone know how much my staff and I learned tonight from Jim's Conference Call and to say that everyone should consider joining in on these calls. We learned so much. My staff was excited and ready to close the next customer only it was 9.30 pm and the shop was closed by the time Jim finished his presentation. It is amazing to me how this man can take so much information and make it not only informative but also fun to learn. A Big Thank You out to Jim!"
—Mary Feeley, Mary's Bridal, Annapolis, Maryland

"Thanks, Jim. I was enthralled over your presentation. Thank you for sharing so beautifully. I have so appreciated receiving the CD's and written training material from Jim Butler of Arizona's Bridal Warehouse. It's inspiring, insightful, and applicable."
—Cheryl Allen, Charlotte's Bridal Fashions, Aiken, South Carolina

"Thank you Jim for all your help. We had a meeting on Saturday with all my staff and everyone is excited to start using the new ideas on how to overcome the objections. I think this year is going to be our year."
—Terry Ortega, Bridal Elegance, Colorado Springs, Colorado

"I really felt empowered to help my staff increase their sales and make their efforts even more rewarding for them. I am anxious to start implementing the training - I know I couldn't have given them the opportunities they will now have without your excellent presentation. I am anxious to get started with the flash cards. I truly feel this will be our best investment for our staff for the year. Thanks."
—Sue Rosenberger, Fantastic Finds, Lansing, Michigan

"I just watched the "Basic' DVD which is meant for new hires and it is amazing. I can't wait for all my consultants to see this. There is no doubt in my mind that the consultants that are good will get better. The term "Basic" is a misnomer. Robin watched with me and she said she loves the "approach" in that she feels anyone who is into self help will gain from this DVD... I have seen most selling DVD's that are available and, in my opinion, none come near these in content value for the bridal industry. Jim has a very successful store with an average 70% closing ratio. His high rates of closings are not accidental. He knows his stuff and no one but a bridal retailer with his level of knowledge and expertise could produce training DVD's that can do what we need to make us successful. I am encouraging stores to get these because I know this type of training is essential and those BBG members who came to Tampa heard and saw first hand that what this retailer has to offer us is essential and desperately needed."*—Jon Saltzman, Jon's Bridal, Tampa, Florida*

"Great info...gained lots of great ideas to incorporate....I know it will bring good results. Thanks so much."—*Karen, BeDazzled Bridal, St. George, Utah*

"THANK YOU SOOOO MUCH FOR THAT CONFERENCE CALL!! I learned a ton!"
—*Dana Southerland, Bridal Gallery, Goldsboro, North Carolina*

"The conference calls are absolutely fantastic. I find your insight, organization, and suggestions very intellectually stimulating. Having been always interested in a quest for knowledge, I have subscribed to many motivational seminars, speaking events, and employed several consultants, but no-one really addresses our bridal issues like you do. The thing I like most about the seminars is the ability to play your CD both on the way to and from work. It is a 'buffer' for thought and actions the next day, how to think in new ways and in general be more creative....Playing the CD while driving gives me a productive solice and those precious quiet moments can turn into many new ideas to implement. Believe me, we are implementing quite a few."
—*Erik Russell, Bridal Superstore, Indianapolis, Indiana*

"I LOVED my conference CD. I am buying them all."
—*Rhonda Shemwell-Shelton, Bridals of Regiss Park, Glasgow, Kentucky*

"The conference call was fabulous. I couldn't believe the hour passed so quickly and was so enjoyable. You really have a gift for speaking and presenting information that is useful. Being an owner, we get pulled in so many directions, the information was helpful and inspiring. Yesterday, I did plan for 15 minutes, and felt more in control as the day took its turns. There were a number of items I know I can implement easily and reap great rewards! It certainly was a boost. Thanks for sharing your wealth of knowledge."
—*Joni Oakey, Margene's Bridal, Boise, Idaho*

"Jim has been instrumental in helping to build our bridal business. The creative ideas and step ahead of the competition is invaluable."
—*Shannon Lindquist, The Bridal Shoppe, Eau Claire, Wisconsin*

"The ideas and implementation of Jim's bridal selling strategies have transformed our store. Our profits have skyrocketed. My focus has become fixed on working on our store, not just working in our store."
—Lisa Brumm, Co-owner, Formals of Litchfield, Litchfield, Illinois

"Thank you so much for sharing of your time and experience with my staff. They were so excited after your training seminar. They each learned from your presentation and each took with them different ideas on how to be better at what they do. My newest and youngest consultant had been having trouble closing sales and we had been analyzing and discussing her sales approach, but something you said just made sense to her. She could not wait to try it the next day. She used your closing method with her first bride and made the sale. She was singing your praises. Another consultant immediately began using the three questions you told them worked for your consultants with great results. Jim, I think you have a real gift for presenting information in a very positive, easy to understand way. The fact that you also work with brides and encounter the same challenges and situations as we do everyday certainly adds to your credibility with my staff. Jim Butler's ideas and training seminars have truly changed the way I do business. My store has become so much more profitable by implementing Jim's ideas and by his using his training material for my staff."
—Brenda Norman, Norman's Jewelry and Bridal, Lebanon, Missouri

"Jim Butler has inspired me in so many great ways in the bridal business. The bridal industry is so fortunate to have this great bridal business person directing us to a better bridal future!"
—Diana Ellingson, The Wedding Chapel, Crystal, Minnesota

"Since I have been working with Jim in his Quantum Leap program, my sales have more than doubled. His ideas are fresh, inviting and very helpful."*—Joy Salyards, Reflections, Harrisonburg, Virginia*

About the Author

Jim Butler and his wife Heather started their bridal business in Mesa, Arizona in the fall of 2001. They grew their business from $0 to over $1,000,000 per year in sales in three years. In addition to growing their own business using the techniques explained on the numerous training materials (CDs, DVDs, workbooks, etc.) available at www.bridaltrainingsystems.com, Jim has helped some of the most respected and largest bridal stores across the country to grow their sales and shatter their previous sales records. Jim has become an expert in the bridal industry and currently speaks to groups of hundreds of bridal stores giving them training and coaching to improve their businesses. He has appeared several times as a panelist and speaker at the Wedding MBA, Las Vegas market, and Better Bridal Group seminar. He offers a monthly coaching and tele-seminar program to bridal stores where he trains and gives sales and business insights gleaned from his own successful bridal store in Arizona. He loves the bridal business, is excited about its future and loves helping individuals and businesses reach their true potential. He and his wife Heather have five children.

MAXIMIZE YOUR STORE'S GROWTH WITH THESE TRAINING RESOURCES BY JIM BUTLER

Get These Resources Online at: www.bridaltrainingsystems.com

TAKE YOUR STORE TO THE NEXT LEVEL

WITH ONE OF THE FOLLOWING THREE MONTHLY MENTORING OPTIONS:

Silver Membership (Sales & Marketing Secrets Newsletter)
$29.99/month

- **Monthly issue of the Sales & Marketing Secrets Newsletter delivered to your business**

This 16 page newsletter is packed with time-tested and proven sales and marketing secrets that have helped grow Jim's bridal store even in difficult and challenging economic times. Each issue contains a hard hitting look at what is working now with informative articles, real world examples, and specific tactics that will help your business grow by leaps and bounds as it is implemented. In addition to an expanded feature article each month, the newsletter will also show you real examples of marketing campaigns Jim has done with one important element taken out. There will be a contest each month to determine who can notice the fatal flaw in the promotion. Each issue will also be packed with specific marketing tips, a detailed description of one marketing promotion that is working now and some lessons he's learned from running the promotion. Three other sections will round out the newsletter including online marketing strategies, a leadership corner and some final thoughts and mind stretching exercises to help you think about your business differently.

For a Free Trial Just for Owners of *Bridal Profit Explosion*, Sign Up Online at: www.bridaltrainingsystems.com/freetrial

Gold Membership (Monthly Coaching & Conference Calls) $97/month

Monthly Coaching and Conference Calls – includes 75-80 minute monthly topic conference call with Q&A session immediately following – each month you will receive a copy of the CD and notes for you to use in your training meetings (there is enough material for one training meeting each month at less than $25/month to have your training meetings taken care of) PLUS a monthly implementation call to help you use the ideas you learn.

Diamond Membership (Sales & Marketing Secrets Newsletter + Monthly Conf. Calls + Monthly Interview Calls) $197/month

- **Includes all benefits of Silver Membership including monthly issue of the Sales & Marketing Secrets Newsletter delivered to your business** (Value $29.99/mo)
- **Includes all benefits of Gold Membership including Monthly Coaching and Conference Calls** (Value $97/mo)
- **Monthly Best Bridal Retailer Interview Call - 80 minute live interview with the opportunity to ask questions and receive a CD copy of the interview for your reference.** (Value $97/mo)

For a Free Trial Just for Owners of *Bridal Profit Explosion*, Sign Up Online at: www.bridaltrainingsystems.com/freetrial